Politics a

Why is primary education so high on the political agenda, and so contentious?
Why is the performance of primary schools so often in the media spotlight?
Why should primary teachers trouble themselves with the politics of their work?

Politics and the Primary Teacher is an accessible introduction to some of the thorniest aspects of a primary teacher's role. It aims to support your understanding of the constant changes in education policy, give you confidence to engage critically with current political debates, and consider how you might shape your response accordingly.

Including questions for reflection, and selected further reading and resources, it examines the complex interface between the work of a teacher and the world beyond the classroom walls. Key issues explored include:

* assessment, testing, league tables and national accountability measures
* the media's impact in shaping both local and national views about education
* political implications of new policies such as academies and free schools
* conditions of work in the classroom and 'workforce remodelling'
* the curriculum, its purposes and structure
* pedagogy and teaching methods
* education for citizenship, health and well-being.

Politics and the Primary Teacher is essential reading for all education professionals who want to think more deeply about primary education, what it offers, and how children, families and communities are served by the primary school.

Peter Cunningham is Bye-Fellow of Homerton College, Cambridge and Visiting Fellow at the Institute of Education, University of London.

The Understanding Primary Education series
Series editor: Dominic Wyse, Institute of Education, University of London, UK

The *Understanding Primary Education* series offers a fresh approach to key topics in primary education, combining compelling practical writing with rigorous theoretical and evidence-based argument. Breaking new ground in both established topics and essential topics which have been less well-covered previously, the series emphasises the importance of research evidence, theory and reflection on practice in primary education. The series will be invaluable reading for all those engaged with initial teacher education and professional development who want authoritative accounts of issues central to working in the primary classroom.

Titles in the series:

Assessing Learning in the Primary Classroom
Sandra Johnson

Politics and the Primary Teacher
Peter Cunningham

Managing Behaviour in the Primary Classroom
Roland Chaplain

Child Centred Education
Sue Rogers

Creating the Curriculum
Dominic Wyse, Vivienne Marie Baumfield, David Egan,
Louise Hayward, Moira Hulme, Ian Menter and Carmel Gallagher

Politics and the Primary Teacher

Peter Cunningham

Routledge
Taylor & Francis Group

LONDON AND NEW YORK

First published 2012
by Routledge
2 Park Square, Milton Park, Abingdon, Oxon OX14 4RN

Simultaneously published in the USA and Canada
by Routledge
711 Third Avenue, New York, NY 10017

Routledge is an imprint of the Taylor & Francis Group, an informa business

British Library Cataloguing in Publication Data
A catalogue record for this book is available from the British Library.

Library of Congress Cataloging in Publication Data
Cunningham, Peter, 1948-
Politics and the primary teacher / Peter Cunningham.
p. cm. – (Understanding primary education series)
1. Elementary school teaching–Political aspects–Great Britain. 2. Elementary school
teachers–Professional relationships–Great Britain. 3. Education and state–Great Britain.
I. Title.
LB1556.7.G7C86 2012
372.11020941–dc23
2011030325

ISBN: 978–0–415–54958–5 (hbk)
ISBN: 978–0–415–54959–2 (pbk)
ISBN: 978–0–203–13589–1 (ebk)

Typeset in Times New Roman
by Keystroke, Station Road, Codsall, Wolverhampton

MIX
Paper from
responsible sources
FSC
www.fsc.org   FSC® C004839

Printed and bound in Great Britain by
TJ International Ltd, Padstow, Cornwall

To Carey, Jim and Matt,
and to hundreds of thousands of primary teachers who patiently,
conscientiously and creatively turn policy into practice.

'A distinctive and much needed analysis of primary teaching as political activity, Dr Cunningham's new book is scholarly and stunningly well written. It shows how such apparently technical tasks as assessment, curriculum development, and school relationships are intrinsically political, and so challenges the traditional insulation of primary schools from the larger social and economic pressures that shape their practices. Compelling reading that should transform our conceptions of contemporary primary professionalism.'

Jim Campbell, Emeritus Professor of Education, University of Warwick, UK

'This excellent book provides a fascinating account of the evolution of primary education policy but also offers an enlightened vision for the future. A must-read for anyone concerned for our children's wellbeing.'

Maurice Galton, Emeritus Professor, University of Leicester, UK

'This book enables readers to confront critically the year zero/educational amnesia too characteristic of current and recent policy-making. It gives the reflecting student and the seasoned primary professional the necessary historical and political knowledge to analyse how primary education came to be as it is and to consider possible options that lie open in future.'

Colin Richards, HMI (retired), Emeritus Professor, University of Cumbria, and Honorary Professor, University of Warwick, UK

Contents

Acknowledgements

Fellow teachers at schools in Oxfordshire, Leicestershire and Cambridgeshire taught me by example and developed my understanding of what it is to be a primary teacher. George Baines, Julia Christy, Isabel Craig, Peter Dagget, Julie Hatton, Ann Holt, Paul Keates and Ann Price amongst those that I've known and admired for their skilful and demanding work carried out with resilience and good humour, and an overriding interest in and care for the children they teach. Many colleagues have helped me explore the relationships between education, politics and history through their writings and personal friendship over a long time and across several continents. These include Brian Simon in Leicester, Harold Silver in Oxford, Roy Lowe in Birmingham, Richard Aldrich and Gary McCulloch in London, Bill Reese in Madison, Wisconsin and Yoko Yamasaki at Mukogawa Women's University, Nishinomiya. Other intellectual influences will be evident from references and bibliography in the chapters that follow. At Cambridge, Cathy Burke and Phil Gardner have been supportive and stimulating colleagues. Gary Foskett, Director, 3Di Associates and former headteacher was especially helpful in his thoughtful comments on draft chapters. Carey Bennet, a critic and true friend, responded knowledgeably with her feet on the ground, implementing education policies in interesting times. None of these friends and colleagues would agree with everything I've written below.

Homerton College and the Faculty of Education at the University of Cambridge, and the Institute of Education in London have been congenial and challenging environments in which to share and question ideas about politics and education in the present and the past. My editor, the energetic but infinitely patient Dominic Wyse, commissioned this book. At Routledge, Anna Clarkson, Helen Pritt, Claire Westwood and Rhiannon Findlay figure amongst a skilled team who help keep teachers and educationists thinking and well informed by enabling them to share their research and ideas, and by providing an independent platform for critical review of education policy and practice.

Abbreviations

ACCAC	Awdurdod Cymwysterau, Cwricwlwm ac Asesu Cymru (Qualifications, Curriculum and Assessment Authority for Wales)
ASCL	Association of School and College Leaders
ASPE	Association for the Study of Primary Education
ATL	Association of Teachers and Lecturers
CACE	Central Advisory Council for Education
CATE	Council for the Accreditation of Teacher Education
CCEA	Council for Curriculum, Examinations and Assessment, Northern Ireland
CCMS	Council for Catholic Maintained Schools, Northern Ireland
CEA/CE	Cambridge Education Associates/Cambridge Education
CPD	Continuing Professional Development
CPS	Centre for Policy Studies
DCELLS	Department for Children, Education, Lifelong Learning and Skills, Wales
DCLG	Department for Communities and Local Government
DCMS	Department for Culture, Media and Sport
DCSF	Department for Children, Schools and Families
DENI	Department of Education, Northern Ireland
DES	Department of Education and Science
DFE	Department for Education
DFEE	Department for Education and Employment
DFES	Department for Education and Skills
ECM	Every Child Matters
EIS	Educational Institute of Scotland
ELB	Education and Libraries Board, Northern Ireland
EPA	Educational Priority Area
ESTYN	Schools Inspectorate for Wales
EYFS	Early Years Foundation Stage
GLC	Greater London Council
GM	Grant Maintained
GTC(E)/(W)	General Teaching Council (England)/(Wales)
GTP	Graduate Teacher Programme
HCCSFC	House of Commons Children, Schools and Families Committee
HCEC	House of Commons Education Committee
HCESC	House of Commons Education and Skills Committee
HEI	Higher Education Institution

HLTA	Higher Level Teaching Assistant
HMI/HMCI	Her/His Majesty's Inspector(ate)/HM Chief Inspector
ILEA	Inner London Education Authority
INSET	In-Service Education and Training
LEA/LA	Local Education Authority, after 2004 known as Local Authority
LMS	Local Management of Schools
MTL	Masters in Teaching and Learning
NAHT	National Association of Head Teachers
NAPE	National Association for Primary Education
NASUWT	National Association of Schoolmasters/Union of Women Teachers
NCC	National Curriculum Council
NCSL	National College for School Leadership
nef	new economics foundation
NFER	National Foundation for Educational Research
NLE/LLE/SLE	National/Local/Specialist Leader of Education
NLS	National Literacy Strategy
NNS	National Numeracy Strategy
NPHA	National Primary Headteachers' Association
NQT	Newly Qualified Teacher
NUT	National Union of Teachers
Ofsted	Office for Standards in Education
Ofstin	Office for Standards in Inspection
ORACLE	Observational Research and Classroom Learning Experience
PANDA	Performance and Assessment data
PGCE	Postgraduate Certificate in Education
PICSI	Pre-Inspection Context and School Indicators
PNS	Primary National Strategy
PPA	Planning, Preparation and Assessment
PSH(C)E	Personal, Social and Health (and Citizenship) Education
PSRDG	Primary Schools Research and Development Group
QCA	Qualifications and Curriculum Authority
QCDA	Qualifications and Curriculum Development Agency
QTS	Qualified Teacher Status
SCAA	School Curriculum and Assessment Authority
SCDC	School Curriculum Development Committee
SCITT	School-Centred Initial Teacher Training
SEAC	School Examinations and Assessment Council
SEAL	Social and Emotional Aspects of Learning
SIP	School Improvement Partner
SPCK	Society for Promoting Christian Knowledge
TDA	Training and Development Agency
TTA	Teacher Training Agency
UNCRC	United Nations Convention on the Rights of the Child
VA/VC	Voluntary Aided/Voluntary Controlled

Series Editor's Preface

'I just want to learn how to teach, I'm not interested in politics.'

'Politics affects everything I do as a teacher.'

'Politics has no place in the classroom.'

If the issues that these questions raise have, however fleetingly, been on your mind then this may be the ideal book to read. Peter Cunningham's powerful exploration explains why politics and history are important to teachers and their pupils, and why direct engagement with political processes is more important than ever.

As I wrote this Preface the news had just been reported that teachers' contributions to their pensions were set to rise year by year from 2011 to 2015. This came at a time when the banking sector had brought the country to the brink of financial disaster, was rescued by the Government using public money, but then seemed to carry on largely as before. On a more positive note, at about the same time the *Observer* newspaper reported a forthcoming new play by Stephen Poliakoff that was to celebrate the teaching profession. Perhaps what these two seemingly unconnected examples reveal is the powerful place that education has in society, and it is education's place in our society and culture that brings it into the political sphere.

Peter's book quite rightly begins with the observation that the work of teachers is often underestimated and misunderstood by outside observers. I have lost count of the times that I have heard people confidently offer their opinions about education when they would be more tentative about the work of doctors, lawyers and a range of other professionals. In my view this is mainly because so many people are simply unaware of the knowledge that is required to be a good teacher. But when these opinions are held by people in government who take decisions that are uninformed by appropriate evidence it is unforgivable.

The book's portrayal of history and politics is notable for the close links made with the practice of teaching, for example, in its chapters on curriculum and pedagogy. Although the power to devise their own curricula was taken from teachers in 1988 (as a result of the Education Reform Act), there was a view that pedagogy, including teaching methods, was for teachers to decide. But even teaching methods are now prescribed by government in England. I say England, because another of the book's strengths is its attention to Northern Ireland, Scotland and Wales, that are increasingly useful sources of comparison. It is not only the facts of recent political change that the book offers but a much deeper understanding built on a proper appreciation of the history of primary education.

I had the pleasure of working with Peter at the Faculty of Education, University of Cambridge. The book was written as a result of Peter's outstanding lifelong attention to primary education, its history and its politics. I know it will engage readers, but I hope that it might also *enrage* you a little! Anger is sometimes a powerful motivation to directly confront the dubious aspects of educational policy that successive new politicians implement with scant disregard for history. I share Peter's vision of the best kind of teacher:

> Our aspiration should be for primary teachers as confident professionals able to make their own decisions about curriculum and teaching method, ready to analyse policy in place of unthinking acceptance, involved in union and other collaborative activities to resist mere imposition, initiating or engaging with opportunities for consultation and democratic debate.

Dominic Wyse, Professor of Early Childhood and Primary Education,
Institute of Education, University of London, UK
October 2011

Chapter 1

Introduction: exploring primary politics

Being a primary teacher is rewarding and demanding. The rewards lie in a sense of worth, the value of your work to the young child, to the family and to the community. This sense of worth is realised when you see children learn, when you watch them develop as individuals and as members of a group, as you observe young children enjoying their achievements in all sorts of activities that you, as a teacher, make possible. The demands are huge, of course, and the frustrations are many. Good teaching requires creativity, determination and patience on a scale much underestimated by outside observers. The critical insight, the empathy and the resourcefulness that you deploy on a daily basis in intensive contact with the children you teach is not well understood beyond the school walls. That lack of outside understanding about the reality of the job is where the politics of primary teaching begins to reveal itself.

Political pronouncements and popular opinion often seem wide of the mark. Perceptions of primary schools by those who work inside them are generally more complex and nuanced than the simplistic diagnoses and remedies proposed by government and media. Teachers' work is everyday, continuous and not confined to the periodic crises that make headline news. So why should busy teachers of young children trouble themselves with the politics of the work? Surely there is more than enough to think about already? The institutional demands of the school, the intricacies of the curriculum, planning lessons, managing colleagues, assessment and record-keeping, preparing for parent interviews or governors' meetings, are all tasks that press for immediate attention. Yet all of those tasks are reflected in the pages that follow, precisely because they are all political. They all involve the interface between the work of a class teacher and a world beyond the classroom walls, a world that instituted the primary school in the first place and perpetuates it as a key social institution. It is the world beyond the classroom that funds and controls the school, defines the role of primary teachers, determining the parameters within which they work. From the enormous superstructure of government and governance down to the expectations of individual parents, carers and families for the progress of their children, the context of primary teaching is innately political.

It might also be argued, however, that primary teaching has been excessively *politicised* over the last thirty years or so, as education has taken centre stage in government policy. Parents and carers, school governors, educational administrators and politicians can also gain from reading this book. Addressed in the first place to teachers, it is nevertheless intended to be useful to all who are concerned with primary schools, and who will benefit from critical reflection about its political dimensions. We can hardly avoid the politics of education when education features almost daily in political debates. Encountering the politics is almost inevitable, but thinking politically about the work of the primary school is not so common. Yet we all need to engage critically, to keep abreast of the arguments and to stay well informed. This book aims to provide support in critical thinking about policies and provision of primary education, what they offer, and how, to children, families and communities served by the primary school.

Political ideologies underlie a continuous adjustment of education policy to the prevailing social, economic and cultural climate. This book is written in the wake of a general election, as a new Government at Westminster, a coalition of Conservatives and Liberal Democrats, replaces the preceding Labour Government, presenting new policies that claim to demarcate a fresh approach, differentiated from what went before. Though much of the argument will be illustrated by events in England, there are important divergences and parallels in other parts of the United Kingdom to be considered. Indeed, the varied experiences of England, Wales, Northern Ireland and Scotland signal the ways that politics affects the primary school and offer instructive comparisons. This book considers ideological argument in Parliament and the media, and the ways in which research, both the work of independent academics and government-directed research, is invoked in those debates. It reflects on the role of pressure groups and bodies of public opinion. It questions the frequently deployed notion of an 'education establishment', often caricatured as self-interested and left-leaning, when inevitably the primary teaching role involves commitment to the well-being of others and demands heavy investment of the self.

As well as observing events as they unfold, the politics of education involves studying change over longer periods of time, and history gives us the privilege of hindsight. Any political theory we apply to current events will be drawn from our understanding of previous events, and any predictive value in theory will draw on analysis of the outcomes of earlier educational policies. Teachers in mid-career are most familiar with the relatively recent past, developments they have observed for themselves or know at second hand from the experiences of older colleagues. The experiences of the previous two generations of teachers are likely to be most closely related to the situations we face today, but the more remote past has its explanatory value, too, in understanding the deeper roots of present dilemmas, continuities and discontinuities over time, and the dynamics of longer term social, economic and cultural change.

Using this book

Outline of chapters

Chapter 2 outlines the nature of politics and political theorising, then introduces a longer historical perspective, standing back and seeing the primary school from its origins as a political institution. This perspective gives a valuable sense of continuities and contrasts. Looking back helps us to see more clearly, not just differences and similarities, but also how ideas were constituted as practice, as ways of teaching, how discourse shaped the work of the teacher. We need to be inquisitive and questioning about the historical evolution of primary policy and practice, as different versions of the past are presented by politicians to justify current policies, and we need to remain sceptical about those justifications. A timeline supports this account of major events from the eighteenth century to the time of the Plowden Report on primary education in 1967.

The following chapters are then arranged thematically to survey in more detail the forty years since the Plowden Report, representing the career span for teachers still working or recently retired. Events described may trigger personal memories and experiences that can provide good material for critical reflection. Each of the chapters is prefaced by quotations that introduce controversial perspectives, and it is hoped that these will provoke an immediate response and a critical frame of mind towards each chapter's theme.

Curriculum is one obvious site that, only in the last twenty-five years, has become a critical policy issue, developments that are discussed in Chapter 3. Curriculum continues under government review and attracts a lot of media attention as a hot topic of popular controversy. Within the curriculum, citizenship and well-being are highlighted in Chapter 4 as predictable sites of contestation. However effectively national identity may or may not be cultivated through the school curriculum, its meaning for an ethnically diverse and globally mobile population provokes a heated debate; health and well-being are also seen as aspects of citizenship education that raise difficult questions about the relationship between the state and the individual. Less predictably than citizenship, the primary teacher's pedagogy and way of working with pupils came to the centre of political controversy, and Chapter 5 explores the implications for professional autonomy and children's learning. A lively debate continues as the new government repositions itself in relation to national strategies for teaching literacy and numeracy, apparently loosening some of the former tight controls, but prescribing for the first time 'set books' for young readers.

Teachers and their conditions of employment have always stood in a clear relation to government policy, as one of the major costs in providing a national education service, and unions were formed to give the teachers strength in negotiating with such a powerful employer. Chapter 6 looks at political drives to reform teachers' working conditions, at struggles for control over teachers' professional training and development, as well as at organisations formed to voice professional opinion on primary curriculum and pedagogy. Testing and league tables have been strategically deployed by politicians in holding primary schools and their teachers to account, especially effective in media debates where catchy statistics grab headlines, as seen in Chapter 7. Publicly challenging the reliability and relevance of these accountability measures will be a constant task for the teaching profession in order to offer parents, voters and taxpayers an alternative understanding of the nature and potential of primary schooling. Politics in its fullest sense is also central to the relationships formed between a school and its local community and, more obliquely though no less importantly, to the way that adults and children interact within the community of the school. Chapter 8 examines some aspects of this, with the implication that a sound democratic education within the school might pave the way for a more balanced and less histrionic national politics of education in the future.

One way of reading this book would be to turn from here to the final chapter. Looking forward, Chapter 9 draws together threads of argument and presents some concluding propositions that might equally be read as a preface to the more detailed studies. The order of chapters does not imply a necessary sequence for reading. Chapters 3 to 8 address in turn distinct political dimensions of primary teachers' work, and might be read selectively in any order. Chapter 2 places these in a longer historical perspective, so that the deep roots of the challenges we currently face may be understood, and also offers some reflections on politics and political analysis. Readers most immediately concerned about a particular aspect such as curriculum, pedagogy, working conditions or governance can turn to any one of the relevant chapters before exploring the longer history. Using the book whichever way seems best, its purpose is to enable and encourage a critical, reflective and more informed approach to the politics and practice of primary teaching. A chronology of key events is provided in the Appendix and this list may be supplemented from personal memory or from individual research using some of the literature and internet sources listed below.

Questions for reflection and further reading

At the end of each chapter questions prompt the kind of discussion that might be valuable in further professional development, so are posed with teachers in mind. The questions address issues covered in the chapter from different angles. They are pitched at three different levels, to take account of career stage. At the first level, questions aim to respond to the experience acquired by a teacher in initial training, or a newly qualified teacher. Second-level questions cater for class teachers with more extensive experience, while questions at level three assume the interests and responsibilities of teachers in senior management roles. Independent learning tasks are also suggested.

For each chapter, selected further readings are listed. Constraints of space limit the more extensive treatment deserved by important issues raised; however, this book is intended as an invitation to explore dimensions of individual interest through further reading, reflection on personal experiences and discussion with colleagues.

Both shorter and longer historical perspectives will be drawn on here. The overriding aim of looking in a practical and critical way at the present prevents this book from going into too much detail about the distant past, but useful literature and web sources for historical events are suggested. For recent and current events, websites and books will provide plenty of relevant information and commentary. The following can be used to identify particular themes and provide contrasting political and professional perspectives which could then be used as texts for critical reflection and discussion with colleagues.

Media and websites

The *Times Educational Supplement* is useful for professional perspectives, the *Guardian*, *Independent*, *Telegraph* and *Times* (especially their education sections) for in-depth coverage of educational controversies from a range of political angles, and the BBC website for news coverage and features. Tabloid newspapers can also be a useful source for critically reviewing popular media representation, inevitably offering less depth and detail in analysis. Searching on keywords will enable creating an archive of reports and commentary on any given topic going back over the last few years.

Mike Baker's blog: Mike Baker was the BBC's education editor for nearly twenty years, and an education columnist for BBC News Online and the *Guardian*. His energetic and knowledgeable coverage of education issues and his incisive analyses provide many valuable texts for discussion of primary education and its political dimensions (www.mikebaker education.co.uk).

Academic journals are many and various, and three can be identified as especially useful for analysis of primary education, politics and policy. *Education 3–13* offers empirical research articles and theoretical analysis of many policy issues. *Forum for promoting 3–19 comprehensive education* regularly engages with political debates, with a strong emphasis on primary education. *Oxford Review of Education* frequently addresses aspects of policy and politics, covering the whole range of educational provision, in lengthier articles. The contents of all three journals can be searched online and are accessible electronically or in paper copy through academic libraries.

The History of Education in England is a website authored and maintained by Derek Gillard, former primary school teacher, middle school teacher and headteacher, and writer on education with special interests in politics, policy and administration of education. The site is a treasure trove of useful material for individual research and discussion, including an extensive chronology, many articles and original sources, such as the full text of the Plowden Report and commentaries on its subsequent political significance and impact, together with many more recent official publications on primary education policy (www.educationengland. org.uk).

House of Commons Education Committee Reports are available online (including the former Children, Schools and Families Committee (July 2007–April 2010), Education and Skills Committee (July 2001–July 2007), and Education and Employment Committee from 1995. Some of these reports are referred to in chapters following on topics such as curriculum and accountability. Individual reports on such topics make valuable reading, and especially the minutes of evidence to the committee which represent points of view from professional and parental interest groups, from think tanks and specialist pressure groups, and across the political spectrum. Extracts of the reports and of the evidence on which they are based make valuable texts for discussion (www.parliament.uk/business/committees/committees-a-z/commons-select/education-committee/publications).

Education interest group websites

National Education Trust: An independent foundation dedicated to improving the quality of education nationwide, shaping its future, and working to help close the achievement gap, their website has many links to news items of current concern and relevance to primary education (www.nationaleducationtrust.net).

Progressive Education Network: The Network was officially launched in 2010, as a platform for a coalition of school leaders, teachers and governors. It argues that despite much to celebrate in reforms and their intent since 1997, the next phase of continuing change needs to be driven by practitioners, government and local communities in partnership (www.progressive-education-network.org).

Teacher union and professional organisation websites offer useful commentary on current political issues and links to relevant resources and publications. Examples include:

Association for the Study of Primary Education (ASPE)	www.aspe-uk.eu
Association of Teachers and Lecturers (ATL)	www.atl.org.uk
College of Teachers	www.collegeofteachers.ac.uk
Educational Institute of Scotland (EIS)	www.eis.org.uk
National Association of Head Teachers (NAHT)	www.naht.org.uk
National Association for Primary Education (NAPE)	www.nape.org.uk
National Union of Teachers (NUT)	www.teachers.org.uk

Personal and professional memory

This comprises a rich and immediately accessible source of 'collective memory'. This book encourages engagement with colleagues in discussion, to share recollections and perceptions, to argue and debate about the way politics has influenced, and continues to influence, primary education practice. More formally, research could be conducted around a particular policy or set of issues by structured interviewing of a sample of teachers, and indeed parents and past pupils, comparing perceptions and evaluation of policy and practice with written records in media and political sources. It is hoped that the chapter texts and the timeline in the Appendix might be a trigger to this kind of discussion and research (see, for example, Cunningham 2007, Warwick 2007b, Warwick and Cunningham 2006).

Key books for reference

Alexander, R. (ed.) (2010) *Children, Their World, Their Education: Final Report and Recommendations of the Cambridge Primary Review*, London: Routledge, contains summary reports of extensive research into many aspects of primary education in England with particular reference to the impact of government policies over the course of the past two decades.

Bangs, J., MacBeath, J. and Galton, M. (2011) *Reinventing Schools, Reforming Teaching. From political visions to classroom reality*, London: Routledge, offers fascinating and highly readable accounts drawing on personal testimony from many of the key politicians, advisers and administrators who contributed to devising and implementing education policies in the past thirty years. It is a resource worth dipping into for insights into educational policy that are both thought-provoking and entertaining.

Chitty, C. (2009) *Education Policy in Britain*, 2nd edn, Basingstoke: Palgrave Macmillan, provides a recent, well-informed and politically critical account. Its chapters include accessible overviews of education politics in successive phases of the later twentieth century, studies of policy-making, curriculum, citizenship and diversity, and privatisation.

Chapter 2

The primary school
as a political institution

What is political about primary teaching? We may like to think of the work as politically neutral, concerned principally with helping young children to become interested and capable learners, well-rounded and happy individuals. Yet current and recent events impress on us, especially in the wake of a change of government, the constant revision of policy that attempts to finely adjust primary schooling to changing perceptions of national needs, and the staking of political reputations on particular solutions to the problems identified. For curriculum, the Rose Review was insistently promoted and implemented by New Labour in 2009, to be rejected and abandoned by a new coalition government the following year, instigating yet another 'major' review. A broad view of pedagogy was implicit in the Every Child Matters (ECM) policy from 2004, reflected in a radical renaming of the government department to one for 'Children, Schools and Families' (though it continued to be accompanied by a centralised Primary National Strategy dictating how teachers should work in the classroom). With a change of government in 2010 the Department of State promptly reverted to a 'Department for Education' and the terminology of ECM was abandoned. The professional status of teaching has been subject to political manipulation by successive governments, with the creation by New Labour in 1997 of a General Teaching Council in England and Wales albeit under close government supervision, and its subsequent abolition thirteen years later in England (but not in Wales) by the Conservative–Liberal Democrat coalition. Moreover, as a further slight to professional status, the latter's flagship innovation 'free schools' was relieved of the statutory requirement to employ professionally trained teachers. In respect of national accountability, school inspection was exploited by the incoming Secretary of State in 1997 as a means of 'naming and shaming' 'failing schools'. Whether or not this policy contributed to improving standards remains debatable and politically contentious. A later programme of 'extended schools' promoted more responsiveness to the needs of local communities, but the introduction of 'academies' contradicted the principle of local accountability by reducing community representation on governing bodies, which could henceforward be dominated by independent sponsors.

Despite complaints about education having quite recently become 'a political football' this chapter will explore, by looking through the long perspective of history, how primary schooling is innately political and has been since its origins. It begins with a brief discussion about the nature of politics and continues by surveying the way that politics has shaped the education system as a whole, and primary education in particular, in respect of curriculum, human resources, finance and control.

Politics

Politics is a process of decision-making by groups, most commonly within civil governments, but the process can be observed in all human group interactions, including all corporate and academic institutions. It relies on social relations involving authority or power and is characterised by the methods and tactics used to formulate and apply policy.

In the western world nation states grew alongside the spread of Christianity, from the Christianisation of the Roman Empire in the fourth century through the Middle Ages, and England became a nation with an established church (the Church of England, of which the monarch is supreme governor) and the state in intimate alliance; Wales, united with England from 1536, shared this situation, though it was also a centre of nonconformist religion from the eighteenth century; Scotland, similarly united with England under one monarchy from 1603 and with a united Parliament under the Act of Union from 1707, though its Presbyterian national Church of Scotland is not a state church; and Northern Ireland became part of the United Kingdom following the establishment of the Irish Free State in 1922, with Roman Catholics the largest single denomination, though a protestant majority composed largely of Presbyterians and Anglicans were the dominant political group. From the nineteenth century schools were provided first by religious denominations assisted by government funds and later complemented by non-denominational state schools. This 'dual system' of state and church provision in Britain is still a live political issue, where other nation states such as Germany, France and the USA moved to a clear separation of church and state in elementary schooling.

In the late nineteenth century parliamentary representation moved ever closer to allowing a vote for every adult and a major function of the school system was seen as producing an educated and responsible electorate. With urban growth following industrialisation, local government was instituted to provide services such as roads, drainage, welfare and education, and the democratic principle was applied to both central and local governments, including elected 'school boards' that later became 'Local Education Authorities' (LEAs). Democracy was limited in practice, as women were denied the franchise in national elections but could vote and stand as candidates in School Board elections.

The principle of majority rule underlay formation of governments at national and local levels and a party system emerged to represent political ideologies and to present alternative political candidates to the electorate. A system of opposition provided effective criticism of the government in power. A mainly two-party system (with one or more minority parties) evolved, with alternative policies for education as for other affairs of state.

Over the last hundred years politics has divided into right and left wings, with the notion of centre ground as a middle way between right and left. The idea of right and left dates from the French Revolution, when members of the National Assembly who supported the republic, the common people and a secular society sat on the left and supporters of the monarchy, aristocratic privilege and the Church sat on the right. The meanings behind the labels right wing and left wing became more complicated with the emergence of socialism and communism. Marx and Engels' *Communist Manifesto* proposed a proletarian revolution to overthrow bourgeois society and abolish private property, believing this would lead to a classless society. Right and left differ in significance between different countries and at different times, but the right generally values tradition and social stratification while the left tends to value reform and egalitarianism, with the centre seeking a balance between the two, as in social democracy or regulated capitalism. One kind of political analysis argues that the left believe in attempting to eradicate social inequality, while the right regard most social inequality as the result of ineradicable natural inequalities and attempts to enforce social equality are seen from the right as utopian or authoritarian.

Also originating during the French Revolution was the notion of ideology, a set of ideas proposed by the dominant class within society to offer either change, or conformity to a set of established ideals. Ideologies are normative systems of thought applied to public matters and are thus central to an understanding of politics. Marxists understand it in terms of class struggle and domination where the ruling class controls the means of production and determines a justifying ideology, while sociologists might take a more neutral view of ideology as a necessary part of institutional functioning and social integration. In either view, education or formal schooling has provided a principal vehicle for instilling ideology, and within capitalist societies liberalism and social democracy are identified as dominant ideologies. For the purposes of an introduction to the politics of education, however, this book refers to two political scientists who take a pragmatic rather than an ideological approach to their subject. Kenneth Minogue and Bernard Crick are of particular interest in our context as both were actively involved in advising recent governments, with particular reference to education. Minogue is a libertarian conservative and former director of the Centre for Policy Studies, a think tank founded in 1974 to promote economic liberalism, advising the Conservative Party in opposition and in government. Crick was a democratic socialist who advised the Labour Party in opposition under the leadership of Neil Kinnock from 1983 to 1992, and was commissioned to advise on citizenship education by New Labour in their first term of office. From opposite sides of the party political divide, both Minogue and Crick are pragmatists who are suspicious of ideology.

Minogue saw Margaret Thatcher's Government in the 1980s as more pragmatic than ideological. He argued that in the post-war era liberal democracy had developed a welfare state that had become economically unsustainable with the inflationary effects of the oil crisis in the 1970s, at the same time as British economic supremacy was being challenged by the new economies of Asia. Minogue placed more emphasis on these practical considerations than on any ideological commitment to classical liberalism and the free market. It was economic realism that demanded a reduction of government expenditure and enhancement of economic vitality, and he recognised the paradox that these policies led to more state intervention rather than less. Minogue's suspicion of ideology led him to describe politics as 'in part a theatre of illusion', and to warn that a price of freedom is constant vigilance towards political rhetoric: 'The beginnings of wisdom in politics is attention to signs of change. As a theatre of illusion, politics does not reveal its meanings to the careless eye. Reality and illusion are central categories of political study' (Minogue 2000, 5).

A sceptical view of political rhetoric is necessary, but the critique of educational politics needs to go further in recognising the significance of 'discourse'. In a very real sense the language that is used in political debate on education constructs the way individuals reason about their participation and their identity. More radical discursive theorists observe how distinctions between language and reality are dissolved, and how powerfully the language used in policy shapes the ways in which teachers, pupils, parents and carers understand and perform their roles.

Crick saw political thinking as the antithesis of ideological thinking and looked for a 'politics of action' as opposed to a 'politics of thought'; for him, 'politics is ethics done in public'. He described politics as

> ... not a necessary evil, but a realistic good, a way of ruling in divided societies without undue violence. It is conservative insofar as it preserves the minimum benefits of

established order; liberal as compounded of particular liberties and requiring tolerance; socialist in providing conditions for deliberate change by which groups come to have an equitable take in the prosperity and survival of the community.

(Crick 2000, 140–141,145)

A democratic socialist, he explained that what most people mean by democracy is not its literal sense of 'power to the people', but rather 'political rule', a system of governing that allows for peaceable compromises to be made between ever-present conflicts of values and interests. Modern democracies are marked by characteristics such as voluntary and individual participation with allegiance given to a government by popular consent on utilitarian grounds. Democratic societies are characterised by a large middle class as wealth in the hands of a few threatens democratic processes, and extremes of poverty remove people from the normal polity and threaten political order. Crick illustrated the need for care in defining democracy with regard to schools, where teachers and adults make decisions on behalf of children:

> I have heard well-meaning people demand that schools should be democratic. That is, alas, Rousseau-like nonsense: that innocence is superior to knowledge, or is itself a form of knowledge. But I have argued strongly elsewhere that schools should be more democratic than they commonly are. I see citizenship education as a democratic impulse, but a democratic school is a contradiction in terms.
>
> (Crick 2002, 92)

Crick and Minogue are introduced here as political scientists offering a way in to engaging with the everyday experience of politics and its impact in the primary classroom. But ideological analysis will also be represented throughout this book with reference to critical writers on education such as Stephen Ball, John Beck, Clyde Chitty, Ken Jones and Brian Simon cited in the chapters that follow.

While the everyday life of the primary school is full of interest and constructive potential, even enjoyment, it also presents a good deal of challenge and frustration. National policies, local politics and the internal governance of the school, all in their different ways constrain as well as enable what teachers seek to achieve. What this book seeks to draw out is the politics that underlies the everyday life of the school, a way of thinking about and analysing the situations encountered by primary teachers. Examining the politics of primary education demands constant vigilance towards the illusions identified by Minogue but also towards the power of discourse. It also calls for reflection on the nature and limits of democracy, at national and local levels, and within the school itself, bearing in mind Crick's 'ethics of action' and seeking to balance conflicting demands of security and order, individual liberty and equitable treatment. A democratic school needs to foster participation and tolerance of dissent and progressive change to meet continually changing needs.

Political representation in democratic systems is a means of controlling the danger of arbitrary interference by the state. An increase of state activity, such as the development of a compulsory and ever-expanding education system, went hand-in-hand with extension of the franchise, and could therefore be interpreted as the product of popular will. But a 'nation' in the sense of a community of people, sometimes described as an 'imagined community', is not the same thing as a 'state'. State activity is not necessarily for the good of the nation and there are no hard and fast rules to limit state administration. Even in modern democracies, state and nation are never identical and where 'universal suffrage' prevails, the fact remains that extending state administration means increased interference in the lives of some groups by others, limiting freedom of action.

In the twentieth century, and perhaps especially in the period following the Second World War, extension of state administration was based on an assumption that civil servants must prove more effective than private enterprise in providing public services. A basic difference between business administration and public administration is that the first aims at profit while the second aims at the public good, though both require ethical conduct to maintain a stable and sustainable relationship between business and labour or between the state and its administrators. This ethical conduct, and the many specialist areas of expertise in which it must operate, such as education and health, require a high level and high standards of education for managers and workers, as also for politicians and public administrators.

Political development of primary education

How did primary education become political in the national context? 'Primary' indicates education for younger age groups, the first stage of schooling, compulsory and provided free by the state for almost a century and a half. A look back at the origins of state provision, at the rationale for this kind of intervention and how it might have changed through 150 years of history, reveals its political implications.

The language used to describe schools is significant. What is now known as 'primary' in the UK was once more commonly called 'elementary', and 'elementary school' remains standard terminology elsewhere in the English-speaking world. British state elementary education in its origins was often described as 'working-class education' on an assumption that the middle classes provided for themselves through the private sector. 'Basic education' is often used in the context of developing countries to imply the foundations of literacy and numeracy. 'Working-class', 'elementary' and 'basic' therefore all bear meanings for the evolution of 'primary'. Whilst the education of all children is compulsory in Britain from age 5 to 16 (raising of the participation age for education or training is currently projected to age 17 from 2013 and age 18 from 2015), parents have the option to pay for private provision, and private schools for the younger age group are customarily distinguished by the title 'preparatory' with its emphasis on preparation for the secondary phase. Terminology has also reflected the age-span of stages within primary, with 'infant' and 'junior' and 'first' or 'middle' schools. Structures of school provision at any one time and place are outcomes of policy informed by educational principles but driven more fundamentally by cultural and economic considerations.

To make sense of the political development of primary education over time and the legacy it has left us in the present, key features will be identified and grouped under three broad headings:

- The *content* of primary education, expressing the aims and purposes that underlay the evolution of a state system of universal basic education (further developed in Chapters 3 and 4).
- The means of providing primary education in terms of *human resources* (teachers and other adults) and the *teaching methods* (pedagogy) they were expected to adopt (further developed in Chapters 5 and 6).
- The means of provision and administration in the form of *finance*, *control* and *accountability* (further developed in Chapters 7 and 8).

To introduce this thematic account of the long historical development, the following timeline includes major events referred to below, providing a chronological framework for reference.

Table 2.1 Politics and primary education – a long history

	Politics	*Education*
Late 17th century	'Glorious Revolution' Bill of Rights	Society for Promoting Christian Knowledge Scottish parochial schools
18th century	Industrial development and urbanisation with political implications	Charity Schools Irish 'hedge schools'
1776	American independence	
1789	French revolution	
1791	Tom Paine *Rights of Man*	
1811		Church of England monitorial schools
1814		Nonconformist monitorial schools
1830	Whigs and radicals in government	
1832	Electoral reform: political representation for industrial employers' interests Continuing industrial and urban growth and commercial economy	
1833		Government grant for church schools
1839	Committee of Privy Council on Education (state administration)	Her Majesty's Inspectorate (HMI)
1846		National pupil teacher scheme Church colleges for teacher training
1859	Conservatives and liberals dominate Parliament	
1861		Report of Royal Commission on 'popular education' (Newcastle Commission)
1862		Revised Code for education: 'payment by results'
1867	Electoral reform with votes for all male householders	
1868	Liberal Government	
1870	Education Act Locally elected School Boards	State elementary schooling to 'fill gaps' left by church provision National Union of Elementary Teachers
1872	Education Act Scotland	
1880	Liberal Government Education Act	Universal compulsory schooling
Late 19th century	Expansion of state bureaucracy Extensive growth of commerce	
1895		End of payment by results
1899		School leaving age raised to 12

Table 2.1 Continued

	Politics	Education
1900	Emergence of Labour Party	Pressure to improve working-class education
1902	Education Act Board of Education (government department for elementary schools) Local Education Authorities (LEAs)	Denominational schools funded by local government Municipal teacher training colleges
1905		Board of Education *Suggestions for teachers . . . in elementary schools*
1906	Liberal Government	School meals and school health service
1914–18	First World War Coalition government and elections suspended	
1918	Growth of Labour representation	School leaving age raised to 14
1919		Burnham Committee on teachers' pay
1920s		Growing interest in child development
1926	General Strike – Labour unrest threatens political instability	
1927		Abolition of Elementary Code New edition *Handbook of Suggestions* BBC schools broadcasting
1929	Economic crisis and depression	Cutbacks in education spending
1931		Hadow Report *The Primary School*
1933		Hadow Report *Infant and Nursery schools*
1939–45	Wartime coalition	Evacuation of school children Expansion of nursery education
1944	Education Act Ministry of Education	'Elementary schools' replaced by primary education for all from age 5–11 'Dual system' of state and church schools continues
1945	Labour Government	
1951	Conservative Government	
1950s	'Consensus politics' Economic recovery after war	Growing resistance to 11+ selection Audio-visual aids and Schools' TV Teacher training course (Teachers' Certificate) extended from two to three years
1963		B.Ed. degree proposed
1964	Labour Government	
1965		Plans for comprehensive secondary schools End of 11+ selection envisaged
1967		Plowden Report *Children and their primary schools* First B.Ed. degrees awarded

Curriculum content

Religion

Historically the state was pre-empted by churches in providing popular education. In the late seventeenth century, a new constitutional monarchy had been formally established in the 'Glorious Revolution', when parliamentary democracy replaced absolute monarchy in 1688, and a Bill of Rights the following year laid down the rights of Parliament, with regular elections. Just ten years later, members of the Church of England established a Society for Promoting Christian Knowledge (SPCK) to publish and distribute the Book of Common Prayer, and to open the first schools for poor boys and girls. These 'charity schools' flourished and expanded throughout the eighteenth century. Industrialisation and urbanisation posed threats to traditional Christian piety and morality, and to meet the needs of a rapidly expanding population Anglicans and nonconformists promoted systems of 'monitorial schooling' from the early nineteenth century, as a way of teaching large numbers of children the basic literacy skills needed to read sacred scriptures and pious literature. Scotland had a long tradition of parochial schools going back to the seventeenth century, where landed proprietors were obliged to build schoolhouses in every country parish. Ireland had 'hedge schools' in the eighteenth and early nineteenth centuries, peripatetic teachers who gave lessons in the open air or in farm buildings such as barns, especially amongst Roman Catholics who otherwise, under the Penal Laws, had to convert to the Anglican church to receive an education.

The British Government, rooted in the Christian religion, from 1833 began to make small grants of money to support denominational schools in England, Wales and Scotland. In less than fifty years this minimal state intervention led to the building of secular schools intended to supplement provision by the churches. By 1900 the churches were educating 3 million pupils in 14,000 schools, while 2.6 million pupils were taught in 5,700 state schools. The fact that 'voluntary' religious schools continued with public funding alongside state schools was a politically contentious matter that has been bitterly debated ever since, especially in 1902 and again in 1944. In Ireland a system of multi-denomination national schools was established from 1831 where children of all faiths had to be accepted whatever the individual school's religious patronage, and parents had the right to remove their children from periods of religious teaching if it conflicted with their own beliefs. Although we might be tempted to discuss primary schooling in predominantly secular terms, religion has never been far from the centre of its project. In fact it has returned with greater force in recent decades.

The state's partnership with churches in providing schools has continued to the present day, and a political dimension of primary schools continues to be their relationships with religious faiths. Where the established Church of England and the Roman Catholic Church are major providers within the state system, in recent times this dominance has been challenged and other faiths have claimed equal rights and privileges to set up schools with state support. Of the 20,000 or so maintained schools (primary and secondary) in England, almost 7,000 are faith schools, of which nearly 70 per cent are Church of England and 30 per cent Roman Catholic. Just fifty-eight maintained faith schools are associated with non-Christian religions. Jewish schools account for thirty-eight of these. Until 1997 only Christian and Jewish schools could receive state funding, but following a change in the law, there are now approximately eleven Muslim, four Sikh and at least one Hindu school. Provision of faith schools in relation to demand continues to be a highly charged political issue.

Citizenship

'Citizenship' might be seen as a secular reconfiguration of the moral purpose that originally motivated Christian churches to set up schools for the working classes in advance of state provision. Social conditions in the industrial revolution stirred religious society to provide education for the poor, and political threats represented by revolutionary movements in the USA (1776) and France (1789) further heightened the moral panic. At the same time, events in America and France sowed the idea of education as a political right. The radical philosopher Tom Paine stated, in *The Rights of Man* (1791): 'A nation under a well regulated government should allow none to remain uninstructed. It is monarchical and aristocratical government only that requires ignorance for its support' (Conway 1894, vol. II, 490). Writing in defence of the French Revolution, he argued that popular political revolution was permissible when a government failed to safeguard its people, their natural rights, and their national interests. The British North American colonies had won their war for independence and Paine looked to the American model of a written constitution and national assembly as preferable to hereditary rule.

In Britain, representative government developed slowly, but two important electoral reforms in 1832 and 1867, responding to political and social unrest, gradually extended the franchise, and the second of these meant that a limited proportion of working-class men could vote. Just three years later, as the state first moved to 'fill the gaps' left by the denominational provision of elementary schools, its rationale for doing so was to educate the new voters. Here lay the roots of policies that continue today to see schools as a medium for cultivating political stability. Universal compulsory schooling emerged by stages during the 1870s, and as the state began to assume the role of major provider, citizenship or 'civics' remained implicit if not always so explicitly articulated as other curriculum aims. Most recently the promotion of citizenship has featured prominently in educational politics of the twenty-first century.

This secular and civic aim affected the elementary school curriculum directly and indirectly in a variety of ways. There was, for example, a strong temperance movement in the early state elementary schools, aimed at the health and well-being of individuals and of society as a whole. Physical education for all, but especially for boys, was to strengthen military power in defence of the nation. Classes for girls in cooking and laundry were aimed at improving the physical quality of the population. And subsequently the new Liberal Government of 1906 introduced measures for providing school meals and a school medical service, aimed at developing the health and fitness of citizens. Following each of the World Wars, in 1918 and again in 1944, the discourse of educational reform implied a rewarding and reinforcing of loyalty to the nation and commitment to democracy.

Citizenship education, in its attention to rights and duties, reminds us that when compulsory attendance was first enacted, it was resisted by many parents and by political critics as unwarranted interference by the state in individual liberty and family life. The *state's right to enforce* schooling and school attendance as a legal duty was quite rapidly accepted, however, and embedded within cultural norms. A century later compulsory education came to be construed as the unequivocal *duty of the state* to protect a fundamental *human right*, the right to an education, embodied in the 1989 United Nations Convention on the Rights of the Child (UNCRC), a striking contrast between the political contexts of the late nineteenth and twentieth centuries.

Basic skills

Whatever the deeper intentions of personal development, whether as children of God or as citizens of the state, a basic prerequisite of that development was literacy, at least in the most limited sense of learning to read. Reading skills were for acquiring knowledge of established thought, in sacred and secular texts. The skill of writing might seem to follow as a natural development from reading, though writing was often viewed with suspicion for the facility it offered to develop and disseminate alternative and subversive ideas. However, writing was also a skill needed by workers in the burgeoning commercial economy of the mid-nineteenth century, and in the growing ranks of state bureaucracy. So, too, was numeracy. In this way a basic curriculum evolved: 'the three Rs' of reading, writing and arithmetic, and the fourth 'R' of religion.

Though the basic skills of literacy and numeracy were taught and acquired in a religious context for personal salvation, and in the political context for citizenship, they were also intended for employment in industry, commerce and public administration. Britain's industrial revolution entailed rapid development of transport, generated huge growth in banking and insurance, in wholesale and retail trading. Office work and shop work was a major occupational destination for adolescents leaving the elementary schools at the minimum leaving age of 12 by 1899, and 14 after the First World War. (In Scotland, by 1899 most children were already staying at school to age 14.) So, in addition to citizenship, a further justification for universal compulsory schooling was economic. Although in 1870 national economic planning was a thing of the future, universal schooling was certainly directed at equipping a skilled labour force. Economic planning became a trend in the years between the two World Wars, and in the aftermath of the Second World War educational expansion was firmly established as a form of national investment in commerce and industry.

The 1944 Education Act saw the introduction of 'secondary education for all', and with all children moving on to a further stage of education, the task of preparing young people for immediate entry to work was removed from the elementary school, now significantly renamed the 'primary' school. On the other hand, a segregated system of secondary education, with grammar, secondary modern and (a few) technical schools, meant that the process of selection at the age of 11 now became a major preoccupation of primary schools. The 'Eleven Plus exam' would decide the kind of secondary school children were to attend and was therefore a major determinant of their future job prospects, what might now be called 'high-stakes testing', the stakes being on the individual child as much as on the school.

Moreover, responsibility for grounding children in 'basic skills' remained that of the primary teachers. The 'skills agenda' is perhaps the most prominent in current political discourse, and the most politically persuasive in justifying public expenditure on provision of schooling for all. Education, regarded in this light as a form of economic investment, is aimed at producing a supply of labour equipped for employment in the kinds of enterprise that will secure national prosperity for the future. Agriculture now only employs 2 per cent of labour throughout the UK and service industries, including tourism and the financial sector, have eclipsed traditional heavy industries such as coal, steel, shipbuilding and textiles, with newer hi-tech industries such as electronics, telecommunications and pharmaceuticals taking their place. A hugely increased proportion of young people are expected to undertake not just secondary schooling, but also to go on to higher education as preparation for the workforce. With increasing emphasis on economic forecasting, governments anticipate economic developments and plan educational provision in terms of the labour market.

Human resources

Teachers

A universal system of elementary schooling needed an adequate supply of teachers. For the eighteenth-century charity schools and their successors – the Anglican and nonconformist voluntary schools of the nineteenth century, members of the denominational community would provide an obvious source of teachers, the principal qualifications being faith and piety in addition to the basic literacy skills that were to constitute a significant portion of the curriculum content. Ability to manage large numbers of children was also required, but to some extent this was secured through the rigid drills and procedures embodied in 'monitorial schools', established in the early nineteenth century following the inspiration of Andrew Bell (for the Anglicans) and Joseph Lancaster (for the nonconformists). The monitorial system was devised as a way of schooling large numbers of children by means of monitors under the supervision of a single teacher, in the spirit of factory production that was at the heart of the industrial revolution. The teacher would teach children of higher ability, who would then pass on their knowledge and skills to groups of lower ability children, and Joseph Lancaster boasted that in this way 1,000 children were taught by one teacher in his school at Borough Road, Southwark.

Once the state had begun grants-in-aid for denominational schools in 1833, attention turned to teacher training. In 1846, James Kay Shuttleworth, the civil servant responsible for administering the grants, devised a two-tier structure of teacher training. The first tier was a pupil-teacher scheme, an extended apprenticeship for a few of the most able elementary school pupils from the age of 14, under the mentorship of selected headteachers. Their pro-gramme included extending their own personal education as well as assisting the work of teachers, and their progress was monitored by inspectors. By this route they could achieve a basic qualification to teach awarded by the state, or they could enter the Queen's Scholarship examination to compete for entry to the second tier, college training. Colleges were denomi-national institutions but subsidised by government, so that the courses, examinations and qualifications were prescribed and awarded by the state. Churches vetting students for entry to colleges ensured appropriate attitudes and aptitudes. From 1902, LEAs began to set up municipal colleges free of church connections, and in the 1920s and 1930s there were tenta-tive moves to bring all training colleges under the academic supervision of universities. The 1950s saw the development of a more sophisticated teacher training curriculum with increas-ing emphasis on scientific and theoretical principles such as developmental psychology, and teachers' certificate courses were extended from two to three years. In 1963 a report on higher education recommended the introduction of B.Ed. degree courses, beginning in 1967.

Appropriate social class origins were problematic in recruiting teachers for working-class elementary schools. On the one hand it was a low-status job, beneath most middle-class aspirants and perhaps requiring a common cultural background to communicate effectively with working-class pupils. On the other hand, state education administrators sometimes expressed regret that working-class teachers lacked the necessary high culture to civilise their charges. These working-class teachers were in a double bind, working to civilise children of their own social class, but open to criticism for seeking to rise above their station by aspiring to such skilled, non-manual work. As they began to organise within their occupational group in the later Victorian period, trades unions were the favoured form of association, appearing to align them with the skilled working classes. Thus in 1870, the year of the first Education

Act, a National Union of Elementary Teachers was formed, from 1889 renamed the National Union of Teachers (NUT). Though presenting itself as an advocate for education, as well as protecting members' pay and conditions, the implication of a 'trade union' might be that they positioned themselves as antagonists to their paymasters, who were of course the government of the day. Alternative kinds of 'professional association' such as the College of Preceptors founded in 1849 (now known as the College of Teachers) tended to provide for teachers in private schools, and predominantly secondary teachers, both groups seeking to distance themselves from the lower status work of the elementary school teacher.

Teachers constituted a large public sector labour force, and the negotiation of their salaries was highly political. Following the First World War, in 1919 they were generously treated by the establishment of the Burnham Committee to negotiate pay, on which central government was outnumbered by representation from teacher unions and local authority employers combined. Behind this generous treatment lay recognition of the influential role of elementary teachers as educators and 'civilisers' of the working classes, in a period when Britain faced the threat of political unrest. Pay and conditions were to prove a matter for confrontation between governments and teachers at several points over the course of the twentieth century, and a long-term issue was teachers' aspiration to full professional status. Levels of qualification and training rose steadily over time and teaching came to be perceived as a middle-class occupation. But as a numerous body of state employees, teachers have never acquired the independence enjoyed by the more elite established professions of law and medicine.

Teaching quality

Once conspicuous public expenditure was being made on education, quality of teaching came under the political spotlight. Politicians insisted on value for money and governments had to find ways of demonstrating this. The monitorial system had set a precedent for seeking efficiency and economy, but also for systematising teaching skills through formal training in the role. Denominational training colleges, as we have seen, were subsidised by government, and churches selecting students for entry ensured the requisite qualities and disposition. The standardised courses and examinations for certification secured some consistency of teaching method and teaching quality in schools. After gaining the college certificate, teachers were inspected annually by Her Majesty's Inspectors (HMI) for a number of years, and this continuous monitoring of teacher quality could be seen as maintaining standards as well as controlling career progression to ensure staff development and efficient running of large schools.

Following parliamentary concerns over quality and cost-effectiveness of elementary schooling, a Royal Commission (the Newcastle Commission) was appointed to enquire into 'popular education'. A Code of Regulations for elementary schools prescribed curriculum content, and as a result of the Newcastle Report, a system of payment by results was introduced in 1862 under the notorious Revised Code. Pupils were tested in the 'three Rs' during an annual inspection of schools, the results of which determined the level of grant, and therefore the teacher's salary. An inevitable consequence of this system was 'teaching to the test', routinised, mechanical and dull methods of teaching. Payment by results was relaxed in 1895, and with the dawn of a new century the introduction of an official *Handbook of Suggestions* (1905), published by the Board of Education and written by a new breed of enlightened and progressive HMI, encouraged elementary teachers to take more initiative in responding to the needs of their particular children.

The only uniformity of practice that the Board of Education desire . . . is that each teacher shall think for himself, and work out for himself such methods of teaching . . . best suited to the particular needs and conditions of the school.

(Board of Education 1905)

This official trend towards more teacher autonomy in pedagogical matters was reinforced in the 1920s when a revised edition of the *Handbook of Suggestions* in 1927 continued to relax the primary curriculum and laid even more emphasis on teachers working 'with the grain' rather than against it, nurturing self-discipline in pupils more than imposing it. Significantly for the theme of this book, that move towards granting teachers greater responsibility for their teaching can be linked to political circumstances of the time. Labour unrest in the General Strike of 1926 appeared to echo the events of the Russian Revolution that had produced a Communist (Soviet) Government. This threat may have encouraged right-wing politicians in Britain to place more curriculum authority in the hands of teachers than to risk its determination by a future socialist state.

Another factor, often overlooked in the long historical development of primary teaching method, was schools' broadcasting. This arguably had political significance. The new media of radio, and later TV, were organised by the state as a form of public service under the BBC, nominally independent of government but subjected to careful supervision. Its educational potential was evident from the start and radio broadcasts for schools were developed from the late 1920s, but its impact can be viewed in different ways. On the one hand, progressive primary teachers and educationists broadcasting through schools' radio produced imaginative and creative lessons, extending the curriculum and providing valuable professional development for teachers. On the other hand, it signalled a tendency towards national standards for primary teaching methods. The historical example of school broadcasting and its contradictory effects anticipates the way information technology in the modern era has provided opportunities for individual creativity by teachers and at the same time facilitated centralised control through government websites and Teachers TV (relaunched as SchoolsWorld online service in May 2011).

Provision and administration

Finance

Finance is clearly a central aspect of the politics of schooling. In 1833, when elementary education began to be seen as being in the state's interest, the cheapest and most convenient solution was to support the voluntary agencies (churches) already making provision. So the principle of 'grant-in-aid' from central government's exchequer was established, matching voluntary effort with government subsidy. Costs grew rapidly as schools expanded, and within twenty-five years politicians began to question the value of this expenditure. Parliament ordered a Royal Commission in 1858 to examine the effectiveness of education thus supported, launching a concern about 'value for money' that has permeated political discourse on education ever since. An immediate solution was devised in the principle of payment by results, described above. It was promised that 'if it is not cheap, it shall be efficient, if it is not efficient, it shall be cheap'. Schools could claim 4 shillings (20p) per year for each pupil with a satisfactory attendance record, and an additional 8 shillings (40p) was paid if the pupil passed examinations in reading, writing and arithmetic.

Following the Newcastle Report, it also became evident that the number of schools pro-vided by the churches was inadequate to meet the growing demand for education. Local government was at that time emerging in the towns and cities as a provider of public services such as roads and policing, so an alternative possibility of funding schools was identified in the form of local taxation. The 1870 Education Act provided for locally elected School Boards to identify the gaps left by provision in their own areas and make them good by building, maintaining and staffing additional elementary schools. School Boards in England and Wales could also impose compulsory attendance between the ages of 5 and 10. The 1872 Education Act in Scotland went further by providing universal compulsion from ages 5 to 13. In 1880 a new Education Act for England and Wales made compulsory elementary schooling universal. By the 1902 Act, School Boards were replaced by LEAs, which carried on the responsibility for funding both municipal and denominational schools in their area, through a combination of central government funds and local revenue. In an increasingly secular society, the state subsidy to church schools was hotly contested at that time and at subsequent points during the twentieth century. The funding of faith schools by the state is still a controversial issue with educational and political implications.

By the late 1960s national spending on education reached a notable turning point as it began for the first time to outstrip the national defence budget. Various formulae were adopted for sharing the cost between central and local government. The ultimate source of both national and local funds is the taxes that electors pay, and over the course of the twentieth century electors became more vocal about the ways in which their money was spent, so the total quantum of educational funding and its effectiveness became a cause of popular political contention. Within the education system, a finer point of detail also contested was the proportion of funds allotted to the primary sector as distinct from secondary schooling, further and higher education, reflecting different perceptions of the relative importance of each sector and its relative contribution to the national good.

Control and accountability

'Who pays the piper, calls the tune' is an old adage expressing a conventional expectation. The principle that control follows funding appears simple enough, but in practice the finance and regulation of public services is highly complex. The first administrative body for state education in the mid-nineteenth century was a committee of the Queen's Privy Council, the Committee of Council on Education. This nominally implied an element of independence from the elected government of the day, though in effect the Committee of Council acted as a department of government. These were early years in the evolution of a state administra-tion that was to grow rapidly over the mid-nineteenth century, and the bureaucratic struc-ture was still quite small. The secretary appointed to this committee, in effect the first senior civil servant responsible for education, was a medical doctor by the name of James Kay Shuttleworth, already known for his research and advocacy of education as a means to the improvement of public health. He was highly committed, energetic and imaginative.

Several years after the first grants to schools, an inspectorate (HMI) was established in 1839, to ensure value for money first and foremost in the church school buildings that were erected with public funds. With the introduction of publicly funded teacher training in 1846, the inspectors' remit expanded to monitoring the quality of teachers and their work in the schools. The title of 'Her Majesty's Inspectors' carried some suggestion of independence from party political control. That feature was to become important in the early and mid-twentieth century, but crucially abandoned in the 1990s.

As elected School Boards grew and raised further funds from local taxation they became responsible for administering their local schools. Scotland, starting from its strong base of parochial schools, had 980 School Boards, one in every parish and burgh. School Boards in large cities became powerful bodies and a struggle for control between national and local government began to emerge. This struggle was epitomised in a legal challenge to the London School Board from central government over its offering adult education in evening classes, allegedly exceeding its authority to provide *elementary* education (defined as exclusively for *children*). A celebrated court judgment found in the Government's favour, leading to a statutory overhaul of the system in the 1902 Education Act. From 1902, the numerous School Boards (more than 2,500) were replaced by about 300 LEAs in the interests of efficiency. These were much larger bodies, in effect subcommittees of the County and Borough Councils that had grown with responsibility for providing a range of local services, of which education was now just one. In Scotland this transition was made rather later, in 1918.

Over the course of a century there thus developed a structure in which local government was mainly responsible for the governance and development of 'maintained' schools, but shared the governance with churches for 'voluntary aided' or 'voluntary controlled' schools in its area. By the early 1960s the UK was covered by two-tier administrations, based on counties and a mixture of sub-administrations including municipal boroughs, county boroughs, rural districts and urban districts. The education service was administered by the higher tier of local government.

Government of education includes distributing funds and specifying how the funds are to be used. Mechanisms of monitoring, accountability and inspection are introduced to ensure that political intentions for education are realised. Between the national and local levels these functions have sometimes overlapped in the past and led to conflict. National and local governments may often be dominated by opposing political parties. Even within a single party there may be ideological differences, as well as differences of perspective about national needs and local needs. A historic example cited previously was the London School Board, wanting to provide evening classes for adults, against the national government's narrower definition of elementary education. More recently a notable and long-running conflict between centre and localities arose over the policy of comprehensive reorganisation, abolition of grammar and secondary modern schools and their replacement by non-selective secondary schools, which affected primary teachers in relation to 'Eleven Plus' selection and the way it dominated curriculum and teaching methods in the last two years of primary education. Some LEAs conflicted with the Labour Government's 1965 policy of non-selective comprehensive secondary education, affecting the speed and completeness of this change and its unevenness in many localities. In effect, two levels of political control came to be exercised, one national and one local and often in conflict. In the closing decades of the twentieth century, with the major source of funding being the nation state, central government exerted increasing control over the character and quality of education provided by LEAs.

Conclusion

This chapter has offered a long historical perspective as an overview of how political and cultural change affects primary education. Long-term evolution of policy results from large-scale social, economic and cultural change. History allows us to compare long-term trends and short-term policy changes, and to speculate about the operation of cause and effect and processes of change and continuity over time. In recent decades education policy has responded to ongoing change in demography, family structure and lifestyle as well as to economic fluctuations and their impact on manufacturing, trade and employment. In the shorter term, our attention turns to the policies of single parties and individual governments, and in the following chapters primary education will be examined within that political framework. From the Labour Governments of 1964–70 and 1974–79 punctuated by a Conservative administration from 1970 to 1974, across the eighteen years of Conservative rule under the leadership of Margaret Thatcher and John Major, through thirteen years of New Labour Governments from 1997 and a Conservative–Liberal Democrat coalition installed in 2010, both continuity and change can be traced in national policies.

Key questions for reflection

- In what ways is a primary teacher's work political?
- Taking any single aspect such as curriculum, human resources or provision and administration, what political debates do you identify in the present and how do these reflect situations inherited from the past?
- Compare the effects of political, economic and cultural changes on primary education in your own experience as a pupil and as a teacher.

Independent learning tasks

Adopt any one of the above questions as a focus for personal research, and/or the basis for discussion with colleagues.

Analyse your own school, making notes on some of its political dimensions: the work it does, its relationships with nation state and the local community, and your own roles and responsibilities within it. A framework for analysis could prepare for reading this book by using its structure: curriculum (Chapters 3 and 4); pedagogy (Chapter 5); workforce (Chapter 6); and accountability (Chapters 7 and 8). Select one category for reflection, perhaps using questions as prompts.

Curriculum: What is political in curriculum content, in the knowledge and values presented for children to learn? What aspects of the knowledge and values might be politically controversial? What recent policy developments have raised issues about the content or organisation of the curriculum?

Pedagogy: What political implications arise in the way learning and teaching is organised for individual children and groups of children within your classroom, across the school and extending into the community? How does government policy influence the way you teach and the way children learn? Does class size or the balance of whole class teaching to individual work and small group work reflect political decisions? What views do parents express (if any) about the way their children learn, and do these views reflect public debates and political controversies in the media?

Are teaching methods viewed simply in relation to the effectiveness of children's learning, or do they arise from decisions about resourcing, or from ideological positions about discipline and order?

Workforce: What different roles are involved in supporting children's learning? What kinds of training and qualifications are required for different roles and how is this affected by government policy? What career structures are available to different personnel and how do concepts of professionalism, skill and autonomy apply? How far is management and decision-making determined by national policy?

Accountability: How is the school's responsibility to the state and to its community exercised? To whom are teachers accountable and how is that accountability implemented? How is the school monitored and evaluated and to what extent are these processes 'politicised'? Are there political tensions in how a school responds to the needs of parents, carers and families of children, to local government and to national government?

The chapters of this book are intended as a prompt to continue reflecting on first-hand experiences, the different schools you've known, and the policy changes you've experienced.

Further reading

Alexander, R. (2000) *Culture and Pedagogy: International Comparisons in Primary Education*, Oxford: Blackwell.
Chapter 6 (120–153) gives a detailed description of the origins and development of elementary and primary education in England, its cultural context, mechanisms of government control, and distinctive legacies and identities.

Chitty, C. (1992) 'The changing role of the state in educational provision', *History of Education*, 21, 1: 1–13.
A succinct analysis from a Marxist perspective, bringing various historians' accounts of the long history of state intervention in Britain to bear on an understanding of the politics of education in the later twentieth century.

Crick, B. (2002) *Democracy: A very short introduction*, Oxford: Oxford University Press.
A democratic socialist interpretation, Chapter 6 (91–103) discusses the conditions of modern democracy to include individual liberties, human rights, economic progress and social justice; Chapter 7 (104–120) examines rights and duties in democratic citizenship, contrasting radical republicanism and liberal democracy.

Cunningham, P. (2002a) 'Primary education', in R. Aldrich (ed.) *A Century of Education*, London: Falmer, 9–30.
An account of the way in which primary education acquired high visibility in educational policy-making in the twentieth century, including factors such as demographics, health, technology and tension between teachers and the state.

Gearon, L. (ed.) (2002) *Education in the United Kingdom*, London: David Fulton.
Chapters 1–4 describe school structures and organisation in England, Northern Ireland, Scotland and Wales respectively, providing a helpful overview of policy and provision for any one of the four constituent countries of the UK.

Minogue, K. (2000) *Politics: A very short introduction*, Oxford: Oxford Univesity Press.
A libertarian conservative view of politics, Chapter 6 (41–48) examines the origins of the modern body politic; Chapter 9 (68–75) discusses political parties and their doctrines; and Chapter 12 (91–98) distinguishes ideology from politics seen as a means of reconciling conflicting interests and beliefs.

Chapter 3

Curriculum: the politics of subject knowledge

The four main purposes of the National Curriculum

To establish an entitlement
The National Curriculum secures for all pupils, irrespective of social background, culture, race, gender, differences in ability and disabilities, an entitlement to a number of areas of learning and to develop knowledge, understanding, skills and attitudes necessary for their self-fulfilment and development as active and responsible citizens.

To establish standards
The National Curriculum makes expectations for learning and attainment explicit to pupils, parents, teachers, governors, employers and the public, and establishes national standards for the performance of all pupils in the subjects it includes. These standards can be used to set targets for improvement, measure progress towards those targets, and monitor and compare performance between individuals, groups and schools.

To promote continuity and coherence
The National Curriculum contributes to a coherent national framework that promotes curriculum continuity and is sufficiently flexible to ensure progression in pupils' learning. It facilitates the transition of pupils between schools and phases of education and provides a foundation for lifelong learning.

To promote public understanding
The National Curriculum increases public understanding of, and confidence in, the work of schools and in the learning and achievements resulting from compulsory education. It provides a common basis for discussion of educational issues among lay and professional groups, including pupils, parents, teachers, governors and employers.

(QCDA National Curriculum website)

The mistake we have made in recent years is that there has been a tendency for Ministers, when something comes up, to think that we can impose new regulation through the National Curriculum. . . . This constant changing of the curriculum . . . is politicisation in the negative sense, as opposed to the positive sense that politicians should have a say on what goes on in our schools.

(David Hargreaves, evidence to HCCSFC 2009)

Introduction

Primary teaching is an awesome political responsibility and the curriculum is the means we have to carry it out. The curriculum offered to young children is critical in developing their understanding of themselves as individuals and as members of their society, in forming their views of the world and their values. Along the scale of curriculum objectives, at one end is personal fulfilment and at the other the entire nation has a stake in the curriculum's contribution to generating a stable political order.

This chapter begins by discussing what is inherently political about curriculum, and why it has become so *politicised*. It then takes two sets of contrasting conceptions that characterise political discourse, the first about the *purposes* of a curriculum in the context of universal and compulsory primary schooling: should it aim mainly at personal fulfilment, the development of a well-rounded and harmonious individual, or should its main focus be on preparation for economic activity in the world of work? The second set relates to curriculum *structure*: should it comprise a hierarchy of traditional disciplines, or a more holistic pursuit of understanding through an interdisciplinary approach? With regard to purposes and to structure, these sets of alternatives tend to polarise opinion along political lines. Finally, the chapter looks at how these kinds of curricular debates have played out in recent political history.

What is political about curriculum?

For everyday use in primary school, the word 'curriculum' is specific and relatively unproblematic. Curriculum is contained in a set of published documents bearing the authority of the government of the day and lays out in considerable detail the range of subject knowledge to be taught to children between the ages of 5 and 11. Clear and comprehensible, it is structured in progressive stages. The Early Years Foundation Stage (EYFS) runs from birth through to the end of the Reception year, but is not formally part of the National Curriculum. Key Stages 1 and 2 are described by means of conventional and recognisable 'subjects', and these subjects are classified as 'core' (English, maths and science) or 'foundation' (the rest), a two-tier distinction reinforced by the introduction of highly prescriptive numeracy and literacy strategies.

Underpinning these specifications are explicit values and purposes, set out on the National Curriculum website:

> Education influences and reflects the values of society, and the kind of society we want to be. It is important, therefore, to recognise a broad set of common values and purposes that underpin the school curriculum and the work of schools.

> Foremost is a belief in education, at home and at school, as a route to the spiritual, moral, social, cultural, physical and mental development, and thus the well-being, of the individual. Education is also a route to equality of opportunity for all, a healthy and just democracy, a productive economy, and sustainable development. Education should reflect the enduring values that contribute to these ends. These include valuing ourselves, our families and other relationships, the wider groups to which we belong, the diversity in our society and the environment in which we live. Education should also reaffirm our commitment to the virtues of truth, justice, honesty, trust and a sense of duty.

> At the same time, education must enable us to respond positively to the opportunities and challenges of the rapidly changing world in which we live and work. In particular,

we need to be prepared to engage as individuals, parents, workers and citizens with economic, social and cultural change, including the continued globalisation of the economy and society, with new work and leisure patterns and with the rapid expansion of communication technologies.

(QCDA 2010)

This comprehensive and positive statement is an ideal to be welcomed. Its concern with the society in which we live is inevitably political. Consensus about 'the kind of society we want to be' or a 'broad set of common values' cannot be assumed, and politics works, as Crick has explained, to negotiate between conflicting ideologies. Individual well-being takes many forms that can be accommodated by a liberal and tolerant society, but legal protections and institutional structures have been slow to take account of changing cultural practices, so that many individuals encounter specific disadvantage or prejudice in the conduct of their lives. Equality, productivity and sustainability are all relative concepts, the application of which, in practice, reflect relations of power. For all the opportunities of globalisation, communication technologies and leisure, obstacles include structural unemployment resulting from mismatch in the labour market and factors such as age, gender, location and skill that are beyond individual control, with or without the aid of education. These are all political realities that we have to confront, even in the earliest years of schooling.

There is, then, a wide political, economic and cultural context to the curriculum. Adults can draw on their own experiences as former pupils to recognise immediately that 'curriculum' in practice extends well beyond the formal, prescribed curriculum. Reflecting on our individual experiences of primary school reveals that we learned as much from our relationships and everyday exchanges with other children and with teachers and support staff as we did in formal lessons. Some of our sharpest childhood memories may be of 'breaks' and playtimes, of the games we played with our peers and the places where we played them. These, we know, were as formative as formal teaching. Our knowledge, understanding and attitudes will have been heavily influenced by the ethos of the school and by its physical environment. This recognition suggests that there is also a local politics of curriculum to be considered. Even the National Curriculum website describes the relationship between national and local as follows:

> The school curriculum comprises all learning *and other experiences* that each school plans for its pupils. The National Curriculum is an important *element of* the school curriculum [my emphasis].

(QCDA 2010)

As an official description of the curriculum, this description of aims and values might be regarded as an example of Minogue's 'political illusions' (Chapter 2), for undoubtedly the prescribed curriculum has been far more dominant and narrowing in its effect on the life of primary schools than merely an 'important element' as officially stated. The main concern of this chapter will be national political debates about curriculum and the impact of public curriculum discourse on the work of primary teachers.

In the research literature, we find definitions of curriculum that attempt to encapsulate its breadth and complexity:

> Curriculum is a socio-historical construction which is expressed through general systems of knowledge characterization and hierarchy; these systems are in turn translated and

transformed into legislative and administrative regulations, academic achievement standards, textbooks and teaching aids, and the practice of teaching and learning in class-rooms and schools.

(Gilbert 2010, 510)

Writers on curriculum in practice have taken the term to embrace also pedagogy and assess-ment, or at least to recognise that these three distinct elements of the process of schooling are closely interconnected. For the purposes of this book, in order to distinguish the aspects of political ideology and strategy that inform pedagogy and assessment, we return to these in Chapter 5 and again in Chapter 7 under the heading of accountability. In the present chapter it is the 'socio-historical construction' of 'systems of knowledge' and their hierarchies, 'trans-formed into legislative and administrative regulations' that occupies our attention.

Here and now, confining ourselves to a consideration of 'subject knowledge', we should enquire how the formal curriculum structure and content becomes political. Any prescribed curriculum in a state system of education will, by definition, be political, but as governments have come to 'micro-manage' primary school teaching, so the politics of subject knowledge has been starkly evident. The school curriculum may be seen as having political implications in the way it determines relationships among individuals, institutions and the nation-state through establishing a status hierarchy of knowledge and skills, and through publicly grading children according to their levels of success in acquiring these. Values such as inclusiveness, excellence, quality and entitlement are subject to different interpretations and emphases with considerable scope for debate.

In broad terms, education for personal fulfilment and education for employment might be identified as competing paradigms, each with political implications. Sorting curriculum content into specific categories, we might identify a humanistic conception of liberal educa-tion that values knowledge and understanding for its own sake, with a range of subject matter to foster self-understanding and moral agency. Contrasting with that, though often over-lapping in specific content, might be curriculum subjects with potential vocational relevance for the individual, including life skills and economic relevance for the wider society. Areas of learning designed to specifically promote citizenship, health and welfare, with their very specific political aims, will be left for more detailed consideration in the next chapter.

The school curriculum remains a site of competing influences. Chapter 2 revealed a histori-cal succession of interest groups such as churches, political parties, a social and intellectual elite represented by state bureaucrats and educational administrators. That list of interest groups can be extended to include the universities who receive as students a proportion of the highest academic achievers from schools, employers who look to the education system to provide a labour force equipped with appropriate skills and attitudes, trades unions and professional bodies representing the interests of different groups of workers, and teachers' organisations with their interests in the feasibility of curriculum requirements. All these have definable vested interests in the curriculum. Beyond these institutional groups are the parents and carers who have hopes and expectations for their own children. Their interests, as well as those of many of the wider groupings mentioned, may be represented by one or more of the think tanks and pressure groups that cohere around a variety of ideological and political positions to express opinion and exert influence on curriculum development.

Purpose: personal development or vocational preparation?

The creation in 1944 of a primary sector for children aged 5 to 11, with progression to secondary school for all, relieved what had previously been the elementary schools' task of preparing children for immediate entry to the world of work. This new freedom allowed for a more 'child-centred' approach, informed by the research of developmental psychologists such as Jean Piaget over the previous twenty years. The developmental needs of the young child became the dominant focus for the primary curriculum and vocational education could be left to the secondary schools. By the mid-1960s, the Plowden Report on *Children and their Primary Schools* gave a powerful endorsement to this emphasis in what became its most quoted and best-known statement: 'At the heart of the educational process lies the child' (DES 1967).

That simple statement seemed obvious enough to many teachers and parents. The Plowden Committee was appointed in the final years of a post-war political consensus, with general agreement on the need for expanding education and improving its quality. The Report was commissioned by a Conservative Minister of Education in 1963 and received just three years later by a Labour Secretary of State for Education and Science. It was not long, however, before its approach to curriculum came under challenge from both right and left, in heated terms that will be discussed later (Halsey and Sylva 1987). Before embarking on a narrative of political events, some political implications of these polarised positions on curriculum need to be examined.

As we have seen, as early as 1791 Tom Paine identified education as a human right, and this right was echoed 200 years later in the United Nations Convention on the Rights of the Child (UNCRC). The UNCRC as a universal charter should be seen as fundamental to the politics of curriculum. Children's rights cover a range of entitlements to protection, health and welfare, and some of these impinge directly on the work of the school, specifying, in effect, the kind of experience that the school should provide. A fundamental right elaborated in the convention is one of personal fulfilment. Article 28 enshrines the right to education: 'All children and young people have a right to a primary education. . . . Young people should be encouraged to reach the highest level of education they are capable of.' The character of that education is developed in Article 29: 'Education should develop each child's *personality* and *talents* to the full' (my emphasis). This then is the goal of self-fulfilment, a supranational statement of right, regardless of any national government's drive to provide schooling for employability. The case for personal fulfilment as a pre-eminent curriculum aim can be elaborated in political, psychological and other ways, but is made here in the context of the government's obligations under this international convention on children's rights.

Article 29 continues by encouraging children to respect their parents, and their own and other cultures. The universal right to primary schooling is therefore seen as a platform to progression through education for personal fulfilment and for cultural understanding. That aim is reinforced by one of the most basic requirements (Article 3), stating that: 'All organisations concerned with children should work towards what is best for each child.' This wide-ranging entitlement clearly puts the child and her or his own interests at the heart of education and welfare provided by government. The political reality is that this supra-national obligation imposes duties on a national government that may well exceed its own political inclinations. Though almost all nations have endorsed the Charter after its agreement by the United Nations in 1989, commentators continue to identify how governments, including those of wealthier nations, fall short of fulfilling its requirements. The UN Committee last examined the UK Government in 2008 and levelled criticisms in several respects to be noted later (UNCRC 2008).

As so often in educational policy and practice, rights extended to minorities are helpful in indicating the extent of the state's obligations to all children. Thus, the UNCRC recognises that children who have any kind of disability should have special care and support so that they can lead full and independent lives (Article 23), a case where treatment of special needs shows the way for treatment of all children. Similarly, respect for the individual is embedded in a specific right for neglected or abused children to receive special help in restoring their self-respect (Article 39). Article 30 respects the child's own culture by asserting a right to learn and use the language and customs of their families, whether these are shared by the majority of people in the country or not.

Finally, with regard to the school curriculum, Article 31 takes the state's obligations well beyond the process of formal teaching and learning, in that all children have entitlement to relax and play and to join in a wide range of activities. One finding of the UNCRC Report of 2008 was that in the UK, with the sole exception of Wales, the right to play and leisure was not fully enjoyed by all children, especially due to poor play infrastructures and notably for children with disabilities. While this right may be fulfilled beyond the boundaries of the school, it can also be taken to suggest that within a system of compulsory schooling, relaxation and play has a significant role. In the primary school, our traditional terminology of 'break' or 'recess' still reveals its functional origins, in a timetable designed for maintaining control, curbing inattention or disruption by enabling children to exercise their pent-up energy or 'let off steam' outside the classroom. In fact the playground or schoolyard was often little more than a bare, contained space to allow this to happen. But as teachers and psychologists began to understand the formative value of play, especially in the primary years of a child's development, so play became more central to the curriculum and facilities for social and constructive play were provided. Only recently have children begun to be consulted about the kinds of play facilities they wanted. The political implications of school providing play are important, as 'play' often features in public discourse about education, when a 'progressive' advocacy of happiness and enjoyment at schools, or even 'learning through play', has been traduced by 'traditionalists' who see this emphasis as somehow antithetical to the hard work and discipline required for 'real' learning.

Personal fulfilment and vocational preparation are by no means mutually exclusive. Fulfilment, satisfaction and enjoyment will, in the majority of cases, eventually include some form of paid employment. It might be argued that to distinguish rigidly between personal development and preparation for the world of work is artificial, and certainly these two objectives can be reconciled within a broad and balanced curriculum. However, the intense focus by New Labour on literacy and numeracy strategies, and the pressure on primary schools to drive up standards to meet national targets, led to a serious and widely recognised loss of breadth and balance at Key Stages 1 and 2 (Brehony 2005). Schools were permitted to cut back on subjects such as art, PE and music. Research revealed how these creative subjects were being squeezed, with up to half of the school week being spent on English and maths, and even modes of creativity such as ICT enquiry, problem-solving and practical work were suffering. Employers, who had been vocal about the need for improvement in the 'basic skills' of school leavers, were now also emphatic about the need to cultivate creativity in preparation for an entrepreneurial world of employment.

Structure: subject centred or integrated?

Bernard Crick described politics as conservative, insofar as it seeks the minimum benefits of established order as against a quest for deliberate change. It is an observation that applies to curriculum change. Extension of elementary education to all working-class children was dominated at first by skills and knowledge to make them more employable in an era of rapid economic change. But there was also the important aim of preserving an established political order. This latter aim meant inducting children into an established culture, a culture conservatively defined in a curriculum that had evolved originally for the education of the upper and middle classes who held political power. Their 'public school' curriculum was rooted in language and mathematics, and focused on the classical civilisations of Greece and Rome, a curriculum that became highly conservative, dedicated to the preservation of the past. The status acquired by classical learning encouraged looking to the past rather than to the future.

Although a diet of classical learning was not considered appropriate for working-class children, as the elementary curriculum began to broaden, a more enlightened and liberal view was encouraged by a few HMI, notably the poet Matthew Arnold. Arnold argued for 'culture' as knowing the best that has been said and thought in the world. So a humanities curriculum for elementary schools began to emerge in the early twentieth century defined in terms of literature, along with history, geography and aspects of the natural sciences. Science additionally had its utilitarian applications with 'object lessons' that explained industrial processes, 'domestic science' taught girls with housewifery and mothercraft in mind, while history and geography carried commercial and nationalist relevance at the height of Britain's imperial age. Thus, for cultural and vocational purposes, a structure of discrete subjects or disciplines was firmly embedded as a way of organising curriculum. State secondary or 'grammar' schools were established in the 'public school' mould, and an 'educational ladder' was made available in the form of competitive scholarships from the elementary to the secondary school for a select few to progress, a narrow path to university or the professions. Curriculum organisation might therefore also have been biased to some extent to favour the needs of the academically most able, rather than the majority who would leave elementary school for immediate employment.

An alternative view of curriculum structure was gradually accepted in the two decades following the Second World War. Attention turned to teaching through topics or themes rather than through discrete subjects. The integrated approach had been advocated by educational philosopher John Dewey and other progressive educationists for forty years or more, but insights from developmental psychologists such as Jean Piaget about young children's learning gave it renewed authority in primary education. There followed in secondary schools during the post-war decades advocacy of a more integrated curriculum that would encourage the young school leaver to adopt an enquiring and critical interest in the world they were about to enter as adults, requiring a more thematic approach that crossed conventional subject boundaries.

In favour of integration was the value for children of applying their skills to 'real' problems, taking an interest in their local environment, drawing on first-hand evidence, seeing relationships between different methods of enquiry and experiencing opportunities for collaboration. Teachers might generate enthusiasm and focus where they had particular interests and knowledge, and scope was opened up for collaborative team teaching, where a group of teachers might contribute their individual interests and expertise to a thematic investigation. Curriculum structure, as we saw earlier with curriculum content and aims, tends again to polarise attitudes along a political spectrum. On the right, a 'traditionalist' or 'conservative' view is that a body of knowledge defined by time-honoured subjects should articulate the curriculum. Towards the left or 'progressive' end of the spectrum the view is that traditional subjects are arbitrary concepts, that careful integration of subject matter through topics related to children's lives and to the world around them will encourage them to see meaning and relevance in curriculum knowledge, and to motivate their learning through interest.

Curriculum politics from Plowden to Rose

Advice, lobbying and micro-management

Chapter 2 observed how the politics of primary curriculum was rooted in a longer historical setting. More recent history, bearing directly on current political and curricular debates, must begin with the Plowden Report of 1967. Following two post-war decades when the new secondary schooling dominated the political stage, primary education stepped into the limelight through a report from the Central Advisory Council for Education (CACE) in England chaired by Bridget Plowden. With extensive media coverage, it generated political weight and even a good deal of consensus around improving the school experience of younger children. Plowden did much to raise popular consciousness of primary curriculum and pedagogy (Halsey and Sylva 1987; Cunningham 1988, 2007).

Plowden was an exclusively English report. An Advisory Council Report in 1946, heavily influenced by the teachers' organisation, the Educational Institute of Scotland (EIS), and followed twenty years later by a 'Primary Memorandum' issued by the Scottish Education Department in 1965, put Scotland in advance of England in advocating a child-centred primary curriculum. The cultural and political tensions underlying this are subtly explored by Paterson (2003, 109–116). In Wales, a touchstone of devolution was the Gittins Report on Primary Education, quite separate from but parallel to Plowden. It shared common threads with Plowden in correlating educational attainment with social background, and stressing that primary schools and the primary curriculum played an important role in compensating for social deprivation, but it also made political claims in advocating Welsh language as an essential part of the curriculum (Jones and Roderick 2003). The Plowden Report however attracted widespread international interest.

A key feature in Plowden's representation of primary schooling was the implied independence of teachers and schools in constructing the curriculum. This relative freedom from political control was evident too in the work of the Schools Council for Curriculum and Examinations. Established about the same time as the Plowden Report, the Schools Council reflected the power of organised teachers to resist early attempts by departmental civil servants to intervene in curriculum reform. The Schools Council provided a forum for curriculum development and innovation led by teachers rather than by government administrators, and though much of its work was initially concerned with the secondary curriculum, during the 1970s it went on to promote important primary developments, for example, in communication skills, drama, religious education, integrated geography and history, as well as conducting innovative research into primary teachers' aims. Separate concerns of Wales were recognised in the establishment of a powerful and widely representative Schools Council committee, hailed as being 'a parliament for education in Wales' (Evans 1985, 94).

The progressive and child-centred approaches advocated by Plowden aroused controversy, and heated debates ensued, fuelled especially by a notorious series of 'Black Papers' on education, ensuring a high profile for the primary sector. In these controversies, educationists and professional practitioners engaged publicly with politicians, and political alignments began to colour the educational debate. Popular interest in education aroused by the Black Papers was reflected in the relatively new phenomenon of think tanks and pressure groups. A prominent early example was the Centre for Policy Studies, founded in 1974 by Conservatives Sir Keith Joseph and Margaret Thatcher to champion economic liberalism. Margaret Thatcher had been Secretary of State for Education 1970 to 1974 and Keith Joseph was to take responsibility for education in her Cabinet during the years 1981 to 1986. The Centre for Policy Studies promoted the case for small, less intrusive government with greater freedom and responsibility for individuals.

Other think tanks campaigning and publishing influentially on educational issues include the right-wing Politeia, a 'forum for social and economic thinking about the role of the state in individual lives' and the non-partisan and classic liberal Civitas. Left of centre are Demos, the 'new economics foundation' (nef) which challenges mainstream thinking on social, environmental and economic issues and proclaims its interest to be 'economics as if people and the planet mattered'. These groups are mentioned in various contexts elsewhere in this book. Interest groups with particular concerns in social policy can be traced back to the early formation of political parties, such as the socialist Fabian Society founded in 1884, predating the Labour Party itself and continuing today as a major left of centre think tank. New groups formed from the 1970s onwards were characterised by research and publication on aspects of social and economic policy and by the publicity they generated for their ideas through media coverage. Research conducted and published by these bodies introduced a new dimension to political and educational discourse; ostensibly independent of government, many were ideologically driven, often associating themselves with a political party. Think tanks also drew on academic research that might support their arguments, so that the inevitable contradictory findings and disagreements between academic researchers began to find their way into partisan debates on education. This state of affairs represents a continuing difficulty for the ways that educational research may inform policy making at the present time, as we shall consider below.

When Keith Joseph was appointed Secretary of State, among his first acts was to abolish the CACE, the body that had produced the Plowden Report, which had come to symbolise progressivism in educational policy as well as an expanding role for the state in education. This abolition was a symbolic act, as too was Joseph's termination of the Schools Council, which had stood for professional control of curriculum development. In 1981, in response to public curriculum debate, the Schools Council had published *The Practical Curriculum*, advocating a child-centred, active and relevant curriculum, including the observation that teachers had too often emphasised 'the content of subjects instead of their importance as ways of experiencing and knowing the real world' (Schools Council for Curriculum and Examinations 1981, 19). The ineluctable drive of government policy towards a national curriculum was nevertheless acknowledged in one of its last publications, *Primary Practice* (Schools Council for Curriculum and Examinations 1983). These Schools Council 'working papers' represent the last independent discussion documents on the primary curriculum before legislation for a national curriculum. Following its abolition it was replaced by a new body, the School Curriculum Development Committee (SCDC), constituted to be much more closely under government control.

A deliberate shift in curriculum policy had been marked by the Department of Education and Science (DES) at the outset of the new Conservative Government in 1979 under Margaret Thatcher. The Department published a guidance document entitled *The School Curriculum*

(DES 1981) which opened with a tendentious paraphrase of Plowden's celebrated statement. It stated that 'The school curriculum is at the heart of education' and went on to add a further deliberate emphasis that appears to place national over individual need: 'Since school education prepares the child for adult life, the way in which the school helps him to develop his potential must also be related to his subsequent needs and responsibilities as an active member of our society' (DES 1981, 3). From here onwards it was clear that curriculum would be specifically a matter for central government, and if this appeared contradictory with the general political direction of diminishing the role of the state, it would be argued that education was seen as principally concerned with national economic success, far too important to be left to the schools, teachers or educationists.

The aims of education had been defined by statute in the 1944 Education Act as 'To promote the spiritual, moral, mental and physical development of *the community*' (my emphasis). Almost half a century later, the 1988 Education Reform Act and successive Acts have added 'social' and 'cultural' development to the list, these additions reflecting a growth of social scientific understanding over the intervening decades, as well as the greatly increased cultural diversity that has also marked British society over that period of time. But this statutory educational aim is now explicitly targeted only at *pupils* rather than at the community as a whole, and is supplemented by the aim to 'prepare all pupils for the opportunities, responsibilities and experiences of life'.

A radical break with tradition in the 1988 Act was its specification of a National Curriculum. The state was now to determine what would be taught in schools, a political practice that had been previously shunned for its association with totalitarian regimes of Nazi Germany and the Soviet Union. It also appeared contradictory alongside more neo-liberal policies aimed at reducing the role of the state and introducing more scope for individual choice. It was decided that the curriculum should progress in four key stages, as a seamless experience from the age of 5 to 16. This was in sharp contrast to the notion that had prevailed from 1944 of primary education as a distinct phase, focused on development of the young child, a phase that was distant from entry into the labour market. But with the new 5–16 structure, as Brehony has observed, preparation for employment has become a key determinant of the primary curriculum in recent years (Brehony 2005). The hallmark of this National Curriculum was its definition in terms of traditional subjects, a specifically neo-Conservative agenda. Conventional subjects, however, left evident gaps in a curriculum for the modern world, which the National Curriculum Council (NCC) then attempted to fill by non-statutory cross-curricular themes such as economic and industrial understanding, environmental education, citizenship and health education.

In Scotland, a National Committee on Primary Education had, in 1983, proposed a balance of subjects and also a balance of 'skills, activities, social experiences'. When the National Curriculum was introduced there, it was described emolliently as 'guidelines'. The relative autonomy of the policy process in Scotland allowed modification of the Westminster Government's approach in ways that would be acceptable to Scottish teachers and parents, conforming to at least a partial child centredness in Scottish educational culture (Paterson 2003). Under the 1988 Act, Wales was granted its own Curriculum Council (known as ACCAC, the acronym of its Welsh title), but it seemed from a Welsh perspective that the welcome new principle of a minimum entitlement curriculum for all children was overshadowed by the emphasis on state control (Jones and Roderick 2003).

The Education Reform Act brought education policy to the centre of political contention. It constituted the flagship of party policy following a general election in 1987 that saw the

Conservative Party under Margaret Thatcher win its third continuous term of office. Secretary of State Kenneth Baker associated himself personally with the legislation that crowned his career in politics. Subsequent Secretaries of State sought to emulate him by putting their personal stamp on education policy. Kenneth Clarke acceded to the post in 1990, when continuing debate about standards of primary education led him to commission a report on *Curriculum Organisation and Classroom Practice*. All three authors of the report, Robin Alexander, Jim Rose and Chris Woodhead, dubbed the 'three wise men', continued to play influential roles in educational politics, and the report's observations on curriculum deserve citing here for the unresolved tensions they revealed.

> The vast majority of primary schools organise the curriculum in terms of subjects and topic work. A topic is generally understood to be a mode of curriculum organisation, frequently enquiry based, which brings elements of different subjects together under a common theme. A small minority of schools organise the whole of the curriculum in terms of separate subjects; virtually no primary school works solely through topics. HMI report that about 30 per cent of work in primary schools is taught as single subjects. Music, physical education, most mathematics and some English are usually taught as separate subjects. The other foundation subjects are very often taught, entirely or largely, as aspects of topic work.
>
> (Alexander, Rose and Woodhead 1992, paragraph 62)

> If it can be shown that the topic approach allows the pupil both to make acceptable progress within the different subjects of the National Curriculum and to explore the relationships between them, then the case for such an approach is strong on both pedagogic and logistical grounds. If, however, the result is that the differences between subjects are extinguished, then the strategy is indefensible.
>
> (Alexander, Rose and Woodhead 1992, paragraph 67)

So, contrary to media caricature and political invective against primary schools for their allegedly progressive practice, subject work was still much in evidence (30 per cent). To the 'three wise men', topic work was acceptable, but only as long as it wasn't seen to hinder progress in the subjects. The passions aroused in such debates, especially on the political right, are reflected in the pamphleteering conducted by such think tanks and pressure groups as the Centre for Policy Studies and Politeia. Alarmist and prolific authors on education in the later 1980s and early 1990s included Sheila Lawlor, Anthony O'Hear and Martin Turner on topics such as curriculum, pedagogy and teacher training. Secretary of State Kenneth Clarke publicly derided the work of early twentieth-century American educational philosopher John Dewey who had advocated topic work around 'centres of interest'; since Clarke displayed little personal interest in philosophy (and only a limited understanding of education), his likely source was a Centre for Policy Studies pamphlet by the outspoken right-wing philosopher Anthony O'Hear.

By 1992 the National Curriculum, together with its complex system of assessment, was recognisably overloaded and over the next decade attempts were made to reform its content and format. Following Clarke, a beleaguered Secretary of State, John Patten, facing widespread professional and parental dissatisfaction with curriculum and testing, commissioned Sir Ron Dearing, a businessman, to undertake a curriculum review. Dearing's report slimmed down the curriculum, to be implemented from 1995. Critics from the right, such as Sheila

Lawlor, Director of the think tank Politeia, accused him of giving in to the demands of teachers who complained of overwork and over-rigid structures, but teacher unions accused him of not going far enough. Certainly, a number of independent studies in the wake of Dearing established clearly that curriculum overload had not been resolved by his proposals (Wyse, McCreery and Torrance 2010). A School Curriculum and Assessment Authority (SCAA) was formed, with Dearing at its head, to replace the National Curriculum Council.

Dearing also recommended a five-year moratorium on any further change, but within two years of implementing the revised curriculum, and following a change of government, New Labour's introduction of literacy and numeracy strategies created fresh pressures. To allow schools to concentrate more on the targets for literacy and numeracy, government announced temporary deregulation of the Programmes of Study for foundation subjects at Key Stages 1 and 2. This action served to reinforce the distinction between 'core' and 'foundation' subjects that had been a contentious feature of the National Curriculum from the outset, implying inferior status for areas of knowledge and skills outside of English, maths and science.

Change of government from Conservative to New Labour took place in 1997 and substantial revision was undertaken in 1999 under a new Qualifications and Curriculum Authority (QCA) (this body had been formed in the last year of the previous government to replace the SCAA). Schools, teachers and parents might have been understandably bewildered by increasingly frequent reorganisations of the curriculum and its administrative bodies for apparently short-term political objectives. However, by 1999, just ten years after its birth, the revised National Curriculum included for the first time an overt statement of aims and purposes, those appearing at the beginning of this chapter. Self-fulfilment is mentioned, but overwhelmingly the purposes concern themselves with the system, with standards, continuity, coherence and public confidence in the work of schools. At about the same time a curriculum for the early years began to be evolved with official guidance from 2002, and in 2008 the Early Years Foundation Stage (EYFS) emerged as a statutory framework for children from birth to age 5, despite the glaring anomaly that these babies and toddlers remained below the age of compulsory schooling (Drummond 2010).

Evidence from school inspections, and from research studies separately commissioned by the QCA and by the NUT, began to reveal pressures on the primary curriculum and concern for the damage to breadth and balance, given the amount of time taken up by the drive to raise standards in English and mathematics and by the national tests. The observation that enquiry, problem-solving and practical work were suffering, along with other evidence of a decline in creative activities such as art, drama, music and even in ICT, caused the Government to set up an internal committee to review the curriculum. Brehony noted the top-down nature of this review, illustrated by the absence of any teachers as members of the committee (Brehony 2005, 36). This protracted sequence of enquiries and attempts at fine adjustments to curriculum balance led to professional disillusionment with micro-management of the school curriculum by government. Until 2010 in England, the Department retained responsibility for strategic management of the National Curriculum, while development and support was delegated to the QCA, in turn reconstituted as the Qualifications and Curriculum Development Authority (QCDA) in 2009, the closure of which was announced following the change of government in 2010.

Reviews and politics

Politicisation of the curriculum gave rise to three reviews between 2006 and 2009, instructive for the varying degrees of political independence they claimed and displayed. One review was conducted by a team of university-based educational researchers, the second commissioned by government and led by a retired civil servant, and the third was a cross-party parliamentary enquiry.

An independent review of primary education, on a scale to match that of the Plowden Report, was announced in 2006 under the direction of Robin Alexander, Professor of Education at Cambridge. Alexander had researched and written extensively on curriculum and pedagogy, had engaged for twenty years with professionals and politicians and had been one of the 'three wise men' of 1992. The Cambridge Primary Review was a direct challenge to ever-tighter control by government, taking stock of the many policy changes over the previous two decades, and reclaiming a voice for educational researchers and professionals, for parents and children, independent of the government of the day. In this spirit the review collected data and opinions from 'consumers' as well as 'producers', removed from an overtly party-political context. It sought evidence in a variety of forms: an open call for 'submissions' of opinion; an extended series of 'soundings' or face-to-face discussions with children, parents and community representatives as well as teachers and headteachers; reviews of existing research; and surveys of available data, including international comparative data. Its interpretation of the evidence aimed to be balanced and non-partisan, while subjecting to scrutiny current assumptions, policies and conventional wisdom.

Rattled, as subsequent testimony has revealed, by substantial media coverage of the Cambridge Review, in December 2007 Secretary of State Ed Balls invited Sir Jim Rose to pre-empt the exercise by undertaking a 'root and branch' review of the primary curriculum, the first such review to be conducted since 1998. Announced as an 'independent' review, it was in fact highly circumscribed in its remit. The Department for Children, Schools and Families (DCSF) went to great lengths to present Rose as an 'independent expert' and to describe the working practices of his team who spent several months gathering evidence. They drew on the views of over 1,000 parents, nearly 2,000 teachers, took into account the views of 5,000 primary pupils, visited 57 nursery, primary and secondary schools and compared primary schools in England with others in Europe, Asia and around the world. They looked at the latest research, consulted experts and made surveys to make sure that their aims and key findings were supported by teachers and parents. Their review responded to evidence from teachers that the curriculum was too prescribed and that any new curriculum would need to be much more flexible to enable teachers to tailor lessons for individual children and classes. Christopher Schenk has knowledgeably described the timing and press manipulation involved as ministers and civil servants tried to gain advantage and discredit the Cambridge Review, but Schenk also regrets the failure of the Cambridge team to draw constructively on Rose's work (Schenk 2010).

The Cambridge Review called for the reinstatement, after years of attrition, of children's entitlement to a broad and balanced primary curriculum, proposing a new framework of twelve core aims and eight domains of knowledge, skill and enquiry (Alexander 2010). It hoped to abandon the politically inspired antithesis of 'standards' and 'breadth', arguing for the highest possible standard to be aimed at across a broad curriculum. Thus it called for re-integration of 'literacy skills' with a rich English curriculum, and 'numeracy' with the full range of mathematics, and removing the artificial distinction of 'core' and 'foundation' subjects in young children's education. It argued for modification of the *national* curriculum to allow schools and communities to respond to *local* needs and opportunities. Turning its conclusions into recommendations for the General Election of 2010, the Review urged political parties and parliamentary candidates to replace curriculum tinkering with curriculum reform, an entitlement curriculum based on clear and explicit aims, to achieve breadth, richness and contemporary relevance, to secure the 'basics' and much more besides, combining a national framework with a strong local component. The Cambridge Report published in 2009 was broadly welcomed by many teachers, schools and educationists for its thorough and properly independent stance, though not without its critics in the academic community who identified some weaknesses and flaws (Campbell 2010; Drummond 2010).

A complication in the interface between academic enquiry on the one hand and policy-making on the other rests, as noted earlier, in contradictory research findings; politicians, often in pursuit of simple and unequivocal answers to justify policies founded on ideological principles, financial contingency or political opportunism, are frequently impatient of the necessarily complex and provisional conclusions of social research. Governments with short-term agendas and conscious of their public image are tempted to discredit professionals or academics as self-interested or remote from the real world. Ministers and their advisers engage in media spin and a 'discourse of derision'. A press release from the DCSF on 16 October 2009, in response to the Cambridge Review, was terse and defensive. It rejected the findings outright, making no pretence of having studied it in any detail. The DCSF also apparently aimed at distancing primary teachers from the Cambridge Review by praising the outstanding quality of teaching and leadership currently seen in schools (with a whiff of hypocrisy, given teachers had so often been the target of official criticism). The government's main political concern was reflected in its description of the Cambridge recommendations as woolly and unclear on how schools should be accountable to the public.

The final report of the Rose Review acknowledged the Cambridge enquiry but proceeded on its own, more limited evidence. It defended the continuing importance of subjects, and the essential knowledge, skills and understanding they represent, as 'vital' but not 'sufficient'. Subjects would now therefore be complemented by worthwhile and challenging cross-curricular studies providing opportunity for children to use and apply their subject knowledge and skills to deepen understanding. Other recommendations emphasised achievement in literacy and numeracy by age 7 and the introduction of modern foreign languages at Key Stage 2. Thus Rose sought to reconcile 'traditional subjects' with 'broad areas of learning', by defining six areas of learning such as 'understanding English, communication and languages', and 'understanding physical development, health and well-being'. Rose also acknowledged that the curriculum must continually evolve but that some stability was also needed, and therefore proposed a five-yearly review, to prevent continual ad hoc changes.

The Rose Review, like the Cambridge Review, had a fairly positive reception from teachers, insofar as both recommended more flexibility in the curriculum and more scope for teachers' own initiatives. Rose had the natural advantage in this respect of official backing and likely implementation. On the basis of Rose's recommendations, the Labour Government in its last year of office accepted the review and claimed to be putting in place 'the most fundamental reforms for decades following Sir Jim Rose's primary review – to make the curriculum less prescriptive and free it up for teachers', a claim both wildly exaggerated and historically flawed. A new primary curriculum was announced for implementation in 2011 and was positively welcomed by primary schools as a significant prospect of improvement.

The QCDA issued documentation and materials from which schools began planning, often with energy and enthusiasm, but all that work was rendered null and void only eight months later as the new Coalition Government announced that the Rose recommendations for the 2011 primary curriculum would be scrapped and a new curriculum review was to be begun.

Meanwhile, the House of Commons Children, Schools and Families Committee (HCCSFC) had decided in 2009 to examine the working of the National Curriculum on the twentieth anniversary of its introduction. This all-party select committee (from the advent of the Coalition Government in May 2010 re-titled the House of Commons Education Committee) was appointed to monitor the work of a department of state. At that time the Committee had access to Rose's interim report, but were unconvinced by his proposals, which seemed to them unnecessarily complex. Yet they were also disappointed that the Cambridge report, despite its extensive analysis of the problems, did not say enough about what might be done in practice to address them. The Committee's view was that the main purpose of a National Curriculum was to set out clearly and simply a minimum statutory entitlement for every child. They were concerned that in its current form it now accounted for all available teaching time and they argued for a cap to be placed on the proportion of the curriculum prescribed centrally. They saw the need for a slimmed-down National Curriculum designed much more from the learner's perspective, setting out the learning to which children and young people were entitled 'to enable them to operate as effective citizens'. They proposed also that parents should be encouraged and supported to take a greater role in overseeing the curriculum experienced by their child.

The Committee criticised the level of central prescription and direction that had occurred under New Labour and identified a risk that ongoing reform of the curriculum continually demanded more and more time, for example, for modern foreign languages at Key Stage 2. The benign intention of encouraging schools to link the formal curriculum with out-of-school life, and children's activities beyond and outside school, in fact generated considerable overload, and this kind of objection came from both the left and right of the political spectrum. In England, the level of political interference in the curriculum had been striking and the continual meddling by ministers was a target for criticism. The Committee concluded that ad hoc changes and additions to the National Curriculum had often stemmed from Ministerial priorities, and while they accepted the principle of democratic control implied, they objected to the intensity of political interference it revealed as damaging to continuity and coherence in children's learning and to teacher professionalism (see Hargreaves' evidence quoted at the beginning of this chapter). They recommended instead a regular cycle of about five years for curriculum review and reform, avoiding additional change outside the cycle, and stated that the agency responsible for curriculum development would carry more authority if it were truly independent from the Department. The Committee also observed that despite official advocacy of pupil voice in schools, nowhere had the government particularly concerned itself with how the curriculum was experienced by children and young people.

These cross-party calls for reducing politicisation of curriculum development were not heeded with the change of government in 2010. In a mood of party political posturing, and notwithstanding the extensive work already invested by schools and teachers in preparing for the new curriculum, the Coalition Government announced its rejection of the Rose Review. It intended to return the National Curriculum to a minimum national entitlement organised around subject disciplines. Ministers wanted 'to ensure every child has a firm grasp of the basics and a good grounding in general knowledge', though also 'to give teachers more flexibility than that offered by the proposed new primary curriculum' (DFE 2010). A new

Curriculum Review was started from scratch with an advisory committee of political appointees supported by an 'expert panel' of educationists, holding out a promise to loosen the constraints of the national strategies.

Conclusion

Long-term change in curriculum is a continuous historical process, a product of cultural and economic change, as described in Chapter 2. Here the focus has been on policies and the role of politics over recent decades. From this account we can summarise the case for and against state control of the primary curriculum. In justification we can see that public expenditure has to be well targeted and to serve the nation's democratically determined needs, and in the evolution of policy we can frequently observe the necessary process of compromise outlined by Bernard Crick. On the other side of the balance sheet, we have seen the influence of political pressure groups that may be far from representative of children and parents, promoting policies based on ideology rather than on educational understanding and objective research. We have seen increasing manipulation for short-term political purposes, including the passionate commitment of some education ministers to ideologies that may not reflect a broad consensus even of their own parties, or individual ministers making a mark for their own political careers. The media also play a significant role in modern politics, and the short-term view encourages knee-jerk responses to headline news such as a single year's test results or international league tables. Governments' manipulation of the media in the process of curriculum reform vividly illustrates the political theatre of illusions described by Kenneth Minogue. These factors encourage discontinuity and instability, exacerbated by political attempts at micro-management of the nation's and children's education. Fears of totalitarianism that only fifty years ago deterred governments from close involvement in curriculum have been easily forgotten.

Policies and curriculum are both products of economic and cultural conditions; politics is a medium of cultural change as well as a mechanism, an expression of prevailing culture as well as a means of realising or imposing curriculum reform. Culture includes the technology and media through which children acquire knowledge, skills and attitudes both within and beyond the formal curriculum, while politics determines specific agenda that teachers must manage in school. Hence the importance of remaining reflective and critical about the curriculum that we teach, habits of reflection and critique that we hope, through the curriculum, to develop also in young pupils. A fundamental principle at stake concerns the balance between facilitating personal fulfilment and equipping the child for economic self-sufficiency. We seek a curriculum of 'breadth and balance' to encourage creativity and enjoyment of learning as well as providing useful knowledge, but the rationale and arguments about how this may be achieved are inevitably part of a wider political discourse.

Key questions for reflection

- Within a national curriculum, what are the political implications of including some subjects and excluding others, the relative weighting of different subjects especially 'core' and 'foundation', and the stipulation of 'cross-curricular' themes?
- How are current policy statements regarding the aims and purposes of primary education reflected in the organisation of the curriculum in school?

- What freedoms and initiatives do governors and staff exert in designing the school curriculum? How is the curriculum explained to parents with respect to national requirements and local considerations?

Independent learning tasks

Adopt any one of the above questions as a focus for personal research, and/or the basis for discussion with colleagues.

List the most significant aspects of the curriculum that have affected you in your experience as a pupil and a teacher. Map these onto the political history of the period; include changes of government and individual Secretaries of State if possible. What aspects of continuity and change can you identify in this sequence?

Further reading

Campbell, R.J. (2001a) 'The colonisation of the primary curriculum', in Phillips, R. and Furlong, J. (eds) *Education Reform and the State: Twenty years of politics, policy and practice*, London: Routledge, 31–44.

Campbell reviews government intervention in primary curriculum as a process of colonisation in three phases. Adopting a balanced view of the need for state intervention and a measure of teacher autonomy, he concludes by observing a continuing authoritarian emphasis on basic skills and on a social and moral curriculum.

Jones, G.E. and Roderick, G.W. (2003) *A History of Education in Wales*, Cardiff: University of Wales Press.

Chapters 7 (173–197) and 8 (198–233) include a valuable account of distinctively Welsh policy developments in curriculum and other aspects, and also a critical view of English educational policy from a Welsh perspective. Jones and Roderick review the effects of the Gittins Report on primary schools in a primary curriculum for Wales, as well as debate over teaching of the Welsh language, the National Curriculum and its adaptation, arguing for the creation of a statutory curriculum unique to Wales as an educational achievement comparable with political devolution.

Paterson, L. (2003) *Scottish Education in the Twentieth Century*, Edinburgh: Edinburgh University Press.

Chapter 7 (109–127) provides a case study of the politicisation of primary curriculum through an account of Scottish developments in their cultural and political context. It argues the extent and limits of child-centredness in Scotland as deep-seated individualism gave the appearance of freedom but overlaid by a professional concern to socialise children for adulthood.

Simon, B. (1991) *Education and the Social Order 1940–1990*, London: Lawrence and Wishart.

Chapter 7 (342–387) reviews primary curriculum and pedagogy in the years before and after the Plowden Report in their political and ideological context, questioning the myth and reality of a 'Plowden revolution'. Appendices also include a useful list of governments and Secretaries of State throughout the period.

Wyse, D., McCreery, E. and Torrance, H. (2010) 'The Trajectory and Impact of National Reform: Curriculum and assessment in English primary schools', in Alexander, R. (ed.) *The Cambridge Primary Review Research Surveys*, London: Routledge, 792–817.

This survey reviews key empirical studies of primary school teaching and learning pre- and post-National Curriculum, with particular attention to observational studies of classroom life and pupil experience, assessing the impact of political policies.

Chapter 4

Curriculum: the politics of citizenship, health and well-being

[W]e aim . . . for people to think of themselves as active citizens, willing, able and equipped to have an influence in public life and with the critical capacities to weigh evidence before speaking and acting . . . [and] to extend radically to young people the best in existing traditions of community involvement and public service.

(QCA 1998, 7)

Citizenship does not necessarily require a deep love of country; it requires minimally a commitment to the polity (Parekh 2000). It is policy and legislative frameworks designed to promote greater social justice and remove barriers to full participative citizenship which will allow individuals to develop affective ties to the nation. Efforts by nation-states to promote national identity and affinity through education, in response to perceived threats, risk unintended outcomes, provoke concerns about propaganda and threaten, rather than secure, social cohesion and democratic participation.

(Osler and Starkey 2010, 119)

Policy and practice around emotional well-being is promoted enthusiastically by over 70 organisations . . . the therapeutic turn in education promoted by these interest groups has a powerful popular cultural and public resonance. . . . One outcome is an unchallenged orthodoxy that children and young people want a personally relevant, 'engaging' education where adults and peers listen and affirm them. [This] diminished view of the human subject intensifies a deeper political and philosophical attack on a view that humans can be active agents who want to find ways to control their world.

(Ecclestone and Hayes 2009, 385, 372)

Introduction

Chapter 3 raised the political implications of personal fulfilment and employability as curriculum objectives. A more explicitly political objective is citizenship. Education for 'responsible' use of the vote had been a principal reason for the introduction of state schooling, following extension of the franchise, in the newly emerging democracy of Victorian Britain. This constituted a minimal conception of citizenship, defined in T.H. Marshall's (1950) threefold classification as 'political citizenship', to which he added 'civil' citizenship, defined as abiding by the law, and 'social' citizenship, which he thought of as active participation in the community.

The introduction of a minimum standard of schooling necessary for the proper exercise of political citizenship was soon followed in late Victorian Britain by the requirement of physical fitness, since the nation depended on military might to maintain its great empire. Health education was not simply a matter of philanthropy but also the product of social Darwinism, and a sense that territorial and economic competition between industrialising nations would result in 'survival of the fittest'. The sacrifices of the First World War led to promises of a 'land fit for heroes', implying that military success depended not just on technical supremacy but also on the fitness and well-being of our conscript soldiers. Recurrence of total war from 1939 to 1945 reinforced this coupling of citizenship and health as the nation fought to defend itself against invasion and to defend democracy against totalitarianism. National defence relied on conscription but also on commitment to political liberty, and the 'people's war' was fought on the home front, as well as in active combat. Despite apprehension that citizenship in the curriculum might smack of the political indoctrination practised by fascist and communist regimes, post-war educational reconstruction meant imbuing children with a sense of national identity, democratic values, law-abiding behaviour and participation in civic life.

In the later twentieth century, political, social and cultural change generated new contexts for citizenship and health education. Devolution for Scotland and Wales challenged the unitary notion of British identity and the growth of Europe as a political entity compromised traditional ideas of national sovereignty. Geographical mobility and migration loosened local allegiances and an increasingly multi-ethnic population diversified the meanings of Britishness. Family structures became more flexible, and consumerism and leisure produced changes in lifestyle with health implications, for example, obesity and drug abuse. Perceptions of increasing antisocial behaviour saw schools being partly blamed for a declining respect for law and order, but simultaneously expected to provide solutions. Voter apathy was a growing problem in the later twentieth century, with diminishing participation in national and local elections, and again it was anticipated that the school curriculum might contribute to checking this trend.

Citizenship with its extensive implications requires curriculum to be considered in a wider sense than in Chapter 3, embracing not just the formal content of teaching and learning but also the organisation and ethos of the school, power relationships and how they are managed, and pupils' participation in decision-making. This chapter will discuss local and global citizenship, religion, health and well-being within the formal and informal curriculum.

Citizenship in the primary curriculum

The citizenship curriculum goes back many years as a concern of politicians and educationists. An Association for Education in Citizenship was formed in the 1930s, reflecting concerns about the growth of communism and fascism, and during the Second World War all sorts of civic activities in schools contributed to the war effort, a war fought for national survival and for the defence of democracy. Elementary and primary school children collected salvage, to be recycled in the manufacture of essential goods reducing dependence on imports, as well as salvage of metal for the construction of tanks and planes. A National Savings scheme operated in schools. Books and games were collected to send to the armed forces and to civilian refugees. Vegetables were grown in school gardens for self-sufficiency. National and community consciousness was raised in this way through the curriculum.

A sense of 'cosmopolitan citizenship' was also embedded in special events such as 'Aid to China Week' and 'Aid to Russia Week'.

Victory in war, for all its tensions and problems, bequeathed a sense of national superiority. Victory for democracy reinforced a concept of Britain as the 'mother of parliaments'. Britain is also a monarchy however, the 'United Kingdom', and the young Queen Elizabeth II was crowned soon after the war, in 1953. The coronation, performed by the Archbishop of Canterbury in Westminster Abbey, was a vivid symbol of Britain's Christian cultural heritage. Prominent at the coronation were representatives of the commonwealth, a reminder of Britain's role as a world power, her heritage of worldwide economic and cultural ties and a strong sense of duty to economically developing countries. Whilst these national identities were absorbed through the press, through radio and through the new medium of television, they were also conveyed to children at school through curriculum activities and extra-curricular celebrations.

The title 'citizen' evolved to describe membership of a republic, where the more precise designation of British children living under a monarchy is 'subjects'. This dilemma may help to explain a preference for a softer form of 'citizenship' rather than any explicit mention of politics on the curriculum. Post-war education for citizenship was concerned with character, and with the 'foundations of a healthy democratic society' (evoking an association between political order and physical health) by encouraging in pupils 'the old and simple virtues of humility, service and respect', an emphasis on preparing pupils to be citizens with duties rather than rights.

The Plowden Report of 1967 offered a view of teaching primary school children as a wider social service involving the whole community, and its advocacy of school involvement in the community could be seen as promoting social or participative citizenship. Plowden's broad summary of the Aims of Primary Education included:

> All schools reflect the views of society, or of some section of society, about the way children should be brought up, whether or not these views are consciously held or defined. . . . Our society is in a state of transition and there is controversy about the relative rights of society and the individual.
>
> (DES 1967, paragraph 493)

> We can fear that [society in the future] will be much engrossed with the pursuit of material wealth, too hostile to minorities, too dominated by mass opinion and too uncertain of its values.
>
> (DES 1967, paragraph 495)

> For such a society, children, and the adults they will become, will need . . . to be able to live with their fellows, appreciating and respecting their differences, understanding and sympathising with their feelings. They will need the power of discrimination and, when necessary, to be able to withstand mass pressures. They will need to be well-balanced, with neither emotions nor intellect giving ground to each other. . . . They will need to understand that in a democratic society each individual has obligations to the community, as well as rights within it.
>
> (DES 1967, paragraph 496)

Twenty years after the Plowden Report there was growing concern about political apathy amongst young people, resulting in a House of Commons Speaker's Commission on

Encouraging Citizenship. As the new National Curriculum had been constructed from traditional subjects, there was an evident need for filling gaps by cross-curricular themes, two of which were Citizenship Education and Health Education. Others were Environmental Education, Economic and Industrial Understanding and Careers Education and Guidance, themes that were acknowledged to be interrelated and sharing common features such as the discussion of values and beliefs, encouraging practical activities, decision-making and strengthening the bond between the individual and the community. The cross-curricular themes however only ever had low status and restricted time allowed to them, compared with the statutory core and foundation subjects, all of which were new and occupied the energies of teachers in the early 1990s.

Curriculum guidance for citizenship education was issued by the National Curriculum Council in 1990, introduced as follows:

> Education for citizenship is essential for every pupil. It helps each of them to understand the duties, responsibilities and rights of every citizen and promotes concern for the values by which a civilised society is identified – justice, democracy, respect for the rule of law.

> Education for citizenship embraces both responsibilities and rights in the present and preparation for citizenship in adult life. It helps pupils by supporting them as they develop from dependent children into independent young people. It is of paramount importance in a democratic society and in a world undergoing rapid change. Schools must lay the foundations for positive, participative citizenship in two important ways: (i) by helping them to acquire and understand essential information; (ii) by providing them with opportunities and incentives to participate in all aspects of school life.
>
> (NCC 1990b, 1)

Education for citizenship, it was argued, promotes the personal and social development of pupils, encouraging them to develop caring attitudes and the motivation to participate in events happening in the world about them. So the theme of active participation emerged and the ethos of a school could do much to support this. An important role was envisaged for parents, governors, members of the community, religious groups, voluntary bodies, local and national government, local services, industry, commerce and many others, emphasising the place of the school in the community.

With the accession to government of New Labour in 1997 came the commissioning of the Crick Report. Worried by political disengagement amongst young people, David Blunkett, Secretary of State for Education, appointed his former politics tutor, Bernard Crick, to lead an advisory group to report on citizenship education. Its terms of reference echoed T.H. Marshall's triad of political, civil and social: 'To provide advice on effective education for citizenship in schools – to include the nature and practices of participation in democracy; the duties, responsibilities and rights of individuals as citizens; and the value to individuals and society of community activity.' A primary sub-group, including experienced teachers, was formed to consider Key Stages 1 and 2. Models of citizenship education from other countries, notably the Republic of Ireland, Scotland and Australia, were drawn on, as well as initiatives and activities in individual schools and LEAs supported by a number of citizenship bodies and community-based organisations. Britain was one of the last parliamentary democracies in the world lacking a formal citizenship curriculum and in September 1998 the

Crick Report recommended citizenship education as a statutory National Curriculum subject for secondary schools, and to comprise a component of (non-statutory) PSHE in primary education. Requirements were written flexibly to avoid direct government control in such a sensitive area and also to allow for schools to respond to their *local* context (QCA 1998).

Citizenship in the curriculum is riddled with dilemmas, integral to the topic itself and contingent on an ever-changing political context. Understanding democracy must include a critical view of democratic deficits in the current practice of national and local politics, for example. Crick's report raised the responsibilities and problems for teachers in teaching controversial issues, in seeking balance, fairness and objectivity. The Education Act 1996 had legislated against bias in teaching of political or controversial issues, requiring schools and LEAs to forbid the promotion of partisan political views in teaching. School governors and headteachers were charged with ensuring that children are offered a balanced presentation of opposing views on political or controversial issues. Teachers therefore require extreme skill and sensitivity in dealing with controversial issues, which may often leave them vulnerable to misinterpretation. In the first decade of the twenty-first century, the citizenship agenda was formulated and re-formulated in an insistent search for remedies to social and political crises.

Local and global citizenship

Citizenship education seen as a project for reinforcing 'national' identity faces the challenge that it takes place in a European and a global context. A notable feature of globalisation is the ever-increasing migration of people around the world, so globalism may well have a significant local presence for primary schools. The Crick Report acknowledged the long-standing political, cultural and religious diversity of British society and stressed the need for tolerance by a majority population. But critics observed that Crick presented democracy as a completed project, rather than as an ongoing struggle, where race, gender and other inequalities persist. Crick's overwhelming emphasis was on the nation-state with only a passing acknowledgement of European institutions, international human rights and the wider global community.

After the London bombings of 7 July 2005, senior government figures provoked public debate about 'British values'. Concerns about violent extremism and security were added to the list of reasons for teaching citizenship in schools, and the Department for Education and Skills (DFES) commissioned an inquiry chaired by a former headteacher, Sir Keith Ajegbo. Ajegbo's Report (DFES 2007) proposed a new fourth strand to the citizenship curriculum: 'identity and diversity', to include critical thinking about ethnicity, religion and 'race' with an explicit link to political issues and values, thus extending the framework of Crick. Ajegbo noted improvements in attitudes over the past sixty years, but saw society as constantly presenting new perceptions and challenges. It became the duty of all schools to address issues of 'how we live together' and 'dealing with difference', however controversial and difficult they might sometimes appear. Schools, through their ethos, curriculum and work with their communities, could make a difference to those perceptions. Teachers needed appropriate resources and training to give them the confidence to achieve this, and the Report found school leaders placing a low priority on education for diversity, insufficiently heeding pupils' voice on experiences of racism. Audrey Osler nevertheless considered that the Ajegbo Report largely avoided critical examination of the roots of this racism (Osler 2009).

Osler and Starkey have argued that a political emphasis on the evolution of British democracy in citizenship education, inspired by the threat of terrorism, avoids confronting barriers that continue to inhibit democracy such as inequalities and racism. Though policy documents celebrate ethnic diversity, they neglect to address power relationships or differential access to rights and services that have affected social groups in forms of gender, disability or racial discrimination. Osler and Starkey observe that democratic citizenship is usually conceived as *national* citizenship, with citizenship education programmes typically focused on citizens' supposed natural affinity to the nation-state. Government and politicians tend to oversimplify nationality in this way, where teachers, in close touch with their pupils and their community, know differently. Governmental bodies most commonly conceive of citizenship as a status, synonymous with British nationality, but the nationalities of pupils in British classrooms vary widely, including many foreign nationals or children of dual nationality. An alternative conception of the status of all individuals as holders of human rights would be much more inclusive (Osler and Starkey 2010).

Citizenship can be defined as a sense of belonging, requiring more than legal status. It requires social and psychological security, protection against discrimination and a sense of acceptance by others within the community. Citizenship should also be a form of engagement with others to shape the community, most commonly in the immediate locality. Beyond the local, however, this practical engagement might operate at different levels within the UK, in the devolved governmental regions of Wales, Scotland and Northern Ireland, and a further level of identity is available in European citizenship and belonging. There are also issues that generate a sense of global community, such as trade, development and disaster relief.

An alternative concept of 'cosmopolitan citizenship' recognises that many young people have flexible and shifting identities rather than identifying primarily with the nation-state. At local, national, regional and global levels, education for cosmopolitan citizenship responds to the realities of learning to live together and develop a dialogue with those whose perspectives are different from our own. Osler and Starkey argue that citizenship education should take the form of a school's serious attention to human rights in actively working for the dignity of all individuals, respecting diversity and difference, as a source of creativity and strength (Osler and Starkey 2010).

Forty years ago the Plowden Report recognised that:

> A school is not merely a teaching shop, it must transmit values and attitudes. It is a community in which children learn to live first and foremost as children and not as future adults. . . . A child brought up in such an atmosphere at all stages of his education has some hope of becoming a balanced and mature adult and of being able to live in, to contribute to, and to look critically at the society of which he forms a part.
>
> (DES 1967, paragraph 505)

Remedies for recurrent social and political crises are to be looked for less in the formal curriculum than in the organisation and ethos of the whole school. A tentative proposal by Crick was the setting up of Community Forums to include parents, police, teachers and young people. Opportunities were to be made for teaching about citizenship both within and outside the formal curriculum and the development of personal and social skills through projects linking schools and the community, volunteering and the involvement of pupils in developing school rules and policies.

This firm belief in volunteering and community involvement as necessary conditions of civil society and democracy was one of the Crick Report's key principles, and preparation for these should be an explicit part of education. The Report argued that freedom and full citizenship in the political arena depended on a society with a rich variety of non-political associations and voluntary groups described collectively as 'civil society'. That requirement continues to be of key significance from 2010 as the new Coalition Government attempts to shift emphasis away from state welfare provision and towards community and individual responsibility.

Both Crick and Ajegbo gave examples of primary school citizenship projects. Crick's selection included effective pupil councils with free exchange of ideas and opinions that in one case reduced bullying and exclusions. Pupils' engagement with school community and local community led to liaison with local councils including a project to improve a local park. One primary school linked with schools in twinned European towns and another compiled a live news service through the internet with thoughtful and questioning analysis of news stories. Examples reported by Ajegbo exploited the potential of languages at Key Stages 1 and 2 for involving pupils in different cultures, drawing on partnership with parents in learning community languages.

The non-statutory status of citizenship guidelines published in 2002 for primary pupils, by contrast with a *statutory* citizenship curriculum in secondary schools, may have reflected doubts about the interest or relevance that younger children would see in political issues. Research evidence exists, however, for primary-age children's engagement with political concerns. Paul Warwick investigated the perceptions of pupils aged 8 to 11. His focus was children's awareness of and perspectives on their local communities and on wider global issues (Warwick 2007a). The most common issues for children at a local level were community relations, environmental problems and crime and violence, though they also concerned themselves with threats of terrorism locally, transport problems, lack of amenities and health risks. Globally their chief concerns were war and terrorism, environmental problems and crime and violence, followed by social problems, hunger and poverty, animal cruelty and diseases. Major sources of information they reported were TV and news (35 per cent), family (16 per cent) and radio (9 per cent). Teachers and schools as a source of information scored only 5 per cent (sixth out of ten, and just ahead of 'friends and gossip'), offering a sharp reminder that formal education is probably not the principal source of political education. Most significant for the primary curriculum is perhaps the view expressed by children so young that responses of policy-makers were inadequate, a youthful scepticism feeding the adult political disenchantment that citizenship education is intended to allay.

Religion and citizenship

Neither politics nor citizenship education can ignore religion. Chapter 2 recalled the historical origins of state intervention in supporting church initiatives that promoted not only basic skills but also law-abiding dispositions and behaviour. A long-drawn-out and passionate debate ensued about the nature and limits of religious education to be provided in state-funded schools. Our legacy is the so-called 'dual system' of schooling that continues to rely on substantial input by churches, especially in the primary sector (Lankshear 2002; Arthur 2002; Halstead 2002). With successive government policies seeking to 'privatise' the education service, there is renewed debate about the appropriate role of faith schools in the provision of public education. In post-war Britain it was mainly Church of England and Roman Catholic schools that were state funded, with some assistance to Jewish schools. Legislation in the 1980s and 1990s secured continuance of state-funded faith schools and the early twenty-first century saw extension to Muslims and Sikhs, as well as a growth in the numbers of Anglican and Jewish schools. Many teachers teach, and many children learn, in denominational primary schools: in 2007 there were about 4,500 Church of England primary schools in England (accommodating nearly 20 per cent of the pupil population), nearly 1,700 Roman Catholic (with 10 per cent of the pupil population), 26 Methodist, 58 of other Christian denominations, 28 Jewish, four Muslim and one Sikh (McKinney 2008). Government support for faith schools might be seen as a policy of diversity and choice appealing to voters, since faith schools enjoy a public perception of success in their quality of teaching, pupil attainment and hence in parental satisfaction. Yet the long historical precedent of provision for the established church and one or two of the most influential denominations raises questions of justice and fairness, and about their impact on social cohesion, and hence on citizenship.

Church schools have been claimed to enhance social cohesion through their moral ethos. It may equally be argued that they do more to inhibit than enhance, effectively selecting on grounds other than religion, since statistics reveal that poorer children and children with special needs tend to be under-represented in faith schools. A key issue that arises in debate is the appropriateness of public funding to support religious denominations, given their inherent selection and divisiveness as a negative impact on inclusion. However, in view of the long historical precedents that have privileged certain faiths in the funding of their schools, bringing an end to state funding could be construed as prejudicing the historic rights of those groups. A more equitable and socially cohesive policy is therefore to extend state funding to other denominational groups, especially given the changing patterns of religious belief and practice. That policy in turn raises difficult questions about the limits and future scope of funding to faith schools in respect of new religious movements, 'new age spiritualities' or how to distinguish between 'religions' and 'cults'. Social cohesion is a contested concept with various understandings. Whilst it has been argued that in the past, faith schools encouraged religious and ethnic minorities to participate in civic and public life, contributing a particular religious and moral perspective to society as a whole, a common perception is that schooling children within an individual faith will generate greater divisiveness. Problems of sectarianism were vigorously debated in Scotland in 2005 when the Scottish Government launched a number of highly publicised anti-sectarian initiatives. In the debates that ensued over subsequent years, the Catholic schools were particularly targeted as the 'root cause' of prejudice, though the claim has been strongly contested (McKinney 2008).

This latter question hinges on personal experience of denominational schooling and its effects, and the second key issue for citizenship education concerns the problem of ensuring children's rights when they receive a denominational education. Schooling grounded in a given faith or doctrine can be seen as suppressing the personal autonomy that should be the aim of all public education. Rational autonomy is a fundamental objective of education, and the rights of the child to make its own choices in respect of belief are embedded in the UNCRC. Article 14 establishes that children have the right to think and believe what they want, as long they are not stopping other people enjoying their rights. The UNCRC also recognises, however, the rights of parents to guide their children on these matters and Article 29 requires that education should encourage children to respect their parents, as well as their own and other cultures. A hard liberal view recognises only individual autonomy and rejects the communal identity of religious groups, but rejection of faith schools threatens the security of minority religious communities. The alleged divisiveness of faith schools on the one hand, and their perceived success on the other, raises a tension between civic virtues and religious virtues, between public and private virtues, but McKinney (2008) argues that this should be seen as a creative rather than a polarised tension, and that some faith schools create 'good' citizens who contribute to the common good.

Difficult questions are raised by fundamentalist religious schools, such as the Emmanuel Schools Foundation, sponsored by Peter Vardy and part-funded by the state. Critics argue that the faith education they offer is limited and restricting, and difficult to reconcile with liberal ideals of rational autonomy. Muslim schools enable children to achieve and protect them from the effects of minority status and racism encountered in state schools, but may cultivate religious beliefs at odds with Western liberal democracy. A challenge for education policy lies in the complexity of immigrant and post-immigrant identities, and the importance of religion and education for preservation of these identities. Questions may be asked as to how faith schools can address new moral issues that arise with developments in science and technology, though the same questions should equally be directed also at non-faith schools in respect to their commitment to a truly liberal education. The legal obligation for a daily act of worship 'wholly, or mainly, of a broadly Christian character' in state schools is widely recognised as problematic, frequently ignored in practice, and was seriously questioned even by HMCI David Bell in 2004.

Some of these issues can be traced in recent history as policy trends and legal judgments have appeared either to threaten or support the position of faith schools. In 2002, an amendment was proposed to the Education Bill (for England and Wales) that would limit the selection rights of faith schools by requiring them to offer at least a quarter of places to children of another or no religion, to promote inclusivity and lessen social division. That proposal was defeated in Parliament. Since then, similar solutions have been proposed even from within the Church of England, when in 2011 the Bishop of Oxford aroused controversy with a radical proposal that admission for churchgoers to Church of England schools should be limited to 10 per cent. In November 2007, the Krishna-Avanti Hindu school in north-west London became the first school in the UK to make vegetarianism a condition of entry; additionally, parents of pupils were expected to abstain from alcohol to prove themselves followers of the faith. In the same month the Jewish Free School in north London was found guilty of discrimination for giving preference to children of Jewish mothers. And at about the same time, an attempt was made by Monkseaton High School in Tyneside to create the first secular school in Britain when the headteacher proposed to eliminate the daily act of Christian worship. Political principles at stake range from government regulation and secularisation of public education at one extreme, through the need to protect minorities and respect religious diversity, with devolution of educational decision-making and management to communities, to liberalisation, privatisation and marketisation of school provision at another.

In 2005, the Chief Inspector of Schools, David Bell, caused consternation when he pronounced:

> Faith should not be blind. I worry that many young people are being educated in faith-based schools, with little appreciation of their wider responsibilities and obligations to British society. This growth in faith schools needs to be carefully but sensitively monitored by government to ensure that pupils receive an understanding of not only their own faith but of other faiths and the wider tenets of British society.
>
> (*The Times*, 18 January 2005)

He criticised Islamic schools in particular, calling them a 'threat to national identity'. In January 2008 the House of Commons Children, Schools and Families Select Committee raised concerns about the government's plans for expanding faith schooling. The general secretary of the Association of Teachers and Lecturers, Dr. Mary Bousted, commented:

> Unless there are crucial changes in the way many faith schools are run we fear divisions in society will be exacerbated. In our increasingly multi-faith and secular society it is hard to see why our taxes should be used to fund schools which discriminate against the majority of children and potential staff because they are not of the same faith.
>
> (*Guardian*, 2 January 2008)

Health and citizenship

Physical education

In the historical development of government policy, every primary pupil's physical health came to be seen as the state's responsibility. Claims about the Battle of Waterloo being won on the playing fields of Eton may have influenced the elementary school curriculum as physical education was promoted to maintain a healthy race of males for defending the nation and females to breed and rear the young. Citizenship in this way took a physical form. Despite its continuing importance in this respect, education policies and funding constraints have worked together over recent years to reduce the attention paid in primary schools to this aspect of children's development.

Physical education makes substantial demands on curriculum time, but government's increasing emphasis on literacy and numeracy had by 2005 resulted in a typical primary school's offering of one thirty-minute PE lesson per week. PE is also costly in resources. Adequate space is required and the facilities needed have become more complex. A swimming pool on the premises is rarely affordable by primary schools, and travel to public pools incurs considerable transport costs, as do adventurous and outdoor activities. Most activities beyond the school premises also require additional adults to maintain adequate supervision. So the financial commitment needed for this aspect of the curriculum is considerable. As the PE curriculum has become more sophisticated, so, too, the training of all primary teachers to the level of competence required is a further national cost; the failure to make sufficient provision in initial teacher education and the consequent poor quality of much PE teaching in primary schools has been a continuous complaint by inspectors over the past twenty years. In 2005, Ofsted reported negatively on primary PE and called for better support for teachers as well as improved accommodation and facilities.

Ofsted also wished to see in particular a strengthening of focus on 'fitness and health' as against skills and performance. Whilst both general fitness and sporting achievement might be viewed as common goals, these two aspects of the PE curriculum reflect different political objectives, each represented by its own department of state. Funded by the Department of Health, the Health Education Authority advises government on strategy and promotes projects to achieve a fitter and more productive nation; fitness is seen as a good in its own right, but also with the aim of saving public expenditure in the long term on health care and reducing the loss of working days through sickness. To this end, in 1998 they issued a policy framework for physical activity of young people. In 2000 the Department for Culture, Media and Sport published *A Sporting Future for All* advocating sport in the community (mass participation) and sporting excellence. Subsequent policy statements have included *Game Plan* (2002), published in collaboration with government's Social Exclusion Unit, identifying sport and physical activity as 'a social instrument to reduce the inequalities of opportunity for citizens to participate in the social structure of British society'. *Playing to Win* (2008) referred to Britain's prospects as Olympic host nation in 2012, encouraging more people to take up sport for the love of it, but also 'to expand the pool of talented English sportsmen and women; and to break records, win medals and win tournaments for this country'. The 2012 Olympics were seen as an unprecedented opportunity to 'unite people at all levels of sport in a new spirit of partnership and common endeavour', but the rationale of specialist sports colleges is concerned with identifying and developing elite performers.

Educationists have regarded these policies as too 'top-down', and Griggs has argued that:

> If Physical Education and in turn sport was to advance in the UK and if politicians want Olympic gold medals and to tackle childhood obesity and sedentary lifestyles, then what needs to happen is a shifting of priorities and resources in the primary sector.
>
> (Griggs 2007, 66)

A 'bottom-up' model, he argues, would involve a PE curriculum offering breadth of experience and flexibility to meet the needs of all pupils. Moreover it would require an acknowledgement that 'core subjects' such as English, maths and science are not to be valued at the expense of all others. Political rhetoric and exhortation must be tested against the detail of National Curriculum requirements. The new Curriculum Review launched in 2011 was notable in prioritising PE along with the core subjects of English, maths and science.

Health education

In 1990 health education was identified as one of the cross-curricular themes needed to supplement the National Curriculum. Curriculum guidance published by the National Curriculum Council (NCC) implicitly acknowledged a political sensitivity to the subject given the relationship between home and school in this particular respect:

> Education for health begins in the home where patterns of behaviour and attitudes influence health for good or ill throughout life and will be well established before the child is five. The tasks for schools are to support and promote attitudes, practices and understanding conducive to good health. Insofar as they are able to counteract influences which are not conducive to good health, they should do so with sensitive regard to the relationship which exists between children and their families.
>
> (DES *Curriculum Matters 6: Health Education from 5 to 16*, 1986, cited in NCC 1990a)

Its social significance was emphasised in recognising that healthy living was a vital issue when society was affected by 'one health crisis after another', one of the most recent at that time being HIV/AIDS. People's health was 'one of the most important products that any society can create' and 'one of the most important resources for the creation of any other kind of wealth'. Everyone was exposed to potential health risks, but individuals could do much to reduce the risks and to improve the quality of their lives and their environment. It was noted that the twentieth century had seen a shift over time away from infectious disease that historically had been the major cause of mortality, towards non-infectious disease, fatal accidents and specific patterns of unhealthy behaviour. These were factors over which individual citizens could exercise personal control. Hence the components of a health education curriculum were identified as: substance use and misuse; sex education; family life education; safety; health-related exercise; food and nutrition; personal hygiene; environmental aspects of health education; and psychological aspects. For teaching health education, as for citizenship, curriculum guidance emphasised the wider aspects of school life, school ethos, and collaboration with governors, parents, families and the community.

Definitions of health education have been refined over the twenty years since 1990 to be grouped with 'personal and social education' as PSHE or even PSHCE, thereby expressing its continuity with citizenship education. Most recently the costs to the nation of poor diet, tobacco and alcohol consumption and drug abuse have prompted a range of new initiatives. Political dilemmas arise, however, from ideological objections on the right to a 'nanny state', seen as debilitating and oppressing some individuals at the expense of taxing others.

Growing obesity and its long-term costs to individual welfare and to the health service led to a succession of campaigns on the quality of school meals. A 2007 report indicated that nearly 60 per cent of the population would be obese by 2050, and in 2008 nearly 14 per cent of children aged two to 10 were classed as obese with a further 14 per cent classed as overweight. In 2005, celebrity chef Jamie Oliver's TV series on school dinners received great publicity and persuaded government to require higher standards of nutrition. Better nutrition was advocated not only for its physical benefits but also as improving behaviour, academic performance and attainment. Ofsted evaluations of that scheme early on showed that in many schools the changes turned pupils off school lunches, but emphasis was laid on the need for parental and community education, and the project was bound to be a long-term one. Primary schools were better placed than secondaries to achieve positive results. In January 2008 the education and health departments launched a £372m healthy living strategy, in which cooking was made a compulsory part of the national curriculum.

A further concern by 2008 was the way rising food costs affected the poorest families, coupled with worries that the current system of free school meals labelled poor children and made them vulnerable to bullying; nearly 16 per cent of children at primary schools (660,000) qualified for free school meals on the grounds of low family income, but more than one-third of eligible children failed to take them up, and child poverty campaigners explained that many felt stigmatised. The Secretary of State for Health launched a £20m experiment to provide all children in two Local Authorities with free school meals. The scheme, run jointly by the Departments of Health and Children, Schools and Families, together with the local authorities, was to examine whether free school dinners reduced obesity, changed eating habits at home, improved pupils' concentration in schools, raised academic standards and boosted health and well-being. Councils and primary health care trusts contributed a further £20m in local funding.

In 2010, Ofsted reported that schools had made encouraging progress by promoting healthy eating, raising nutritional standards and making good meals affordable, but take-up remained low amongst poorer families with overall take-up just under 40 per cent in primary schools. One obstacle to better participation had been children's preference for junk food, suggesting a need to listen more sensitively to pupils' views, to provide more attractive places for eating and more attractive presentation of food. In its last month in office, the New Labour Government announced an extension of a pilot project to provide free school meals to half a million children from low-income families, but in June 2010 the new Coalition Government abandoned the previous government's plan.

Well-being and citizenship

The concept of primary schools as agents of welfare has a long history going back more than a hundred years, but for present purposes might be conveniently identified in the 1967 Plowden Report, recognising the primary school's role in its community setting. Its specific recommendation of Educational Priority Areas (EPAs), where additional funding was provided to schools in deprived areas to fulfil this aspect of their work, echoed the contemporaneous policy in the USA of an 'educational war on poverty' in President Lyndon Johnson's 'Head Start' programme.

More recently, a succession of policy measures under New Labour produced an emphasis on well-being that constituted in effect a maximal interpretation of citizenship. Alongside the government's obsession with standards and performance, assessment and league tables, and physical health, ran concerns about the effects of social exclusion and the protection of children. Social breakdown and its impact had been epitomised over a number of years in horrific and highly publicised events such as the abduction and murder of the infant Jamie Bulger by two primary-age pupils, the racial murder of Stephen Lawrence in 1993, the abuse and torture by her carers of Victoria Climbié in 2000 and the murders of Jessica Chapman and Holly Wells by a school caretaker in 2002. Every Child Matters (ECM) originated as a Green Paper in 2003 following an extended review of issues raised by the Climbié case. A new Children Act in 2004 provided more joined-up and accessible services for the needs of children, young people and families, and the Government published *Every Child Matters: Change for Children* as guidance for schools and teachers (DFES 2004).

This policy may be seen in relation to both health and citizenship education, illustrating a gradual elision of citizenship, health and well-being to combine current ways of working through the formal curriculum and through the wider role of the primary school. The government's aim, it was stated, was for every child, whatever their background or their circumstances, to have the support they needed to: be healthy; stay safe; enjoy and achieve at school; make a positive contribution in the community; and achieve economic well-being. To indicate this wider scope, the Department of State itself was renamed from 'Education and Skills' to 'Children, Schools and Families' in 2007, reflecting its responsibility for issues affecting children and young people up to age 19. Following the General Election of 2010, this title was abandoned and deliberately replaced by the narrower 'Department for Education', appealing to a right-wing lobby that preferred a focus on 'the basics' of formal schooling, but a junior minister was nevertheless appointed with responsibility for 'children and families'. After some deliberation, the office of independent Children's Commissioner was endorsed; this role had been created by the Children Act 2004 with the remit of encouraging adults who work with children to 'think about the needs of children and young people and listen to their views to make their lives better'. The Commissioner speaks especially for children and young people who are neglected or vulnerable, such as the physically less able or emotionally troubled, and those recently arrived in the country, and the Commissioner's work is guided by the UNCRC. The policy drive to integrate education and children's social services encountered considerable problems especially at the local level, with tragic and well-publicised failures in child protection, but the ideal of a joined-up service had considerable resonance for citizenship education in its broadest sense.

The 'five outcomes' of ECM are held to be universal ambitions for *every* child and young person, whatever their background or circumstances. The Ajegbo review *Diversity and Citizenship* (2007) observed how ECM had been effectively used in some schools to value children's diversity, and to promote inclusive citizenship. MacConville's study of inclusion in the same year was more critical however:

> Over the last ten years we have heard much that has been written using the language of empowerment. We have been regaled with words and phrases which have sought to emphasise the central role of children and young people in the decisions taken regarding their educational and social lives: voice, opportunity, listening . . . and so on. While used undoubtedly with honesty and meaning, there is a view, frequently expressed, that such language has been hijacked by politicians, educational opportunists and ideologues. This has resulted in cynicism towards these terms, and their grudging acceptance as yet another checklist or policy which needs to be 'done'. . . . Listening and hearing are of little account unless there is resultant action.
>
> (MacConville et al. 2007, x)

MacConville's edited collection revealed the first-hand accounts of students with autistic spectrum disorder, visual impairment, specific learning difficulties, hearing impairment and physical disabilities. A 'deeply grounded' and 'emancipatory' research project, it noted that for all the rhetoric of pupil voice there was little evidence for how pupils themselves perceive inclusion. Throughout her inquiry pupils emphasised needs of 'social belonging' and 'self-esteem', and the consequent necessity for schools and teachers of understanding disabilities at a psychological as well as a behavioural level. Here she cited Article 12 of the UNCRC, challenging us to reconsider the ways in which we engage with discourse of inclusion, a clear matter of citizenship rights:

> Without the active participation of young people there will be no social future. We need to engage in dialogue, to accept children's right to be included, to look actively for their competence, to give them time to express their views in their own way, and to treat them and their views with respect.

Following its ECM agenda, in 2005 the DFES began promoting a non-statutory programme of Social and Emotional Aspects of Learning (SEAL), a framework and resources for developing social, emotional and behavioural skills, with built-in progression for each year group. The policy, to foster well-being through the school curriculum, was directed in part at specific issues of topical concern such as bullying and attendance. It can be seen as a political programme, not confined to Britain, where governments saw the potential of affective learning in meliorating emotional deprivation and social exclusion and longer term gains in reducing the cost of social welfare. Popular with primary teachers, the programme nevertheless attracted opposition, especially from critics on the ideological right. Amongst the most vocal in this respect have been Frank Furedi, and Kathryn Ecclestone and Dennis Hayes, quoted at the start of this chapter, who attack what they call 'therapeutic education' as both diminishing the human 'subject' and betraying the traditional academic 'subjects' of the curriculum (Ecclestone and Hayes 2009).

Education for well-being has attracted scorn and derision through its translation into political and media discourse as education for 'happiness'. The title 'Happiness Counts' was nevertheless adopted for a project conducted by Action for Children, one of the UK's leading charities committed to vulnerable children; their research partner was the 'new economics foundation' (nef), an independent 'think-and-do tank' whose mission is 'economics as if people and the planet mattered', to demonstrate and inspire 'real economic well-being, aiming to improve life by innovative solutions that challenge mainstream thinking on economic, environmental and social issues' (Action for Children and nef 2009). Their report represents a further stage in the development of education for citizenship, seen both as welfare and as social investment. Crucially for an understanding of citizenship education, it called on the concept of 'social return on investment', aiming to reshape the way society invests in its future through children. The Allen Review seemed to underline the state's concern for all-round development of the individual. Appointed in 2010 to consider the scope for early intervention and prevention in the pre-school age group, and led by Graham Allen MP, its objective was to develop policy for maximising life chances as well as reducing long-term costs in the health and judicial systems.

Schools' engagement with local communities for the purpose of improving children's well-being extends the practice of citizenship education. The policy of Extended Schools promoted this engagement for practical and economic reasons, seeing school premises as a valuable local resource and maximising the use of school facilities for community benefit. More idealistically the principle embodies the practice of citizenship for educational ends in a community setting, offering activities for children, especially deprived children, before and after school, including study support, sport and music clubs, combined with parenting and family support, and access to specialist services such as social workers, housing officers and health services. Originating as a concept in the USA, with British precedents too in the Community Colleges of the 1930s, Extended Schools were promoted more recently in Scotland, with a pilot of 400 schools from 1998, and in Wales the idea of community-focused schools was used to explore similar kinds of provision. In England, a Children's Plan launched in 2006 had £1.3bn allocated for Extended Schools over the years 2008 to 2011, £10m of which went to Northern Ireland where the Department of Education led the development in collaboration with the Department of Health, Social Services and Public Safety, and the Department for Social Development. By 2010 the vast majority of primary schools in England were recorded as offering extended services.

Conclusion

Primary teachers would have no difficulty in agreeing that citizenship education should include a curriculum, pedagogy and a school ethos that teaches by precept and by example the values of democracy, self-respect and respect for others, cooperation, a healthy life-style, well-being and even 'happiness'. David Cameron, as Prime Minister of the Coalition Government from 2010, has promoted happiness as an object of government policy. The implications of citizenship education, and the way it was implemented under New Labour, have nevertheless been subjected to incisive criticism. John Beck identified citizenship education as a highly politicised intervention in the curriculum. He observed how its rationale was based on worries about voter apathy and alienation, but suggested that this apathy reflected disenchantment with the conduct of *official* politics, a critique supported by the evidence of children's views researched by Warwick and cited earlier in this chapter. Whilst there is abundant evidence that British citizens of all ages care intensely about specific political issues, New Labour, whilst overtly championing 'active citizenship', in effect disempowered British citizens in many areas of their lives. Despite a plausible and influential discourse in an appeal to 'shared English values', 'modern patriotism' and 'cosmopolitan citizenship', there were clear contradictions and gaps between proclaimed aspirations and their implementation in practice (Beck 2008, 29, 43–44).

One conclusion might be that citizenship education should be more explicit in a critical treatment of politics and political processes; though that may appear more appropriate for a secondary rather than a primary curriculum, Warwick's research suggests that older primary school children may themselves be expressing the need. Access to news media means that primary pupils are aware of political issues and events, and analytical thinking could be encouraged to question systems of governance at all levels – school, local, national and international.

Citizenship education broadly conceived has been shown to range more widely, to embrace children's rights, health and well-being. Religious education and provision of faith schools are also culturally embedded and complicating factors. Projects for Citizenship and PSHE in the primary curriculum are nevertheless hindered by their low status for assessment purposes in comparison with core subjects, as teachers remain under pressure to improve performance in 'the basics' by which schools are measured. Primary teachers have to attend, however little it may contribute to performance measurement, to children's social development, social identity, religious belief, physical health and well-being, all of which have political connotations. As a vital and rich curriculum field it becomes potentially problematic if governments determine the parameters of citizenship education for their own particular ends. Teachers have a heavy responsibility to be alert to this, to understand and cultivate citizenship in the fullest sense of social development for democracy, to question and resist its narrow prescription or imposition of values by the state.

Key questions for reflection

- To what extent do you see yourself as a teacher of citizenship? What are the political implications and what might be the role of religious education or of health education?
- In your experience how effectively does citizenship education address inequalities, prejudice or racism, and what are the key factors in dealing with these issues?
- How can citizenship education be developed as a whole school policy and what political implications does this have? In what ways can citizenship education be promoted by engaging with the local community?

Independent learning tasks

Adopt any one of the above questions as a focus for personal research, and/or the basis for discussion with colleagues.

Look closely at the UNCRC and match the aspects of citizenship education in your school against the articles of the charter. Look at national reports on the UNCRC website and draft a report on your own school, with recommendations.

Further reading

Beck, J. (2008) *Meritocracy, Citizenship and Education: New Labour's Legacy*, London: Continuum. Chapter 3 (29–50) develops a critique of citizenship education discourse as a call for active citizenship in the form of uncritical 'volunteering' that avoids genuine political participation (defined by Crick as 'civic republicanism'). Beck argues that this official discourse ignores the roots of voter disenchantment, at the same time disempowering sources of organised democratic influence such as local government, trades unions and professions.

Ecclestone, K. and Hayes, D. (2009) 'Changing the subject: The educational implications of developing emotional well-being', *Oxford Review of Education*, 35, 3: 371–389.
This article is suggested reading to illustrate the ideological and political debate aroused by arguments for emotional well-being as comprising a necessary objective and component of primary education, within the broad scope of social and citizenship education, as in the SEAL programme. Ecclestone and Hayes argue that this undermines both the individual human subject and the traditional concept of curriculum subjects.

Griggs, G. (2007) 'Physical Education: Primary matters, secondary importance', *Education 3–13*, 35, 1: 59–69.
Griggs notes the abundant evidence for the poor quality of PE provision in primary schools in England and Wales, despite the fact that this stage of schooling holds the key to lifelong physical activity and proficiency in sport. In arguing for a shifting of priorities and resources, he exposes the political dimensions of policy-making for primary PE and the need to replace 'top-down' policies with a more 'bottom-up' approach.

McKinney, S. (ed.) (2008) *Faith Schools in the Twenty-first Century*, Edinburgh: Dunedin Press.
Chapter 1 (1–14) documents and explores the complexity of debate on faith schools, given the struggle between different understandings of the rights of individuals and groups within the state, and the role or responsibility of the state in upholding those rights. This debate is intimately related to the nature of citizenship education and its provision in state schools.

Osler, A. and Starkey, H. (2010) *Teachers and Human Rights Education*, Stoke on Trent: Trentham.
Chapters 9 and 10 (113–141) offer a critique of citizenship education as conventionally defined, proposing an alternative model of cosmopolitan citizenship and the practice of human rights education in schools.

Warwick, P. (2007b) 'Hearing pupils' voices: Revealing the need for citizenship education within primary schools', *Education 3–13*, 35, 3: 261–272.
This article reports an action research project on the implementation of citizenship education in primary schools, as a way of evaluating the potential of citizenship education to fulfil the intended outcomes of the ECM policy. Hearing pupils' concerns about local and global issues revealed their own understandings of politics and political engagement as a starting point for primary teachers planning for citizenship education.

Chapter 5

Pedagogy: a political issue?

An holistic concept of pedagogy was at the core of [Bruno Ciari's] thinking [at Reggio Emilia]. Parents, as well as teachers and children, were seen as central to the educational process. Pedagogy, therefore, went beyond the particular skills of individual teachers. Children were viewed as strong and rich personalities with a natural curiosity to be exploited in the varied settings of school and community life. Co-operation and communication were seen as crucial and buildings and classrooms were built to exploit this. Teachers worked in pedagogic teams with the support of a pedagogical co-ordinator or *pedagogista*. Observation and research and the need for children to engage in a continuous process of discussion, interpretation and presentation of their work were together seen as key to pedagogical success.

(Leach and Moon 2008, 2)

Those who worship at the shrine of 'the child' argue that the primary classroom should be a place of happy spontaneity in which a teacher and child together explore experiences of mutual interest. Children, they suggest, should discover for themselves rather than be told anything by the teachers. One to one, personalised conversations between the teacher and individual children are better, therefore, than whole class instruction in which the teacher explains things which, on a different view of education, it might be thought every child within their class needs to know.

(Woodhead 2009, 98)

Introduction

Pedagogy might seem at first sight the least political of all the topics dealt with in this book. Engaging with young children in the classroom and the mechanics of communicating knowledge might appear too lowly or too technical to merit detailed attention by politicians. However, there's no question that pedagogy *has* become political. Teaching methods, simplistically represented or crudely caricatured, have been passionately attacked and defended in public debate about primary schooling. This chapter will raise questions about how and why that happened and with what effect. Was it inevitable? Is it so in other national systems and cultures? *Should* it be so?

These questions arise in part because of a narrow conception of pedagogy that has prevailed in Britain. Pedagogy is now truly political in two quite distinct aspects. In the first place, drawing on the narrow definition of pedagogy as classroom practice, its political significance derives from its greater or lesser efficiency and cost-effectiveness in achieving the state's educational objectives. But pedagogy can be conceived much more broadly as a symbolic interaction that represents a set of power relations between the state and the individual, between older and younger generations in society, and in that sense it is innately political. Commentators such as Brian Simon and Robin Alexander have observed our critical reluctance in Britain to adopt a wider understanding found in other cultures and adopted in other nation-states, of pedagogy as a social process that extends well beyond the classroom and the school. In that broader *cultural* sense, pedagogy is bound to be profoundly political, yet might at the same time avoid the posturing of successive governments and individual Secretaries of State that has left teachers and children as pawns on a party-political chequer board.

Enter any primary classroom and what we immediately encounter is pedagogy in the form of activity by teachers and learners, in an environment that vividly reflects the kinds of teaching and learning in progress. Outside the classroom but within the bounds of the whole school, the patterns and character of interaction between children and staff might be seen as an extension of that relatively formal pedagogical encounter. Over the course of a school term we also observe a range of extra-curricular activity and engagement with the community. Parents, carers and other adults assisting in teaching and learning, parents and carers consulting with teachers about individual children's learning, meeting in groups or attending school events, productions and celebrations, are aspects of the wider pedagogy. Visits to the school by community members, and visits by pupils in the local environment or further afield dissolve the boundaries of the school and extend the meanings of pedagogy. The wider concept of pedagogy in a community setting is what makes the Italian example of Reggio Emilia so compelling (as in the quote from Leach and Moon at the start of this chapter). The extended schools programme, described in Chapter 4, has potential for developing this kind of social pedagogy.

To understand the politics of pedagogy as it affects primary school teaching this chapter takes three approaches. First, we need to explore the way pedagogy is and has been understood and discussed by educationists and by a wider public. Second, we should critically trace the steps by which primary school pedagogy in particular has come to be politically directed. Finally, we will home in on the classroom to consider the impact of political debates on the everyday processes of teaching and learning, and the scope that is left for teachers to employ their own initiatives in planning and carrying out their work. While welcoming popular interest that penetrates the mythologies of classroom life, we must defend the space for initiative and responsibility allowing teachers and children to interact constructively and meaningfully without undue political interference.

Pedagogical science and popular understanding

Debates about pedagogy have often turned on whether teaching should be understood as an art or as a science (Robinson 2004). There have been inspired and inspirational teachers, gifted communicators and charismatic individuals, exponents of the *art* of teaching, who can motivate and nurture learners. Such apparently 'natural' teachers have given rise to the platitude that 'good teachers are born, not made'. At the same time, we can trace a long historical trajectory of *scientific* interest in pedagogy. Interest in the psychology of learning emerged in the seventeenth century with the work of J.A. Comenius and John Locke, and grew to be a field of methodical and large-scale research by the later nineteenth century, and the results of those investigations began to suggest and inform systematic approaches to teaching that took it from being a set of craft skills to an applied science. Theorists, experimenters and practitioners whose ideas have been hugely influential include Pestalozzi, Froebel and Herbart, Montessori, Dewey, Vygotsky, Piaget and Bruner. Systematic teaching methods were developed by Froebel and Montessori, and general principles based on scientific enquiry included Piaget's stages of child development.

From 1905, after abandoning the system of payment by results (Chapter 2) the government produced a book of *Suggestions for the Consideration of Teachers and Others Concerned in the Work of Public Elementary Schools*. A new edition appearing in 1927 exhorted the teacher to

> . . . aim at a discipline which arises naturally from a mutual understanding between himself and his pupils.

The teacher's starting point must be

> . . . no rigid syllabus or subject, but the children as they really are: he must work always with the grain of their minds, try never to cut across it.

> . . . to bring into play and gradually develop, direct and refine the children's fundamental interests and instincts.

> . . . The characteristic note of recent educational doctrine or practice has been the insistence on the importance of the individual as distinct from the class.

Ideals of self-discipline and self-education for children went hand in hand with a reliance on the individual teacher's judgement. So, about eighty years ago, government encouraged a pedagogy that would promote children as active agents in their own learning, rather than as empty vessels to be filled with knowledge. This more open stance reflected the concurrent growth of developmental psychology in the early decades of the twentieth century, although the *Handbook of Suggestions* rested its liberal approach on general precepts rather than on psychological theory. That spirit continued in the years after the Second World War up to and including the Plowden Report of 1967. Yet for all Plowden's encouragement of child-centred and discovery methods of learning, supporters as well as critics identified a lack of systematic description of pedagogical processes.

Brian Simon observed that the 'primary school revolution', claimed by some of its more enthusiastic supporters to have been revealed in the Plowden inquiry, was something of a myth, partly wishful thinking by child-centred educationists, partly media hype. In 1981 he published a highly influential article entitled 'Why no pedagogy in England?' (Simon 1981). He observed that the discourse of teaching in England was neither coherent nor systematic, and that no theory had been developed comparable to the continental European 'science of teaching'. As a result, teachers here tended to conceptualise, plan and justify their teaching with a combination of pragmatism and ideology. From his personal involvement in campaigning for educational reform, and from his historical research on state schooling, Simon recognised that all education is grounded in social and political values of some kind (Simon 1991, 1998; Chitty and Simon 1993). But he also recognised the need for professional knowledge based on evidence and on principles distilled from collective understanding and experience. These theories of teaching and learning constituted a pedagogy that should be generalisable and open to public scrutiny.

The Plowden Report, and the debates that ensued, inspired a new wave of research based on close observation of primary classrooms. Research methods became more sophisticated, using qualitative and quantitative instruments for classroom observation. Neville Bennett's *Teaching Styles and Pupil Progress* (Bennett 1976) was one such study, and another beginning in the 1970s was the ORACLE (Observational Research and Classroom Learning Experience) project conducted at the University of Leicester by Brian Simon and Maurice Galton (Galton, Simon and Croll 1980; Galton, Hargreaves *et al.* 1999). In keeping with these developments, HMI adopted a more scientific approach to the gathering and publication of their extensive data from classroom observation in the context of school inspections. Pedagogical research thus progressed considerably after Plowden, and 'the cumulative body of scholarship and evidence about children, learning, teaching and culture, not to mention the collective experience of teachers', began to provide an ample basis for a coherent and principled pedagogy (Alexander 2004, 28–29).

Nevertheless, Robin Alexander (2004) reiterated Simon's argument about the lack of scientific pedagogy in Britain, in a critique of New Labour's policy paper *Excellence and Enjoyment: A strategy for primary schools* (DFES 2003). Alexander saw that this new strategy was in effect a pedagogical statement; given its belief that it could harness enjoyable means to achieve excellent ends he thought it properly ambitious, and because it came from government it had to be taken seriously (Alexander 2004, 27). Following observations by independent researchers, teacher unions and professional groups, and above all concerns expressed by Ofsted, about the effects of the literacy and numeracy strategies that had been operating for the previous five years, *Excellence and Enjoyment* sought to disarm criticism and to secure professional goodwill by relaxing the pressure of government prescription and targets, and by designating a new Primary National Strategy (PNS). Yet despite increasing levels of pedagogical prescription, Alexander identified in the 2003 document a continued absence of serious pedagogical thinking. It persisted in focusing on a procedurally narrow definition of 'what works' in the classroom, as against a societally broad definition of curriculum. Alexander argued that any sense of how pedagogy connects with culture and social structure was ignored. He pointed to unproblematised expressions such as 'common sense' and 'what every teacher knows', together with messianic assertions like 'we believe', 'we want', 'we need', 'Government . . . believes it knows better'. Under a highly centralised and interventionist education system 'the discourse becomes mired in the . . . mendacity and spin of policy-speak, in pragmatism and compliance' (Alexander 2004, 29).

Debates over teaching methods strike a chord in popular understanding, as most people carry good or bad memories of education of one teaching style or another encountered in their childhood. Reminisce with adults of any age about their experiences of schooling and memories emerge about classroom events and incidents, points of interaction between teachers and children; in other words, about pedagogy. Adults will offer firm opinions regarding the good or harm these pedagogical experiences did them. An artificially polarised discourse of 'teacher-centred' pedagogies on the one hand and 'learner-centred' pedagogies on the other acquired ideological significance in Britain, as in North America. The polarisation of political right and left around 'traditional' and 'progressive' approaches to the curriculum was explored in Chapter 3, and perhaps nowhere is the antithesis of tradition and innovation more pointed than in discourse about pedagogy. Reassertion by government of an emphasis on 'teaching' rather than 'learning' was accompanied by ever-more rigorous guidelines for training teachers, and evaluating teaching on a scale of 'excellence, competence or failure'. Teachers' and researchers' deep concerns for the processes of children's learning was derided, for example, by Chris Woodhead (2002) in *Class War*, as the 'lunacy of lear-nacy', and in his *Desolation of Learning* (quoted at the start of this chapter). More recently, the coalition government's education White Paper in 2010 was entitled *The Importance of Teaching* which may be read superficially as a compliment to the teaching profession, but more tendentious is its implication of a transmissional approach to pedagogy; that is, teaching is considered more important than learning.

One of several populists to enter the pedagogical debate is the sociologist Frank Furedi in his book *Wasted: Why Education isn't Educating*. Furedi's attack on what he describes as 'Throw-away Pedagogy' has in fact little or nothing constructive to say about pedagogy, which is not defined, but is instead a repetitive tirade against change and innovation in education generally. Furedi argues for the preservation and transmission of traditional sub-ject knowledge, calling in his defence the eminent political philosopher Hannah Arendt. Nowhere does he confront cultural change, however, ignoring the different contexts in which children now learn, the effects that information technology has had on the distribution of knowledge and styles of learning, unimagineable in the 1950s when Hannah Arendt was writing. Children now, with mobile technology at their fingertips, are de facto independent learners and teachers' pedagogy has to take account of this. Another of Furedi's concerns is 'confusion about adult authority', where he harks back to a lost age when teachers supposedly commanded more respect from their pupils. In fact he offers some appreciation of pedagogy for *motivation*, with reference to John Dewey's advocacy of less rigid and more open-ended teaching methods, but Furedi worries about the abdication of adult authority that this might entail (Furedi 2009, 73–84).

The right-wing think tank Centre for Policy Studies (CPS) has joined in the pedagogical debate over many years. CPS promotes policies 'that provide freedom and encouragement for individuals to pursue the aspirations they have for themselves and their families, within the security and obligations of a stable and law-abiding nation'. Their recent pamphlet *So Why Can't They Read?* by journalist Miriam Gross was published in 2010 following the General Election. Boris Johnson, Mayor of London, contributed a foreword lamenting the level of adult illiteracy in London and the unemployment and criminality to which it leads, highlighting the need to improve basic skills so that London can maintain its economic leadership; he notes that over one-third of children leave London's primary schools with reading difficulties and about 5 per cent can hardly read at all, while 20 per cent leave secondary school unable to read and write with confidence. However, these undoubtedly serious and tragic facts are used specifically to endorse a phonics-based approach to reading, advocated by Gross. Her case is that progressivism imported from America had taken over since the 1960s, that spontaneity and informality had taken priority over order and discipline in the primary classroom. Self-esteem and equality came to receive more emphasis than selection and competition, and teachers were guilty of over-attention to personal and social education and emotional well-being. Gross introduces anecdotal evidence, with a familiar litany of complaints echoing from the Black Papers of the 1970s to Chris Woodhead, whose more recent observations are cited at the beginning of this chapter. Pedagogy, then, despite all the research that promoted teaching from an art to a science, remained a topic of popular discourse, a discourse marked by political dissension, throughout the later decades of the twentieth century and on into the twenty-first century.

Political direction of pedagogical practice

1967 to 1997

The Plowden Report of 1967 stirred public awareness of primary education, and the polarised and sometimes histrionic public debates in its wake generated interest amongst a wider and better informed public. Popular perceptions of pedagogy went hand in hand with heightened political anxiety about the teaching process, and published findings of pedagogical research were commonly seized on by protagonists of one political persuasion or another.

A reading survey undertaken by the National Foundation for Educational Research (NFER) and published in 1974 appeared to show that standards had fallen in the post-war years and prompted a government enquiry into the teaching of English, headed by Alan Bullock (DES 1975). The teaching of reading thus became a site for pedagogical debate. HMI developed a more 'scientific' approach to the gathering and publication of their extensive data from school observation, with a view to influencing government policy, one example being the national Primary Survey published in 1978 as an evaluation of developments in the ten years since the Plowden Report (DES 1978). Over the previous decades individual HMI had been influential in the development of primary policy through informal channels of communication, and now the inspectorate aimed to complement social scientific research and to inform political and professional debate more formally, and by publishing the outcomes of their practical work of observing primary classrooms.

Primary education was to become further publicised and politicised in the mid-1970s by events at William Tyndale School. Although problems at the new comprehensive secondary schools were also attracting sensational media coverage at the time, it was a relatively small north London primary that notoriously provoked a radical extension of state intervention in education. Adventurous and overtly political teaching methods adopted at William Tyndale aroused parental and community concern, and exposed divisions of opinion within the school and in the Inner London Education Authority (ILEA). National exposure of the dispute in newspapers and on TV, and of the subsequent enquiry over several months in 1975 to 1976, gave extended publicity to the school and its problems. Issues raised were not just about curriculum and teaching method, but also about monitoring and control by school governors and by the LEA. The Prime Minister at the time, Jim Callaghan, responded in his 'Ruskin Speech' (delivered at Ruskin College, Oxford) by announcing a government-sponsored national debate on education, and by anticipating the need for closer central government supervision of the work of local authorities and schools.

The consequent increase in central government control is discussed in other chapters in relation to curriculum, regulation of the teaching profession and governance of schools. In the later 1970s and on into the early 1980s, a growing interest in teaching methods was also taken by politicians. The Education Reform Act of 1988 secured statutory force for state intervention in the content of curriculum, but in parliamentary debates about this new principle government insisted that it would not dictate how teachers should teach. In retrospect, however, the Act might be seen as creating a precedent for further intervention, this time in pedagogy. Only four years later, in 1992, an officially commissioned report on primary curriculum organisation and classroom practice by Alexander, Rose and Woodhead initiated a process in which classroom teaching methods were increasingly scrutinised and eventually prescribed by government. Secretary of State Kenneth Clarke launched this enquiry with a reassurance that 'questions about how to teach are not for Government to determine', but his style of politics ensured that their report was given dramatic media coverage. Reporting in early January, the authors were dubbed the 'three wise men' and, in appearing to criticise child-centred teaching and to call for a return to more formal methods, their report touched a public nerve and re-awoke memories of the William Tyndale affair. The immediate effect of all this on practice in schools was illustrated in Ofsted reports which from 1994 to 1998 observed a steady increase in grouping pupils by ability, especially in English and mathematics at Key Stage 2.

National strategies

Following their election in 1997, whole class teaching and setting of pupils according to attainment was encouraged in New Labour's White Paper, *Excellence in Schools*, a distinctive feature being its proposal to launch a National Literacy Strategy (NLS). Alexander (2004) has commented on the tendentious language in which New Labour's education policy was presented, including keywords and phrases such as 'standards' (which were to be 'driven up'), 'underperforming' and 'failing' schools (which were to be met with 'intervention' and 'zero tolerance'), a 'tough new' approach and the 'step changes' (needed to 'deliver' a 'world class' education). New practice was to be 'evidence based', though in the event over the lifespan of these policies the evidence invoked by government was highly selective and carefully trimmed to political spin. Here we can observe the theatrical and illusory traits of political presentation to which Kenneth Minogue alerted us (Chapter 2). Also evident is that despite the proclamation of change by a new government, there was clear continuity with the policies of the political opponents whom the new government had replaced, illustrating the kinds of compromise described by Bernard Crick as integral to democratic politics (Chapter 2). Vaunted as New Labour innovation, the NLS represented a good deal of borrowing from the previous Conservative administration which, only a year earlier in 1996, had launched its own National Literacy Project, funded for five years and involving initially 266 primary schools in a sample of local education authorities. The NLS has been characterised by Brehony as a 'teacher-proof' curriculum, indicating that primary teachers could not be trusted to raise standards without the government's top-down, standards agenda (Brehony 2005, 33).

The NLS framework proposed a 'literacy hour' with a structure of time and class management to reflect its teaching objectives. Although non-statutory, it was nevertheless suggested that the literacy hour should be implemented throughout the school as a daily period of dedicated teaching time, and any alternative framework adopted by schools would require justification to Ofsted inspectors. The details of the NLS had been developed in opposition by a New Labour Literacy Task Force under the leadership of Professor Michael Barber. On taking office, the party established a Standards and Effectiveness Unit within the Department for Education and Skills (DFES) headed by Barber. The significance of this appointment is that he was an educationist turned 'policy wonk', a former teacher, NUT official and professor of education who became a political adviser (Barber 2007). Barber's trajectory was indicative of a new career track for some professional educationists; as governments had become concerned with educational reform over the course of thirty years, they had been advised by career civil servants and HMI or influenced by independent educationists operating through think tanks, but changing styles of government by the late 1990s allowed for hiring chosen specialists on the civil service payroll, expert advisers and loyal party members supportive of government policy.

Commentators have noted the role of Ofsted and its Chief Inspector, Chris Woodhead, advocate of a 'back to basics' policy of whole class teaching, in supporting the new strategies. Woodhead's cynicism about alternative pedagogies is expressed in the quotation that opens this chapter. In literacy, 'back to basics' was associated with a stress on phonics and in numeracy on calculation skills. As the NLS was being planned, a significant shift in emphasis is found in Ofsted reports between 1994 and 1998 from 'purpose and organisation' to 'the mechanics of writing, including phonics and grammar' (Wyse 2003). A National Numeracy Strategy (NNS) soon followed the NLS, arising from the work of a Task Force chaired by Professor David Reynolds. The NNS also hinged on whole class teaching with emphasis on arithmetic. A tripartite structure for the daily mathematics lesson was prescribed, starting with oral work and mental calculation, followed by children working in groups set according to ability, and ending with a plenary.

An initial improvement in statutory test (colloquially known as SAT) scores followed the introduction of the national strategies but began to flatten out after five or so years. A consequent policy rethink, led by the left of centre think tank Demos, suggested a need to move away from a centrally determined and test-driven approach towards individualised learning programmes for all pupils, arguing that the 'knowledge economy' now demanded more curriculum flexibility to foster creativity in the workforce of the future. Schools Standards Minister David Miliband followed Prime Minister Tony Blair in advocating a policy of 'personalised learning', insisting however that this was 'not a return to child-centred theories . . . [nor] . . . a licence to let pupils coast at their own preferred pace of learning'. Personalised learning was included in *Excellence and Enjoyment* (DFES 2003). In 2006, QCA published guidance on a renewed Primary Framework for Literacy and Mathematics for implementation by 2008. The House of Commons Children, Schools and Family Committee (HCCSFC) in its Fourth Report of 2009, noted the Department's claim to have streamlined National Strategies guidance, yet the amount of additional guidance remained considerable, ostensibly crucial to empowering teachers and raising standards. They quoted one witness critical of New Labour's way of working:

> Initially there was a promise to provide guidelines only on what children were entitled to be taught, and there was to be no question of eroding the teacher's responsibility for the how or the particularity of teaching. There can still be no quarrel with that. However, that promise was quickly broken and we now have a totally prescriptive, centrally worked out set of curriculum packages designed for 'delivery' by teachers.
>
> (HCCSFC 2009, Ev 250, paragraph 2 [Malcolm Ross])

The Committee examined aspects of pedagogy (paragraphs 83–86). It concluded that the Department's claims about the non-statutory status of National Strategies guidance appeared 'most notably disingenuous' in respect of synthetic phonics, as schools were offered an 'opt out' rather than 'opt in' set of guidance, and the Minister in his evidence was clear that his Department wished to see more 'consistent use' made of it. This epitomised the problem of National Strategies guidance in that it often promoted a particular approach as the 'one best way', such as the three-part lesson and objectives-led teaching. The Committee saw that as highly problematic, especially as the strategies had typically been supported by selective use of available evidence. The Committee's own earlier inquiry into the teaching of early reading had concluded that a range of approaches could work effectively, so long as teachers were trained and systematic in applying them. The Committee was convinced that a 'one best way' to teach was not supported by the research evidence, that the Department should not place pressure on schools, and should send a much stronger message to Ofsted and local authorities as to the *non-statutory* nature of National Strategies guidance. Following the 2010 General Election, the new Secretary of State Michael Gove responded in contradictory ways to this trend of thought. On the one hand he announced abandonment of the National Strategies. On the other hand a new stage of assessment introduced in the form of a reading test at the end of Year 1 was to be based specifically on phonic understanding.

Assessment

Assessment is a key factor influencing pedagogy. Going back a century and a half, critics of the Revised Code of 1862 and 'payment by results' complained how these policies encouraged 'teaching to the test', resulting in banal and sometimes bizarre practices in the classroom (Victorian inspectors reported children reading books held upside-down, implying pupils had been taught by heart the passages to be tested). Imposition of a national curriculum in 1988 was accompanied by a system of testing. One justification for the statutory tests was that to create a free market in education, parents as consumers needed information about the quality of schools between which they were to choose. This function of government, providing 'market information' in the form of published test results, helps to explain the contradictory policies of a 'free market' accompanied by increased central control.

Exacerbating the situation at the turn of the twenty-first century were the political high stakes attached to assessment. The New Labour Government set targets for school improvement, expressed in terms of test results, and its first Secretary of State for Education, David Blunkett, promised to resign if the targets were not met. By the year 2002, 80 per cent of 11-year-olds were to reach the expected standard for their age in English at Key Stage 2 and 75 per cent were to reach this level in mathematics. Early improvements were found in the Key Stages 1 and 2 results but could be attributed, in part, to sheer novelty, where improvement is prompted by the mere fact of change as much as by the specific effectiveness of new methods. By 2001 it was becoming clear that the rate of improvement in statutory test results was slowing down and the goal of continuous improvement promised by government began to appear elusive. Policy-makers attributed this failure not to the schools and the teachers but to social and cultural factors such as poverty, fractured communities, high pupil turnover and low community aspirations; for political reasons however, statutory tests could not be abandoned and there was no let up in the policy drive towards ever-more detailed assessment.

In 2009 the House of Commons Committee questioned a claim by the Department that testing reflected curriculum and heard a range of evidence on the way that in practice, curriculum followed testing rather than vice versa (HCCSFC 2009, paragraphs 78–81). The Committee also recorded a perception among schools that Ofsted inspection results were largely determined by a school's test scores, with inspectors paying comparatively little attention to wider ECM outcomes. This inspection practice reinforced the potential for testing arrangements to have negative effects on teaching and learning, just as inspection also affected pedagogy directly by encouraging adherence to the National Strategies as the officially recommended means of raising Key Stage test performance – 'teaching to the test'. Such doubts led the English government to pilot other forms of testing and to appoint an 'expert group' for advice throughout 2008 and 2009, but it held hard to the need for statutory tests as a measure of accountability. Teacher union opposition to 'the SATs' became more vociferous and public debate continued.

In other parts of Britain the direction of policy moved away from statutory tests and towards teacher assessment, specifically led by concern for the impact of assessment on pedagogy. The Welsh Assembly Government's concerns about the inappropriateness of educational provision for young children led it to abandon Key Stages 1 and 2 'SATs', to be replaced by teacher assessment. Northern Ireland relies on teacher assessment in Communication and in Using Mathematics at the end of Key Stages 1 and 2. In Scotland a new *Framework for Assessment* of their 'Curriculum for Excellence' was developed in 2009. Here, the main reforms were to allow assessment arrangements that would 'follow and support the new curriculum, promoting higher quality learning and teaching and give more autonomy and professional responsibility to teachers'. Standards and expectations were to be defined in a way that reflected the principles of breadth and depth of learning as well as a greater focus on skills development (including higher order skills) in the Scottish curriculum. A national system of quality assurance would be developed to support teachers in achieving consistency and confidence in their professional judgements. Such variations in policy around the UK should make it possible to compare the impact on pedagogy of different forms of assessment within the British Isles.

To understand the political force behind assessment and testing as it affects pedagogy, we have to recognise the globalised competitive environment in which governments make education policy. The 'standards movement' took hold on a worldwide scale in the 1990s, an outgrowth of what was known in the USA as 'systemic reform' in which the curricula of schools were to be 'aligned' with systems of assessment so that reliable estimates could be made of what children were learning and how well the schools were fulfilling their instructional mission. When David Reynolds chaired the Numeracy Task Force he had recently helped produce a report for Ofsted speculating on the possible causes for the apparent superiority of Taiwanese methods of teaching science and mathematics over those used in England, and in announcing the Task Force, Secretary of State David Blunkett made clear that international indicators showed England too far behind economic competitors in the basic skills of literacy and numeracy. This was accompanied by an official view that traditional teaching methods such as whole class teaching had 'delivered good results in countries like Taiwan'. In the same vein, evaluation of the national strategies' success was commissioned from international evaluators, bringing in a team from the University of Toronto led by Professor Michael Fullan. Their report was less than a conclusive or unequivocal endorsement, finding that investment in a sustained and focused approach to changing teaching methods was an exciting and ambitious undertaking with the clear possibility of improving outcomes; by 2003 they found that the strategies had not yet produced the needed depth of change in teaching, and that LEAs and schools would need to have increased scope and responsibility for such professional learning.

Professional autonomy, teaching and learning in the classroom and beyond

Politicisation of pedagogy has impacted significantly on the professional autonomy of teachers. Stipulation of teaching methods by central government has a marked effect on the professional role. Planning, supporting and monitoring young children's learning remains the core task for primary teachers and a construction of their work as 'delivering' National Strategies distorts and demeans it. Despite, or perhaps even because of the National Curriculum, the 1990s witnessed a flourishing of community resources, parks, nature reserves, museums and theatre groups that enlivened the facilities available to new generations of young learners.

These resources provided interesting opportunities and challenges for their teachers to offer a rich diet of knowledge and skills through activity learning, but at the same time a *dirigiste* approach to pedagogy threatened to stifle creativity in teachers as well as in children. Yet creativity is widely recognised for being as important to national economic success as levels of attainment in the core subjects.

We should now trace some of the principal arguments about how state intervention affects the daily task of teaching. The Toronto evaluation of the National Strategies was generally upbeat in its assessment. Evaluators noted that it was easier to assess the effect of the Strategies on teachers' practice than on pupils' learning. The main changes were listed as a greater use of whole class teaching, greater attention to the pace of lessons and planning based on objectives. Limitations of the top-down approach to policy were also identified, however, as targets that had initially helped mobilise teachers, subsequently skewed their teaching methods and narrowed the curriculum. Ofsted also reported on the strategies and made substantial criticisms, but ironically these were often directed at teachers for following the frameworks and guidance slavishly with too little questioning and reflection.

Announcing the 2003 Primary National Strategy (PNS), Charles Clarke as Secretary of State claimed to be responding to headteachers' complaints about excessive pressure from top-down targets and promised more autonomy for schools in allowing them to set their own targets. But as Alexander noted in his vigorous critique, the promise of autonomy was contradicted by a 'continuing pressure of testing, targets and performance tables and the creeping hegemonisation of the curriculum' by literacy and numeracy, with three-part lessons, interactive whole class teaching and plenaries soon to become a template for the teaching of everything (Alexander 2004). The PNS showed few signs of a serious desire to move away from 'standards' in favour of creativity and pupil-centred curricula. It claimed to increase teachers' autonomy on the grounds that the strategies, though strongly supported by government, were not statutory. What Alexander described as double-speak on professional autonomy was exposed in PNS recommendations for 'Realising the vision' and he italicised keywords to emphasise the contradictions:

> 'We have set out our *vision*, but we want it to be a shared *vision*. . . . We intend to spread the *dialogue* more widely. . . . This document is just the starting point for that vital *dialogue* which will shape the future of primary education. . . . This document begins to offer a *blueprint* for the future' (DFES 2003, paragraphs 8.14–8.17).

> Vision? Dialogue? Blueprint? Elsewhere in the report there is less ambiguous talk of 'the project' (paragraph 8.17). How can it be all of these?
>
> (Alexander 2004, 15)

Alexander saw the PNS as 'patronising in its assumption that teachers will be seduced by Ladybird language, pretty pictures, offers of freedom and enjoyment, and populist appeals to their common sense' (Alexander 2004, 28). Kenneth Minogue's warning about the theatrical illusions of political discourse is pertinent here. Though the strategy was not statutory, it was unsurprising that local authorities dutifully appointed primary strategy directors, fearful as they were for their Ofsted inspection ratings should they not conform.

Resistance remained a possibility. In his research on the pedagogical effects of policy, Maurice Galton quoted a lively and resourceful teacher deciding to substitute for 'literacy hour' a meaningful and interactive task with a Year 6 class:

I don't think it is helpful for children of this age to have their creativity and imagination stifled by having to follow set prescriptions. Learning is best done by doing. And I don't think that banging on about full stops and commas and different kinds of writing genres helps children to develop their minds.

(Galton 2007, 2–3)

On the other hand Galton cited another Year 6 teacher who liked the literacy hour because it gave a firm structure to her teaching and pupils knew what they had to do to succeed. Materials produced by the QCA were seen as useful because they 'Save you the trouble of having to plan lessons. It cuts out the need to think and allows more time for marking.' Thus from his data he neatly illustrates two responses to government policy, two poles in pedagogical style and two opposing constructions of the teachers' role. Each position may be seen as inherently political and responds to a highly politicised policy context.

Galton observed that even limited early gains in the 'basics', claimed by government as proving effectiveness of the literacy and numeracy strategies, had peaked. Meanwhile the strategies had had negative effects on teachers and classrooms that were less newsworthy. Emphasis on a *performance* rather than a *learning* culture in schools – one education minister having told Galton personally that performance was the only acceptable measure of learning – was found to have produced a dip in pupil attitudes, low morale amongst teachers, an impoverished curriculum and restricted pedagogy (Galton 2007, xi). Experienced teachers were antagonised rather than inspired by the 'meaningless jargon and catch-all phrases emerging from the DFES Standards Unit and the PNS', and failed to find value in continual innovations and new initiatives that required the ditching of tried and tested methods. More problematic still for the future of pedagogy was that after ten years of implementation, younger teachers under the age of 30 had known no alternative to the strategies and so had limited alternative experience to call upon.

Throughout the twenty years since the imposition of the National Curriculum and the Dearing Review of 1993, and in response to the advocacy of whole class teaching in the 'three wise men' report, its imposition in the form of national strategies and their subsequent revisions, a succession of researchers has evaluated the impact of these government policies on teachers and on learners. Some of this research has been undertaken by government bodies such as Ofsted, or commissioned by them from independent researchers, some has been similarly commissioned by teacher unions, and some has been initiated and conducted independently by educationists in universities. Given the complexity of researching such phenomena, it is unsurprising that divergent findings emerge. The varied scope and scale of enquiries and the methodologies adopted may themselves affect the outcomes. A survey of such projects was undertaken by Wyse, McCreery and Torrance (2010) for the Cambridge Primary Review where comparison and evaluation of findings are made. Conflicting conclusions from empirical research are a further strand in the web of government policy-making, but a political forum in which competing opinions can be aired and assessed is provided by the Education Committee of the House of Commons.

Teachers' frustration at policies of directed pedagogy is found in evidence heard by the House of Commons Committee in 2009. The promotion of 'one best way' and pressure to follow centrally produced guidance meant some teachers being prevented from using their preferred approach. As one teacher commented:

In 2004, I was not allowed by my local authority to teach children consistently according to the principles of synthetic phonics. I was told I must use the National Literacy Strategy 'searchlights' [approach]. . . . I was also told that I must use the government pro-grammes, Progression in Phonics and Playing with Sounds. These programmes have now been withdrawn by Government and replaced by the synthetic phonics programme Letters and Sounds. In other words, government initiatives were used as justification for preventing me from teaching in a way that was later promoted through new government initiatives.

(HCCSFC 2009, paragraph 84)

Evidence to the Committee from the National Association of Schoolmasters/Union of Women Teachers (NASUWT) observed:

Despite its claims to the contrary, the current inspection system focuses almost exclu-sively on the nature and operation of school processes rather than outcomes. Although the [National] Strategy frameworks are not statutory . . . Ofsted continues to emphasise their importance in the development of effective approaches to curriculum planning and delivery at school level.

(HCCSFC 2009, paragraph 81)

The Committee concluded:

In such a context it seems to us that a local authority or a school would have to be very confident to decide not to 'play it safe' by following centrally-produced guidance: The underlying policy is one of Ministers being relentless in driving up standards and in developing the policies to do so. . . . Time and again one hears of teachers who suspend their judgement and instead follow what the various curricula tell them to do because then they 'can't be blamed'.

(HCCSFC 2009, paragraph 82)

Ewa Allison offered insights from a comparative research study, contrasting English educa-tional politics with the fundamental political change experienced in former Soviet bloc coun-tries (Allison 2010). She compared England's prescriptive approach with the child-directed methods operating in Poland, suggesting how teachers could take ownership of the curricu-lum and its delivery for the benefit of their pupils. Teachers were shown to require autonomy and empowerment to respond sensitively to the needs of children and to adapt their practice for effective learning to occur.

In contrast with the narrow definition of pedagogy as teaching that characterised English policy, Poland aspired to 'social pedagogy'. Bringing up children was not simply about transmitting knowledge, but included learning, well-being and all-round development of the learner. In Poland, 'pedagogy', devoid of 'top-down' pressures, gave learners time, space and varied opportunity to learn how to learn and become independent learners. In England, by contrast, national policy was aimed at standardising teaching, reinforced by local authority advice filtered down from government guidance, generating mechanisms to assess pupils, promoting and monitoring didactic skills-based teaching, instead of empowering pupils.

We can go even further than this with another comparative example, that of Reggio Emilia in Italy. The understanding of pedagogy drawn from there is rich and holistic, as Leach and Moon indicate in the brief quotation that opens this chapter and further developed in their recent work *The Power of Pedagogy* (Leach and Moon 2008). They draw a concept of pedagogy that goes beyond the interaction of children with individual teachers to the development of children's natural curiosity in the varied settings of school and community life, pedagogy as a mode of engagement with social processes, with cooperation and communication as crucial features. The concept of social pedagogy implies teamwork and a collaborative process, a shared responsibility not just of parents and teachers but also of wider society, in the holistic development of children's cognitive, emotional and practical abilities. Elements of government policy straining towards a social pedagogy might be identified in *Excellence and Enjoyment* (2003), and more so in *Every Child Matters* (2004) discussed with regard to citizenship education in Chapter 4, but the official policy remains constrained by an ideological reluctance to acknowledge fully the principles of social pedagogy and constricted by the rigid systems of assessment and testing that continue to be imposed.

Conclusion

This chapter has traced the way the traditionally closed world of the primary classroom has been opened up over the past forty years to public view, to observational research and to political debate. There have been gains in terms of professional understanding and losses in terms of professional control. As technical aspects of pedagogy became the subject of popular interest and politicised in the 1970s, successive governments responded to public concerns by imposing a highly mechanistic model.

Psychological research of the learning process gave rise to new understandings of the teachers' task, including affective aspects such as motivation. Latterly neuroscience has progressed these undertandings at a technical level, yet the symbolic nature of teaching interaction means that politics is still foregrounded. Both the scientific knowledge and the symbolic character and political overtones of the teaching relationship have led governments to attempt to micro-manage pedagogy, to find 'the one best way' and to impose it through national strategies and through testing to generate measurable outcomes.

All this has implications for teachers' work, which will be considered further in Chapter 6. The problem is one of government policies leaving insufficient room for genuinely pedagogical relationships, not just between pupils and their teachers, but in a whole variety of settings beyond the classroom. Approaches to pedagogy are politically polarised and arouse deep passions. The principle we should seek is more scope for teachers to respond to children's learning needs, able to make their own decisions about teaching method in the context of a much broader concept of social pedagogy.

Key questions for reflection

- If pedagogy is a question of purely technical procedures in the classroom, why has the organisation of children's learning aroused such heated political debate?
- Reflecting on your methods of teaching, what aspects are directly influenced or constrained by government prescription? What influence do assessment and targets have in a school's pedagogical practice? What relationship, if any, do you identify between classroom teaching methods and wider social pedagogical aspects of your work?
- What degree of initiative is left to individual teachers in their teaching? What scope should be allowed for teachers' individual professional judgement in the way they teach?

Independent learning tasks

Adopt any one of the above questions as a focus for personal research, and/or the basis for discussion with colleagues.

To reflect on the ways that teaching methods have been politicised and the polarisation of media representation, review examples of the campaigning literature on pedagogy and related press comment, for example:

Miriam Gross (2010) *So Why Can't They Read?* Centre for Policy Studies. Available at www.cps.org.uk (accessed 26 May 2011).

Rachel Williams, 'Primary school "street" talk breeding illiteracy, claims thinktank'. *Guardian*, Monday, 19 July 2010. Available at www.guardian.co.uk/education/2010/jul/19/primary-schools-street-literacy (accessed 26 May 2011).

Max Hastings, 'Ideologues of illiteracy: The terrible damage wrought on our schools by Left-wing educationalists'. *Daily Mail*, 20 July 2010. Available at www.dailymail.co.uk/debate/article-1296126/Ideologues-illiteracy-MAX-HASTINGS-terrible-damage-wrought-schools-Left-wing-educationalists.html (accessed 26 May 2011).

Michael Shaw, 'Marks out of 10 – No place for facts in fiction'. *TES Magazine*, 13 August 2010. Available at: www.tes.co.uk/article.aspx?storycode=6054229 (accessed 26 May 2011).

Alternatively, review a chapter of your own choosing from:

Chris Woodhead (2009) *A Desolation of Learning* (Pencil-Sharp Publishing), or from Frank Furedi (2009) *Wasted: Why Education isn't Educating* (London: Continuum) and compare with any one the articles listed below for further reading.

Further reading

Alexander, R.J. (2004) 'Still no pedagogy? Principle, pragmatism and compliance in primary education', *Cambridge Journal of Education*, 34, 1: 7–33.
Alexander sets out to test the continuing validity of the alleged absence of rigorous pedagogy in English primary education against the government's Primary National Strategy of 2003. Postulating three domains of ideas, values and evidence, it critically assesses the Strategy's account of pedagogy and the political assumptions it embodied.

Allison, E.B. (2010) 'Pedagogy – how is it influenced in primary schools? A comparative study of literature about pedagogical influences in primary schools in England and Poland, with a focus on English primary schools', *Education 3–13*, 38, 1: 55–67.
Allison critically reviews recent empirical studies comparing pedagogical influences in primary schools in England and Poland. The article illustrates the value of comparative research by contrasting cultural constructs of 'classroom pedagogy' and 'social pedagogy', and its analytical model may usefully be compared with Alexander's three domains of ideas, values and evidence.

Brehony, K. (2005) 'Primary schooling under New Labour: The irresolvable contradiction of excellence and enjoyment', *Oxford Review of Education*, 31, 1: 29–46.
Brehony assesses the most significant policies on primary schooling under New Labour, with an inevitable emphasis on pedagogy, in part to determine what these policies revealed about its political project. He notes the dual thread in educational policy of a need to appeal to the electorate and gain electoral advantage, and a genuine attempt to address educational problems, questioning the mantra of 'evidence' as a supposed antidote to ideology.

Soler, J. and Openshaw, R. (2006) *Literacy crises and reading policies: Children still can't read!*, London: Routledge.

Chapter 5 (62–79) examines the reading standards debate of the 1990s for the emergence of a new dominant narrative and media debate that overturned the child-centred vision of primary teachers, replacing it with a technicist description of a pedagogy controlled by market mechanisms. This narrative was then embedded in the National Literacy Strategy.

Woods, P. and Wenham, P. (1995) 'Politics and pedagogy, a case study in appropriation', *Journal of Education Policy*, 10, 2: 119–141.

This article discusses the 'Three Wise Men Report' of 1992 and the public debate it provoked in the press and among politicians, educationists and teachers. Based on interviews with key players and with teachers, the paper is seen in relation to differing interests and different contexts: the political, the policies of the 'New Right' influencing its reception; and the educational, when the policy was implemented through the LEA and appropriated by classroom teachers.

Chapter 6

Workforce and politics

A whole raft of policy initiatives on teacher education appears to have been framed specifically to change the nature of teacher professionalism and to increase a focus upon craft skills at the expense of reflection and professional understanding. By emphasising competencies the dominant discourse of liberal humanism is undermined and replaced with a discourse of technical rationality; technicians are preferred to reflective practitioners whose skills are theoretically underpinned. Whilst central government holds on tightly to strategic control it relies increasingly on intermediary agencies like Ofsted and the TTA, headed up by government appointees, to implement and facilitate its vision.

(Hall 2004, 37)

I am always humbled by the commitment and hard work of staff in our schools . . . and am grateful for everything that you do to help children achieve. . . . Nothing matters more to us than having great teachers and great heads. Everything else that we want to achieve flows naturally from the people working in our schools. . . . So your ideas of how we can improve professional development are particularly important to me.

(Gove 2010)

Introduction

Where Plowden had put the child at the heart of primary education in 1967, to be replaced in 1981 by 'the curriculum' (DES 1981), in 1997 Cedric Cullingford proposed: 'At the heart of primary education is the role of the teacher' (Cullingford 1997, 2). That proposition recognises the key role of a class teacher who takes overall responsibility, throughout a complete school year, for the learning experiences of around thirty children across the whole curriculum. In political discourse 'teacher' is often represented as a unitary occupational category; at the operational level it covers a huge variety of roles. The most obvious variable is the age of children or young people that we teach, early years, primary or secondary. Within the primary school, the role varies according to responsibilities such as management, special needs coordination or curriculum leadership, but most primary schools are characterised by their collegiality, the way staff operate as a close-knit team. Across the differentiated roles of support staff such as teaching assistants, midday supervisors, site manager and office staff, a close collaboration centres on the care and welfare of the pupils.

Politics and policy have impinged on the role of primary teachers, which this chapter will explore in three respects: training and professional development; conditions of work in schools; and the professional associations and organisations that represent primary teachers' views and interests. Policy discourse that describes teachers as a 'workforce' neglects and obscures the blend of vocationalism and professionalism demanded in effective primary teaching. Balancing the vocational and the professional creates tensions, and individual teachers interpret the balance differently, but in every case the investment of self in the role of class teacher and the deployment of specialist expertise are considerable. This complexity of the role makes varied and subtle demands in terms of initial teacher education and continuing professional development, yet training and development are increasingly micro-managed by government. Teachers require a sense of control and ownership in their professional growth, and opportunities to network widely with colleagues who share specialist knowledge and skills. Working conditions need to recognise the demands of the primary teacher's role and to provide the necessary support and facilities to do the job well. Finally, teachers' voices need to be heard and heeded by policy-makers, which requires a more effective engagement with educational politics than is currently achieved by an unwieldy proliferation of professional organisations.

Training and professional development

Initial teacher education

Successive governments in the later twentieth and early twenty-first centuries aimed to improve the quality of education in ways that were seen as essential to industrial development and economic growth. That led to closer control first of the school curriculum, as considered in Chapter 3, and then of classroom teaching, as discussed in Chapter 5. The aim of more closely regulating the educational process at classroom level also led to tighter specification and monitoring of teacher education and training. If the school curriculum had grown into a 'secret garden' over the first half of the twentieth century, it might be said that the teacher training curriculum had also become forbidden territory.

Ensuring teacher supply of sufficient quantity and quality is a necessarily political function in maintaining a state education system. Fifty years ago, for example, training colleges readily complied with government policy in the huge and urgent expansion that was required to satisfy a dramatically increased demand for teachers to meet the post-war baby boom then going through schools. In 1959 however, when teachers' certificate courses were extended from two to three years, and when a Bachelor of Education (B.Ed.) degree was subsequently instituted in the later 1960s, politicians had little or no say in the details of course content. Then in the 1960s and 1970s, as teacher education secured a firm place within the higher education sector, so it acquired the academic freedom from state interference that had traditionally characterised the universities. Subsequent political intrusions from the mid-1980s into reform of teacher training were therefore hotly contested. New policies raised fundamental questions regarding the knowledge and skills needed by teachers, the claims of different interest groups in defining those needs, and the appropriate settings for teacher education and training.

A prevailing assumption for many decades had been that whereas secondary teachers required the subject specialism that could only be gained through a university degree, the broad curriculum coverage required by primary teachers could be sufficiently achieved by a two-year college course, leading to a 'teacher's certificate'. On the other hand, professional training and experience in the classroom, desirable but not absolutely necessary for secondary teachers, was seen as indispensable for those aiming to work in primary schools.

For primary teachers, professional understanding and experience were increasingly informed by the growth of developmental psychology and scientific knowledge about cognitive and emotional growth in younger children. To accommodate these expanding requirements, the teachers' certificate course was extended, and then just a few years later the B.Ed. degree was introduced as a course lasting three, or even four, years. This comprised a degree-level course of academic study, together with the practical experience necessary for gaining Qualified Teacher Status (QTS). In the 1970s, many of the former training colleges, now 'colleges of education', began to be absorbed into their local universities as schools or institutes of education. Higher education had meanwhile been restructured into a 'binary system' with traditional universities on one side, and polytechnics administered by local education authorities as an alternative form of higher education with a more vocational purpose. While some colleges of education moved into their local university, others merged with their local polytechnic. Teaching had at long last been established as a graduate profession in the sense that a university or polytechnic degree would now be a prerequisite for entry to teaching in primary as well as secondary schools.

Underlying this long sequence of enhanced certification and institutional reorganisation was a constantly growing aspiration across the whole of society for university education. In addition, there was rapid increase in the birth rate, and therefore in projected demand for teachers. At work here were some of the dynamics through which teaching became politicised, demographic trends and social aspirations both exerting pressures on state provision of education. Governments need to meet popular demand for education, a costly service, and teachers are a necessary and expensive means to this end. With the economic and cultural crises of the 1970s, successive governments felt impelled to engage actively in reforming the methods of teacher training. From 1970 to 1974, Margaret Thatcher was Secretary of State for Education and Science (about the time that education had become the largest spending government department, overtaking defence) and her will and determination to reform public services and to constrain public spending emerged as a hallmark of her policies. One of her first acts on taking office was to appoint a committee to enquire into teacher training and development, but a fall in the birth rate projected a much reduced demand for teachers so that over the mid-1970s the teacher training system would be severely contracted.

For our present discussion of politics and teaching, the significant questions are not quantitative, but qualitative and ideological. The issue that divides different political standpoints is not 'how many teachers?' but rather 'what kinds of teachers?'. Interest groups include government, teacher unions and the universities, but within each of those groups is found a range of different opinions. John Furlong (2001), in his account of teacher education reform, drew on an extended research project into modes of teacher education. He identified four successive phases: 1976–1984, 1984–1992, 1992–1997 and the fourth beginning with New Labour in 1997. For each phase he described key policy debates and policy 'texts', then examined practice in terms of initial training courses, their structure and content and their links to schools. In 1976 we find a fairly fragmented model of minimal national policy intervention and great diversity of course content between relatively autonomous colleges and universities. The objective was a highly educated individual and 'expert' teacher. By 1997 the aim had become a 'competent practitioner'. This shift followed the government-led demand for a 'modernised' workforce with collective rather than individual values and responsive to changing national policy priorities. It led to strong control of institutions through a specified teacher training curriculum and 'standards', and a specific and substantial contribution to the training process by schools themselves.

Such rigorous specification of requirements for teacher qualification and monitoring of the quality of courses developed from 1983 onwards, when a Council for the Accreditation of Teacher Education (CATE) was appointed by Secretary of State Sir Keith Joseph. CATE exemplified much stricter control of primary teachers and primary teaching, giving government ministers closer oversight of entry into the profession. With only minority representation of teacher training institutions themselves on this council, CATE took on the task of validating college and university courses according to centrally stipulated criteria. These included minimum times to be spent on school practice and a requirement for teacher educators in higher education to acquire 'recent and relevant' experience in the classroom.

Under CATE, all pre-service teacher training courses had to be accredited according to these statutory criteria, progressively refined over subsequent years. A notorious example of specific ministerial interference stemmed from Keith Joseph's personal hostility towards sociology and its alleged tendency to left-wing political critiques of education policy: entry criteria for primary PGCE courses were revised so that only first degree subjects seen as directly relevant to the primary school curriculum were acceptable, thus excluding not only sociologists but also modern linguists, philosophers, economists, lawyers and many other graduates in less conventional disciplines who might have skills and knowledge to contribute in a broad primary curriculum.

Nevertheless, as Kathy Hall (2004) describes, critical attacks on teacher training institutions continued from right-wing think tanks like the Centre for Policy Studies and alarmist articles such as one in *The Spectator,* a conservative political journal, that portrayed teacher educators as subversive Marxists. These campaigns raised the political temperature on issues of teacher qualification. CATE was in status only an advisory body but in 1994 when it began to produce advice that was politically unacceptable to the government of the day, supervision of teacher training and qualification passed to a new body, the Teacher Training Agency (TTA), at once more powerful than CATE and more directly under ministerial control. The shift in terminology from 'council' to 'agency' is relevant in understanding the changing political relationship. The TTA replaced 'validation criteria' with detailed requirements for courses of teacher education, and compliance was achieved by TTA control in allocating funds and places to institutions and courses. Regulation was tightened by specifying 'competencies', later 'standards', that had to be demonstrated by teachers in order to qualify. Hall's quote at the beginning of this chapter brings out the discursive significance of 'competencies'.

Definition of the Key Stages 1 and 2 National Curriculum in terms of traditional subjects, instead of a more thematic cross-curricular approach to primary curriculum, provoked a change in the training of primary teachers. Instead of aiming to produce generalists with professional expertise in assisting children's learning, their training was increasingly orientated towards the production of subject specialists. The New Labour Government from 1997 continued the development of a national curriculum for initial teacher training, a top-down, Ofsted-enforced curriculum with strong emphasis on the core subjects, with the risk that this concentration on 'the basics' would in turn lower the levels of specialist subject knowledge of those achieving primary QTS (Brehony 2005, 31, 35). Introduction of national literacy and numeracy strategies entailed further regulation of initial teacher training. Prescription of methods for classroom teaching of the strategies was extended to prescription of the programmes for student teachers, and under this new national curriculum for intending teachers, students were required to demonstrate the obliged knowledge and skill in methods of teaching the strategies.

Initial teacher education has also seen the evolution of school-based routes into teaching. Political critiques of university and college courses for prospective teachers in the 1980s included their apparent remoteness from the classroom. This critique had roots in the century-old mutual suspicion between 'practitioners' and 'theorists' as well as a more recent justification in complaints by headteachers about inadequate classroom-management skills amongst NQTs, especially in the more challenging conditions that began to present themselves in some inner-city schools. Politically it offered a pretext for attacking the monopoly of teacher training traditionally enjoyed by Higher Education Institutions (HEIs). Alternative models were experimented with, such as School-Centred Initial Teacher Training (SCITT), the Graduate Teacher Programme (GTP) and Teach First, all embodying the principle of 'learning on the job'. Projects of this kind were represented not only as a challenge to 'producer capture' by the academic world of teacher educators, but also as widening access to the profession through diversity of provision, and potentially cost-saving through more economical models of teacher training. Teacher educators in HEIs were, at the same time, seeking closer partnerships with schools through mentoring schemes, whilst criteria for initial training courses demanded an increasing proportion of time spent in professional placements.

Following the change of government in 2010, the White Paper *The Importance of Teaching* announced further moves towards relocating initial teacher education from HEIs to schools. A national network of teaching schools coordinated by the National College for School Leadership (NCSL) would work through teaching school alliances to provide training and development from initial training through to headship. A further new policy direction for entry to teaching was the insistence on high standards of academic excellence with incentives to attract graduates with first class degrees and deterrence of HEIs offering low standards of A-Level entry to B.Ed. courses.

Continuing professional development

As in many other professions, it became widely accepted during the later decades of the twentieth century that initial training and qualification was not an end but a beginning, that professional training and development must be continuous throughout a career. Diverse opportunities for professional development had been offered to teachers earlier in the century by teacher unions, HMI and universities. HMI pioneered specialist courses for primary teachers in the post-war years, which focused on the personal development of the teacher, whether in artistic creativity or in their understanding of maths and science, confident that extended personal education would enhance classroom practice. Attention was also paid to new knowledge about child development. These courses did not pretend to offer any framework of structured or sequential professional development. More structured, with definite curriculum innovation and development in mind, were the courses for primary teachers associated with new curriculum projects such as Nuffield Science and Maths in the 1960s, and then other curriculum innovations produced by the Schools Council in the years following the Plowden Report. A number of local authorities had been prominent in encouraging primary teachers to attend courses, supporting them and providing follow-up in newly established teachers' centres. Local authority teachers' centres became instrumental as providers of in-service training to support Nuffield and Schools Council curriculum projects.

A committee under Lord James, commissioned by Margaret Thatcher as Secretary of State in 1970, proposed a more structured provision of in-service education and training (INSET) for teachers, what we now recognise as continuing professional development (CPD). The

James Report conceived such courses not as ad hoc and optional, but as an integral component of a teacher's professional development, undertaken for at least one term in every seven years. University institutes and schools of education responded by offering Advanced Diploma and Master's courses with significant academic and research content. After 1970, the newly founded Open University played an important role with its modular offering, which allowed certificated teachers to raise their qualifications to degree level through part-time and distance learning, again with emphasis on educational theory or academic subject knowledge. Under this regime, initiative in taking these opportunities remained with the teacher, so that individual responsibility and choice in further professional development complemented the relative autonomy of the primary teacher in her or his classroom.

A significant shift in policy occurred in the late 1990s, however. Introduction of the literacy and numeracy strategies brought further national regulation not only of initial teacher training but also of CPD. Training materials were developed by national government and literacy and numeracy consultants were appointed in LEAs. Time and resources for CPD were allocated to introducing and managing literacy and numeracy, leaving far less scope or resources for independently chosen routes of development. In effect, professional development was thereby determined by political rather than personal priorities. In allocating schools' budgets for in-service training, heads and governors were now expected to have regard to curriculum needs of the school, perhaps as identified by Ofsted inspection reports, so that political priorities mediated through national curriculum requirements or inspection frameworks effectively constrained a teacher's individual growth. For career progression, courses and certification such as those provided by the NCSL necessarily took priority over the pursuit of any specialist intellectual interest by individual teachers. A National Professional Qualification for Headship was introduced in 1998 and became mandatory for headship candidates in 2009. Though it trained over 30,000 candidates in ten years, only one-third of those proceeded to headship, and a substantial revision of the programme was announced in 2010. A scheme for identifying and training Specialist Leaders of Education (SLEs), and Local Leaders of Education (LLEs) was also introduced under the auspices of the NCSL with the aim of raising standards generally, especially in management and leadership and especially in challenging and difficult schools. At the peak of this hierarchy are National Leaders of Education (NLEs), and the 2010 White Paper included a target of designating 1,000 NLEs by 2014.

John Furlong highlighted a fundamental contradiction between political rhetoric and the realities of policy. In its Green Paper of 1998 entitled *Teachers: Meeting the Challenge of Change,* the New Labour Government projected the vision of a 'new professionalism', calling on teachers to take individual responsibility for development of their skills and subject knowledge, and to seek evidence for what works in practice nationally and internationally. Yet the initial training curriculum, as we have seen, continued to restrict any scope for 'extended professionalism' that university-based training could offer, in preference for a rigid 'standards'-based curriculum, while the 'evidence' envisaged for dissemination through CPD drew from a narrowly defined body of research selected to coincide with political priorities.

Most recently the aim of raising the status of teaching from graduate level to a Masters level profession has again been directed as a political project. Hence the introduction of the Masters in Teaching and Learning (MTL) as a government-funded practice-based Masters programme, developed by a rebranded government agency, now the Training and Development Agency (TDA) for schools, and delivered by schools in partnership with HEIs. So the traditional role of universities in pursuit of politically independent critical learning is replaced by that of validating a qualification designed by the state. The MTL is advertised as promoting 'reflective practice, so most of your learning will happen in the classroom while you're teaching', as distinct from the critical reflection that could take place away from the classroom, which received only token and grudging acknowledgement.

> You will need to do some studying in your own time, but the emphasis will be very much on hands-on learning. There will also be opportunities to share experiences with and learn alongside other MTL participants. This may mean spending some time outside the classroom.
>
> (TDA website)

Conditions of work in schools

The conditions under which teachers work in primary classrooms are determined by government policy and call for political critique. There may be questions simply of funding, of how much resource is provided to meet the needs of the job, or more intricate questions of how resources are deployed and what results are expected from them. Conditions of work are underpinned by cultural traditions and assumptions, but at any given point in history, as at the present time, they are the result of official definitions of the primary teacher's role, as well as the level of resources made available for state education. Both factors are outcomes of political decision-making, frequently the subject of political negotiation by teachers' representatives.

Role

In 1987, the Teachers Pay and Conditions Act brought to an end what had been an open-ended teachers' contract. It introduced a much tighter specification by central government of the way that teachers were to conduct their professional tasks, with a contract specifying hours of work under the direction of the headteacher, so-called 'directed time'. As currently agreed in 2010, in addition to the 1,265 hours of directed time, a teacher 'must work such reasonable additional hours as may be necessary to enable the effective discharge of the teacher's professional duties', for example, in planning and preparing courses and lessons, and in assessing, monitoring, recording and reporting on the learning needs, progress and achievements of assigned pupils. Political intervention, with a new and much tighter control of teachers' work, was in keeping with developments in public sector employment generally. It was just one manifestation of wider and deeper economic and cultural changes, and signalled a fundamental shift in the working atmosphere of the primary school.

In the teachers' conditions of work up until that time, there had been no detailed specification of what a teacher was required to do, and contrasting views could be found about the demands of primary teaching. To many outside the profession it was seen as a relatively easy job of teaching compliant young children, with a short working day and long holidays. Contrasting with that, the Plowden Report had in 1967 endowed the role with an awesome and weighty responsibility for 'the whole child', involving hours of careful preparation and review outside the school day in order to cater effectively for individual needs. In the early 1980s, Cedric Cullingford identified on the one hand a continuing invisibility of primary teachers: 'Teachers had autonomy. They seemed to live in private spaces'; on the other hand, many, including parents, had begun to see them as better trained, more skilled, professional and dedicated. But there was also a significant shift of emphasis in the role of the primary headteacher from curriculum leader and colleague to financial controller and chief executive (Cullingford 1997, 3, 9).

What has particularly characterised the primary school and the way it works in practice is its collegiality. Distinguishable from secondary school not only by the age range of pupils and organisation of the curriculum, but also by size, the primary school is typically a much smaller entity, which affects the character of the workplace. The scale of the school community and the dependency of pupils requires closer collaboration between professionals and ancillary staff. Secretaries, site managers, playground supervisors and kitchen staff tend to liaise more closely and informally where their common concern is the welfare of young children. Romantic views of this community, its humour, as well as its scope for personality clashes and internecine warfare, have been represented in popular literary form by Miss Read (*Village School* 1955), Jack Sheffield (*Village Teacher* 2010), and in the long-running radio comedy 'King Street Junior' by Jim Eldridge (1985–1998, 2002–2005) amongst other examples.

Under New Labour, there was a sharp accentuation of intervention and prescription in pedagogy and curriculum. For individual teachers' experiences of working conditions, much depends on the span of political change encompassed by their careers. A teacher retiring in 2010 after forty years of service would recall the degree of autonomy enjoyed in the years following the Plowden Report, rudely interrupted in mid-career by the imposition of a National Curriculum, which removed much of the teacher's discretion, followed by government intervention in pedagogy as whole class teaching became official policy in the 1990s. A regime of high-stakes testing and publication of league tables encouraged cheating by some schools, leading in such cases to annulment of test results, suspension of headteachers, and even in one case in 2003, the jailing of a head. In that case the chair of school governors explained the pressure as their school had been left at the bottom of the league tables and the head worried about its impact on recruitment. With the 2003 policy of *Excellence and Enjoyment* the Secretary of State announced a dropping of externally imposed targets for primary schools in 2004 in response to headteachers' complaints about excessive pressure, and promised more autonomy for teachers and schools in setting their own targets. Teachers currently under the age of 30, by contrast with their older colleagues, have known no alternative to the pressurised regime of strategies, targets and league tables. At any point in time, the teaching staff of a school, depending on their ages and career histories, will have experienced a varied range of training and conditions that inform the different attitudes that individuals bring to the role. Researchers and commentators over the course of the past few governments have observed an infiltration of 'performance culture' into the primary classroom, seeing demoralised teachers 'performing' for the purpose of surviving inspections. Pollard (2001) observed hard-edged performance systems and structures gradually altering taken-for-granted assumptions and ways of thinking. More recently Galton (2007) regretted that emphasis on *performance* rather than *learning* has taken hold in primary school culture.

That the National Curriculum and National Strategies had served to de-skill teachers was agreed by pressure groups to the left and right of the political spectrum. In 2009, the House of Commons Children, Schools and Families Committee observed that 'at times schooling has appeared more of a franchise operation, dependent on a recipe handed-down by Government rather than the exercise of professional expertise by teachers' (HCCSFC 2009). Robert Whelan, representing the non-partisan and 'classical liberal' think tank Civitas (Institute for the Study of Civil Society), rejected the government's view that the National

Curriculum is a light regulatory framework within which teachers can develop their skills as 'a dangerous dream world'.

> [That] is not what we are hearing from teachers. Teachers are very oppressed. . . . I do not accept the view that it is only the poor teachers who say, 'Oh, we can't do this because of the National Curriculum.' It is a genuine excuse: they feel they are so rigidly controlled that they cannot do what they trained to do as teachers.
>
> (HCCSFC 2009, Q 91 Robert Whelan, Civitas)

Over the last twenty years, teacher unions have been active in commissioning research on working conditions, as a means of monitoring the impact of government policies on teachers' working lives. This research has generated a considerable database and literature, and three recent examples can be compared for their different findings. Teachers responding to Galton and MacBeath, investigating for the NUT in 2002, acknowledged that the National Curriculum and the Strategies had had a positive effect on teachers' workloads and on the quality of pupils' educational opportunities. On the other hand, inspection, testing and performance management had increased workload burdens while contributing little to the quality of children's learning experiences. Increased amounts of paperwork generated by testing and inspections were felt by the teachers to call into question their professional competence in managing children's learning, and the loss of control was a major source of stress, especially amongst those with a strong sense of vocation who experienced role conflict as personal values brought to teaching were undermined by the new orthodoxy. Lack of time to spend with individual children, especially for younger teachers, marked the failure of primary teaching to live up to the rewards and motivations they had expected from the profession, and left them disillusioned. A decline in their own sense of creativity had also resulted from the reduced time for teaching more creative areas of the curriculum.

The Association of Teachers and Lecturers (ATL) commissioned an investigation by Webb and Vulliamy, published in 2006, which found that while many teachers felt the policy had 'come full circle' insofar as the Primary National Strategy was beginning to put back into teaching what had been taken away by narrow and prescriptive strategies, retention of narrow Key Stage assessments with results used for a variety of conflicting purposes was likely to continue adversely affecting children's learning and teachers' well-being. Galton and MacBeath, revisiting schools in 2007 that they had researched five years earlier, found a mixed picture. On the positive side, 'workforce remodelling' had provided planning, preparation and assessment (PPA) time, which allowed for more reflection and renewal, making teachers feel valued and having a greater sense of managing their own time. On the negative side its deployment depended on school budget and school leadership, and PPA time was often used to catch up on urgent tasks; remodelling had not reduced the primary teacher's overall workload, as systems of record-keeping became more complex, and more time was now given to pupils' and parents' problems, a consequence of changes in society as well as policy change. Independent enquiries may understandably produce inconsistent or even contradictory results as regards the impact of reforms on teachers' workload, but Wyse, McCreery and Torrance (2010) have attempted a balanced evaluation of a number of these enquiries in their overview for the Cambridge Primary Review.

Gender and ethnicity are significant features of the working environment, factors which vary from one school to another. The primary teaching workforce is predominantly female; in England, Wales, Scotland and Northern Ireland alike, around 80 per cent or more of primary teachers are women and a quarter of all primary schools are reported to have no male teacher. Proportionately fewer women occupy the senior roles of headteacher and deputy head, though the proportion is increasing. A tendency for males to occupy senior management roles has been seen as influencing young children's perceptions of status and authority, ultimately affecting their own career aspirations, although suppositions about young boys' need for male teachers and male role models have been contested. The scope for positive discrimination by gender and ethnicity in recruiting primary teachers is contentious and problematic, and whilst neither aspect of teacher recruitment is currently as high on governments' policy agendas as it should be, that of encouraging ethnic minority students into teacher education and training surely ought be a political priority.

A politics of the workforce in a multi-ethnic society needs to address the experiences of ethnic minority teachers. Important as it is for equality of opportunity in employment generally, teachers have particular significance for their influence on the learning and achievements of children and young people. The potential impact of teachers as role models is great, and a more diverse population of pupils is more likely to identify with an ethnically diverse group of teachers. A disproportionately white teaching force faces challenges in engaging with the black and ethnic minority communities served by their schools. With this in mind, the DFES commissioned research on ethnic minority teachers' professional experiences, published in 2007. African Caribbean, Bangladeshi, Indian and Pakistani teachers in London, the West Midlands and the North West reported a prevailing motive to serve their communities and to provide role models for underachieving students. African Caribbean teachers in particular felt that greater representation was needed at all levels of the profession from class teacher to headteacher. Elements of racism in recruitment procedures, and fear of potential racial abuse prevented most ethnic minority teachers from seeking work in predominantly white areas. National Curriculum requirements were perceived as hindering their ability to support the learning of ethnic minority pupils and as compromising teachers' professional expertise (Cunningham and Hargreaves 2007). Gus John, the first African Director of Education in Britain, in Hackney from 1989 to 1997, has written and campaigned about the professional and the political difficulties black primary teachers have encountered, for example, from black parents and from white colleagues, from policies of teacher unions and of governments (John 2006).

Resources and 'workforce remodelling'

Over the course of the twentieth century the historic model of an isolated teacher in charge of a class of forty, fifty or even sixty children gradually disappeared. Pupil–teacher ratios declined, school buildings became more open-plan, social relationships between children and teachers, and between teachers and parents, developed along more informal lines. The curriculum became more diverse, teaching and learning styles more active, promoting more collaborative engagement between teachers. Team teaching and parental involvement have become more common and attention to individual needs within the mainstream classroom has resulted in the presence of other adults alongside the teacher in the classroom. A reduction in class size has undoubtedly reflected more generous resourcing of primary education. Developments such as team teaching and classroom assistants may enhance the quality of work, but raise harder questions about the relationship between levels of resourcing and teachers' professional role. This has been the case in respect of government policies of 'workforce remodelling'.

At first sight it may seem surprising that the introduction of classroom teaching assistants as a government policy should have been professionally sensitive or politically contentious. A term coined by John Patten, an accident-prone and short-lived Secretary of State for Education (1992–1994), might hold a clue, as he proposed recruiting a 'mum's army' to solve the staffing shortages of primary schools. His proposed policy was questioned from various angles. Was it in the interests of efficiency or of economy? Was it intended to enhance or to undermine the qualified primary teacher's role? A legacy that needs to be recognised in understanding professional suspicion about such a policy was the long history of young 'pupil-teachers' as apprentices, and the use of 'ancillary' untrained teachers in elementary schools, a policy consistently opposed by teacher unions up until the Second World War. In 2003, ten years after Patten's pronouncement, a more focused and constructive policy of 'workforce remodelling' was introduced by New Labour. The discursive power of the term is not to be underestimated however.

This government initiative aimed to reduce teachers' workload, as a means of raising standards in schools. The School Workforce Agreement was signed in 2003 by central government, local authority employers and most of the teacher unions, paving the way for a much bigger role for support staff, and guaranteeing that teachers would no longer have to do many of the customary tasks that had been included in their role, such as covering for absent colleagues, collecting money, photocopying and even preparing classroom displays unless they chose to do so. It also allowed for PPA time, a guaranteed minimum of 10 per cent of their teaching time. The Agreement acknowledged the important role played by school support staff and by 2006 the number of TAs nationally was 150 per cent higher than in 1997, TAs representing a quarter of all teaching staff in schools. Their vital role and the need for specialist training was recognised by the introduction of a qualification for higher level teaching assistants (HLTA). Enhancing the class teacher's role by freeing more time to exercise the professional skills for which they have been educated and trained, they acquire at the same time management of other adults as an additional responsibility.

A *TES* survey in 2008 showed 38 per cent of teachers reporting a small reduction in workload, 10 per cent said it had increased it; 25 per cent said their school had introduced the deal in full, and 47 per cent said their school hadn't. The view of the NASUWT was that where it had been fully implemented it was working well, and that the problems lay with schools that were not complying. An Ofsted report in 2010 showed that the wider schools workforce, including teaching assistants must be effectively deployed, well managed and properly trained, and that the effectiveness of the reforms depended on all school staff being valued and treated as professionals. Research commissioned by the ATL into the role and effects of TAs in English primary schools painted a largely positive picture of increased teacher effectiveness and effective classroom management. In 2006, Webb and Vulliamy recorded a fundamental change in the culture of primary schools following the rapid expansion in numbers and responsibilities of TAs, which demanded of classroom teachers new skills of delegation and mentoring, but also gave them additional status as managers. They concluded that 'The workforce remodelling agenda is viewed both as a threat to teacher professionalism and as a means to enhance it by opening up new possibilities' (Webb and Vulliamy 2006, 95). Bangs, MacBeath and Galton (2011) found a mixed but gloomier picture from the range of research they reviewed and cited research from an industrial relations perspective that found 'workforce reform' in teaching to represent increasing 'separation of conception from execution' elevating the role of managers in designing and maintaining, codifying and policing the work of teachers.

Professional organisations and associations

How primary teachers are represented (literally and figuratively) in public discourse has political repercussions. As education gained a higher political profile over the last fifty years, the role and performance of teachers became increasingly public. A product of the communications and media revolution, this exposure is shared with other public employees like police and social workers, whose work affects the lives of citizens and whose services are paid from the public purse. Teachers are subject to regular scrutiny by central government in the form of inspection. Teachers as an occupational group come into the spotlight as schools' performance is publicised, as questions of educational expenditure, effectiveness and value for money become major political issues, and even as high-profile cases of professional misconduct hit the headlines.

> Political objectives and new values coincided. Government interest prompted media coverage; media coverage prompted government interest. Policy changes are best justified in terms of a deficit pathology; a deficit pathology was what the press were happy to provide.
>
> (Alexander 2000, 145)

In their locality, primary teachers have high visibility because parents of younger children have regular contact with school, and although parent–teacher relationships are generally sympathetic and collaborative within the local community, the national discourse of teaching generated by politicians and the press must also influence parental attitudes. These circumstances have changed the role of organisations that represent teachers and their interests, so any study of politics and primary teaching must take into account the structures and functions of teacher unions and professional groups. Professional bodies have given primary teachers a national voice, raising questions of professional recognition, its meaning and its implications within educational politics.

John Beck (2008) drew on Basil Bernstein's conclusion that professionals are motivated by their pursuit of specialist ('sacred') knowledge, but that in applying this knowledge they have to engage with 'profane' issues of economic existence and power struggles. Historically the established professions of law and medicine emerged with collective autonomy over professional training, conditions of work and practice. Beck argues that professional autonomy operated not only to insulate professions from the pressures of unrestricted free market competition; they also insulated professional knowledge and values from external interference. This autonomy and insulation was a key to the development of

> . . .inner dedication to ends and values which transcended . . . mundane considerations of profit, the demands of powerful clients, etc. Similarly, a sense of genuine ethical responsibility can only arise, among such service-providers, where it is the practitioners themselves who are responsible for the quality of the service offered.
>
> (Beck 2008, 73)

Beck is not blind to abuses made possible by privileged conditions of professional independence, but he insists that the idea of inner dedication is more than a self-serving myth.

Teacher unions developed over the nineteenth and twentieth centuries (Chapter 2) like trades unions in general, as political organisations within the larger Labour movement.

A distinctive feature of the teacher union movement was that it committed itself not just to securing teachers' conditions of service and remuneration, but also to defending and promoting the cause of education. In this sense it laid claim to the kind of professionalism described by Beck as going beyond self-interest. Unions, as we saw earlier in this chapter and in preceding chapters, have commissioned research to provide sound evidence on the conditions of work in school, on curriculum and pedagogy, which are not simply questions of teachers' own rights as employees, but also affect the quality of education received by primary school children. Where the Educational Institute of Scotland (EIS) is a large union that represents teachers across all sectors, the complex history of teacher unionism in England has left a fragmented legacy that has no doubt weakened its power. Some unions such as the NUT and NAHT were proportionately more representative of the primary sector than others such as the ATL and NASUWT that traditionally represented the secondary sector, though these distinctions have lessened over the years.

Robin Alexander has suggested that the professional culture of English primary teachers is subservient and dependent, lacking the strong professional subject interest groups with which secondary teachers can identify (Alexander 2000). It is arguable however that from the 1970s primary teachers gradually became more confident of their status, more articulate and assertive. Increasingly populated by graduates, professional training courses with their elements of educational theory, and especially sociology, may have sharpened critical perspectives. Broader cultural trends such as the decline in deference to authority also encouraged a greater openness within the profession, and teachers, through their unions, learned to respond as education came under attack.

Professional responses to political exposure and increasing research on primary education came together in the formation of special interest groups. An annual Plowden conference was first hosted in 1966 by the Advisory Centre for Education and later by Bishop Grosseteste College in Lincoln. In the same year a Primary Schools Research and Development Group (PSRDG) was founded in Birmingham to give primary school teachers a voice in national debates and a chance to engage in professionally oriented research; from 1973 it published the journal *Education 3–13*. A National Association for Primary Education (NAPE) was formed in 1980 as a campaigning group, its membership to include parents and local councillors as well as professionals engaged in primary education. In 1982 a Primary Education Study Group was formed, based at a Centre for Primary Education at Charlotte Mason College in Cumbria; it was motivated 'by a recognition of the difficulties teachers faced and a wish to understand and disseminate good practice where these difficulties had been successfully overcome' (Cullingford 1997, 1–13). The Association for the Study of Primary Education (ASPE) was launched at a conference in Leeds in the wake of the 1988 Education Reform Act to provide a voice for primary specialists working in schools, LEAs and teacher education, including some HMIs, aiming to help advance the cause of primary education by promoting its study. In 2002 it took over publication of *Education 3–13*. These groups emerged initially from centres of activity based on university institutes of teacher education, attracting the enthusiasm and energy of classroom teachers themselves anxious to make the professional voice heard in political debate, and including alliances of parents and other interest groups.

Examples can be identified of where unions and other professional organisations have collaborated in campaigns on government policy. A 'National Primary Alliance' in 2003 brought together four separate bodies (the National Primary Trust, the National Primary Headteachers' Association (NPHA), the National Association of Primary Education and the British

Association for Early Childhood Education) in collective resistance to statutory tests. Another alliance of chief education officers, school governors and primary and secondary headteachers called for a review of league tables in England, to make national tests more reliable and meaningful. At the same time, the NUT balloted its members on a refusal to administer the tests at Key Stage 1 and Key Stage 2, revealing considerable resistance among primary teachers to national testing, and widespread boycotts of testing occurred again in 2010.

Beck identifies a continuity of policy by successive governments since 1979, radically disempowering sources of organised democratic influence, such as local government, trade unions and the professions, which once had some capacity to act as a counterbalance to the dominance of the centralised state (Beck 2008). He argues that New Labour effectively weakened independent professions and marginalised trades unions, empowering managers and disempowering employees. This was achieved in part through educational discourse, introducing terms such as 'workforce remodelling', prescribing 'best practice' and insistence on the need for 'step change'. That discourse quickly inhabited the everyday currency of professional talk, through dissemination in direct professional development, documents on policy and practice, or through Teachers TV (launched in 2004 by the DFES and privatised in 2011) with connotations of teaching as 'delivering' government policy.

Attempts had been made in the early twentieth century to establish an independent register of teachers and even a Royal Society of Teachers, but both initiatives failed. Teachers aspired to the model of established professions like medicine and law that enjoyed self-government and control over entry to the profession, training and remuneration. The main obstacle for teachers was that the majority were state employees, and governments would clearly resist conceding the independence and professional status that would allow a public workforce, far larger than the medical profession, to make the kinds of costly salary demands that doctors eventually secured on the formation of the National Health Service. Increased state prescription of curriculum and conditions of work in the 1980s encouraged renewed campaigns for some form of professional recognition for teachers, and the New Labour administration in 1997 perceived an opportunity to harness teachers to its educational mission by offering a professional body in the form of a General Teaching Council for England (GTCE) and a separate one for Wales (GTCW).

Far from independence, however, the General Teaching Council for England gave no scope for negotiation of salaries or conditions of service. It was established by the Teaching and Higher Education Act of 1998 with two aims: 'to contribute to improving standards of teaching and the quality of learning'; and 'to maintain and improve standards of professional conduct among teachers, in the interests of the public'. Its role was therefore to guarantee a 'new professionalism' with standards and accountability very much to the fore. It undertook to maintain a register of qualified teachers in England, to regulate the profession, and to provide advice to government on issues affecting the quality of teaching and learning. The GTCE received most media coverage for its disciplinary cases against teachers accused of professional misconduct, so failed to convey a positive image of the profession.

The General Teaching Councils in the rest of the UK presented themselves with more force and idealism. Scotland had its own Teaching Council thirty years in advance of that in England, one of the first in the world. The Council claims a significant role in shaping the teaching profession in Scotland and for the work of its members in raising educational standards. It commits itself to observing the highest standards of impartiality, integrity and objectivity in the advice it provides, to promoting equality and diversity, and in 2009 the Scottish Government declared that GTC Scotland would become an independent profession-led body, a situation towards which it now progresses. Northern Ireland's Teaching Council describes itself as 'dedicated to enhancing the status of teaching and promoting the highest standards of professional conduct and practice'. In Wales, public protection is prominent in the representation of its functions, but also the status of teaching, and provision of educational advice to government:

> The GTCW protects the public by ensuring that teachers are appropriately qualified and that they maintain high standards of conduct and practice . . . and administers Assembly funding for teacher development. . . . The Council aims to provide an independent representative and authoritative voice for the teaching profession in Wales and seeks to provide robust advice to the National Assembly and other organisations on teaching issues.
>
> (GTCW website)

Michael Gove, incoming Secretary of State for Education in May 2010, despite his warm words for teachers that open this chapter, announced very early on his intention to abolish the General Teaching Council for England. The Welsh GTC, which continues in existence, published a statement expressing regret at this proposal, emphasising the respect parents and the wider public have for the teaching profession and the reassurance they have of knowing that teachers are part of a regulated profession.

Conclusion

Initial teacher education and training became gradually more sophisticated over the course of the twentieth century, as the foundational sciences of psychology and sociology, and an extended primary curriculum, made more demands on primary teaching. As primary teaching methods entered the political spotlight, however, governments became more interventionist. The importance of teachers' personal development in their careers was gradually eclipsed by a managerialist and technicist approach. Reforms in the staffing of primary schools poten-tially enabled primary teachers to exercise more effectively their professional skills, though the impact on their role and their working conditions has been mixed.

A change of government in 2010 highlighted the political significance of teachers' work, in almost weekly statements reflecting the role and status of teachers. In close proximity it was announced that £4 million would be allocated to extend the highly competitive Teach First scheme to the primary sector, encouraging bright young graduates to become primary teachers through workplace training, while at the same time funding was to be cut for the training of HLTAs whose work had been promoted as enabling qualified teachers to focus their professional skills where they are most needed in the classroom (*Guardian*, 10 August 2010). The schools minister announced his preference for Oxbridge graduates with no PGCE to qualified teachers with degrees from a 'rubbish university' and premiums were offered for first class graduates undertaking school-based teacher training. Teachers in Free Schools would not need Qualified Teacher Status despite the statutory requirement of QTS in state schools (*Guardian*, 28 September 2010).

The politicisation of primary schooling had variable effects on the patterns of teachers' representation. High-profile debates about the nature and quality of primary education spawned a number of interest groups that provided a platform for informed discussion of professional concerns. The structure of teacher unions continued to be fragmented, however, with competing interests and responses to government policies. Aspiration to professional recognition was notionally conceded by the state in the form of a General Teaching Council, subject to close political control, and although there are signs of some progress achieved by this body in Scotland and in Wales, in England it hardly flourished and has subsequently been abolished.

Primary teachers often encounter a public discourse in political and media debate that is categorical and reductive. It is embodied in policies that define training and development as simply acquisition of classroom management skills that determine conditions through 'workforce remodelling' and that seek to control professional organisation. Active involvement by primary teachers in union and other professional groups may help to counter this trend by asserting a professional voice in policy-making. We might aspire to an alternative vision of primary teaching as a profession, valued for its expertise and judgement and trusted with self-regulation. Achieving that goal in a changeable political climate requires a critical engagement with politics on the teachers' part.

Key questions for reflection

*   How far should the content of initial teacher education be stipulated by government, and what should be the respective roles of universities and schools? For CPD, compare the interests of individual teachers and the schools in which they are employed, and assess the roles of government policy and of independent research in determining priorities for professional development.
*   Compare the contributions of teacher unions and other organisations to maintaining a professional voice and professional status for primary teachers.
*   What considerations apply in effective staffing of primary classrooms, making use of teachers and assistants? What should be the roles of government and of individual schools in deciding these arrangements?

Independent learning tasks

Adopt any one of the above questions as a focus for personal research, and/or the basis for discussion with colleagues.

Map your experiences of the working conditions of primary teaching over the course of your career against changing government policy, including public discourse on the nature and status of the work. Or survey professional websites for representations of primary teaching and identify any political implications.

Further reading

Alexander, R.J. (ed.) (2010) *Children, Their World, Their Education: Final Report and Recommendations of the Cambridge Primary Review*, London: Routledge.
As part of this wide-ranging survey, drawing on a variety of evidence, pages 419–434 (in Chapter 21) deal with recruitment, training and development of primary teacher, and pages 443–455 (in Chapter 22) cover workforce reform and its implications for teachers' roles, professionalism and status.

Bangs, J., MacBeath, J. and Galton, M. (2011) *Reinventing Schools, Reforming Teaching. From political visions to classroom reality*, London: Routledge.
Chapter 4 (47–67) deals with policies for CPD, workforce reform and GTC based on interviews with politicians and policy-makers. It reveals the horse-trading at government and department level between

competing and conflicting policy priorities, the contingencies of funding and the tensions between unions representing different sections of the teaching profession.

Furlong, J. (2001) 'Reforming teacher education, re-forming teachers: Accountability, professionalism and competence', in R. Phillips and J. Furlong (eds) *Education, Reform and the State: Twenty-five years of politics, policy and practice*, London: Routledge, 118–135.
Furlong provides an analytical model of change in initial teacher education and training which makes clear the relationship between policy and practice in a succession of phases over the last decades of the twentieth century.

Galton, M. and MacBeath, J. (2008) *Teachers under pressure*, London: NUT/Sage.
Researching teachers' first-hand experiences, Chapter 1 (4–12) and Chapter 2 (13–22) examine 'intensification' of teachers' work and loss of autonomy as a result of education policies in the UK, while Chapter 9 (93–103) documents this as a worldwide phenomenon. Chapters 3 and 4 (23–42) focus on primary teaching and effects of workforce remodelling.

Hall, K. (2004) *Literacy and Schooling: Towards renewal in primary education policy*, Aldershot: Ashgate.
Chapter 2 (35–50) contains a succinct but detailed and critical account of teacher education and teacher professionalism under the policies of successive governments, Conservative and New Labour, citing a wide range of sociological, philosophical and some comparative research.

Richards, C. (ed.) (2001) *Changing English Primary Education: Retrospect and Prospect*, Stoke on Trent: Trentham. With particular reference to the following chapters: Campbell, R.J. 'Modernising Primary Teaching: Some issues related to performance management' (95–106); Hayes, D. 'Changing Aspects of Primary Teachers' Professionalism: Driving forward or driven backward?' (139–154); Southworth, G. 'Primary School Management' (107–122).
All three chapters reflect on policy developments in the early stages of the New Labour Government and review the impact of policy on teachers through performance management (Campbell), definitions of professionalism (Hayes) and relationships between school and community (Southworth).

Chapter 7

National accountability:
audit and inspection

In theory the new culture of accountability and audit makes professionals and institutions more accountable *to the public*. This is supposedly done by publishing targets and levels of attainment in league tables. . . . But underlying this ostensible aim of accountability *to the public* the real requirements are for accountability *to regulators*, *to departments of government*. . . . The new forms of accountability impose forms of *central control –* quite often indeed a *range of different and mutually inconsistent* forms of central control.

(O'Neill 2002, 52–53)

Managerialism has not passed Scotland by. From 1992, the devolution of budgets to schools provided a context from which local management cadres emerged, and in the mid-1990s, under both Conservative and Labour rule, a spate of Scottish Office documents disseminated ideas and practices concerning 'value for money', performance indicators, customer care and the rest of the managerial agenda. . . . There is a strong emphasis on mechanisms of performance management, as a means by which national agenda can be transmitted to school level, and to this extent, Scotland, with its ambition of achieving a 'world-class' education system . . . is just as recognisable as England in terms of its membership of a global policy community.

(Jones 2003, 155)

Introduction

To whom do primary teachers feel accountable? Most immediately it's the individual children for whom class teachers feel the greatest responsibility. The primary setting gives continued and intensive contact with a group of children whom teachers get to know quite intimately, and accountability for 'the whole child' is both to the child and to their parents or carers. Other accountabilities reach wider. Different teaching roles affect the way these accountabilities are experienced and prioritised, whether as senior management, subject coordinator or a specialist role; for instance, in Special Educational Needs.

Political discourse and its representation in the media makes teachers acutely conscious of the *national* accountability that they carry for a range of public concerns, from the moral condition of children and young people and their future job prospects, to the economic prosperity of the nation. Politicisation of primary education in later twentieth-century Britain has made schools more publicly accountable, and a changing political culture that prioritises accountability has affected all public institutions and professions.

The concept of accountability originated long ago in revolutionary democratic movements to describe the duties of governments to their people; the American colonies, launching their war of independence in the 1770s, demanded of the British government: 'no taxation without representation'. As democratic politics progressed in Britain, the right to vote was demanded on the grounds that a state that taxed its citizens and regulated their lives should be held to account for its actions. In the twenty-first century accountability roles appear to have reversed, with an emphasis on schools' and teachers' accountability to government for the way they carry out their work.

This chapter begins by discussing the national framework for administering the school system through which accountabilities are exercised. Attention is drawn to significant differences in Wales, Northern Ireland and Scotland that reveal positive alternatives to the English regime. It goes on to consider targets and league tables as an accountability mechanism, before turning to inspection, a more traditional means by which primary schools and primary teachers are held to account. The ultimate rationale is that we should be accountable to the children whose life chances depend on the quality of our teaching, and to their parents and carers. But this political imperative of accountability, to have its desired and desirable effect, needs to be balanced by a sense of value and esteem within the profession and amongst a wider public.

National accountability and its context

The history of state involvement in 'working-class elementary education' has been traced in Chapter 2. Universal compulsory schooling was provided free of charge, and the cost to the state continued to escalate not just on account of the ever-increasing child population but also with regular raising of the school-leaving age and the improved quality of provision. Public finance was the imperative for some form of accountability to ensure that funds were being spent judiciously and efficiently, and as education came to be seen as investment in the nation's future, so the effectiveness of its spending needed to be assured. Previous chapters have described ever-closer monitoring of the day-to-day work of schools, in relation to curriculum and pedagogy and to teachers. Data-gathering methodologies and information technologies in the latter half of the twentieth century meant that more intricate measurements of 'output' could be used to hold schools to account.

Education in the UK is now a devolved area of policy with each of the constituent countries having separate systems under separate governments (Gearon 2002). The UK Government in Westminster is responsible for education in England, while the Scottish Government, the Welsh Assembly Government and the Northern Ireland Executive each has its own territorial responsibilities. The distinctive legacy of the educational system in Scotland goes back three centuries and the education systems in England, Wales and Northern Ireland have shown increasingly marked differences in recent policy. Since devolution, education policy in the four constituent countries of the UK has diverged: for example, England has pursued reforms based on diversity of school types and parental choice; Wales (and Scotland) remain more committed to the concept of the community-based comprehensive school. Systems of governance and regulation – the arrangements for planning, funding, quality-assuring and regulating learning, and for its local administration – are becoming increasingly differentiated across the four home countries.

This account begins in Westminster and Whitehall, where the government and administration have responsibility for an English population of about 52 million (84 per cent of the total UK population). Within government a Department of State has particular responsibility for administering the education system. It is headed by a Secretary of State, a senior member of the government with a seat in Cabinet, supported by three Ministers of State with particular responsibilities that include schools, children and families, two Parliamentary Under-Secretaries and a huge administration led by a Permanent Secretary. The function of such a Department is to draft policy consonant with the broad political strategy of the government of the day. Policies requiring major legislation are taken to Cabinet and agreed before being put to Parliament. Legislation is then drafted and when it has been debated and approved in the Commons and Lords, and received Royal Assent, is implemented through means devised by the Department. On less important policies the Department may be responsible for drafting regulations that are not debated in Parliament but after due process can be implemented as 'statutory instruments' ('delegated' or 'secondary' legislation). Other policies may be considered not to require legislation, so non-statutory regulations are prepared by the Department, perhaps in consultation with specialist or professional groups, and implemented through Local Authorities or contracted out to private sector companies for implementation. Another major function of the Department of State is preparing budgets for necessary expenditure that have to be agreed in Cabinet and adopted by the Treasury before being debated and approved by Parliament on a regular basis. Having secured its annual budget, the Department is then responsible for allocating and administering it. The Department for Education is accountable to Parliament for public spending on education in England, for its effectiveness and for the efficiency of the education system generally. It in turn imposes accountability within the education system on local authorities, schools and other bodies, and mechanisms are devised and implemented for carrying out this accountability.

The growing importance of education within a modern state and the large proportion of national expenditure it consumes was reflected in its gradual rise in status. After the Second World War education was seen to be vital to social reconstruction and economic development of the country, and a Ministry of Education was established with a leading politician of the ruling party representing it in Cabinet (Simon 1991). By 1964, education was closely identified with producing the scientific and technological skills that were needed for commercial enterprise and military defence, and the Ministry was renamed 'Department of Education and Science', retaining that name for almost thirty years. Its frequent renaming in more recent years reflects changing political strategies and priorities for education. Policy on science and technology, now seen as too important to leave to the educationists, was removed to another department in 1992, leaving a Department *for* Education. The subtle change of linking word from *of* to *for* was not insignificant, indicating the more managerialist approach that had evolved in the 1970s and 1980s epitomised by a National Curriculum; no longer was education a social function proceeding with support and encouragement from the state, but instead had become one of the principal levers of social and economic policy.

In 1995, on the view that the main purpose of education was to skill the labour force, a short-lived and unhappy attempt was made to merge two Departments as a single Department for Education and Employment (DFEE). By 2001, 'Employment', with its own particular culture and concerns, was once again removed, but the spirit of the earlier merger was echoed in a renamed Department for Education *and Skills*. Within two years, a new policy direction was evident with the government's response to many aspects of social exclusion affecting children, alongside a call to action from the Laming Report on the death of Victoria Climbié (Chapter 4). 'Every Child Matters' argued for 'joined-up' children's services between education, health and child protection, and effectively changed the mindset of providers at national and local levels, so a Department for Children, Schools and Families (DCSF) was created in 2007. This reconfiguration was symbolically reversed only three years later by an ideological rebranding on the return of the Coalition Government in 2010, reviving the title previously used in the early 1990s: Department for Education. The new Secretary of State thereby aligned himself with a traditionally conceived formal process of education divorced from its association with children's and families' welfare, though in practice children's welfare remained within the departmental remit. It is perhaps unsurprising that this kind of political theatre, if not the costs entailed in enacting it, evokes a hint of cynicism in teachers who have to work with the everyday realities of providing for children's learning, and on ever tighter budgets.

Alongside the various transformations of the Department for Education has been an increasing trend from the 1970s onwards for education policy to be decided in the Prime Minister's office (Chitty 2009). The Downing Street Policy Unit began as a means of coordinating government policies across different departments, and with the growth of a more 'presidential style' of government has increased in significance. Tony Blair came to office with his three policy priorities famously expressed as 'Education, education, and education'. Michael Barber, former teacher, NUT officer and professor of education, had been one of his most influential policy advisers and was placed at the DFEE as leader of a new Standards and Effectiveness Unit, almost as a personal representative of the Prime Minister within the Department.

A fundamental change in national accountability for education has grown with the privatisation of education services through public–private partnerships and private finance initiatives (Chitty 2009). The outsourcing of public services has occurred also in other areas of policy such as health and transport. Promoted as a way of 'modernising' government it was not simply to raise capital or to massage balance-sheets, but was also argued as bringing business expertise, efficiency and dynamism, the 'knowledge economy' and 'fast capitalism' into the delivery of education policy. Examples include the contracting out of school inspection with the creation of Ofsted under the 1992 Education (Schools) Act as an 'independent' non-departmental public body (colloquially known as a 'quango') commissioning school inspection services from private companies. Another huge contractor was Capita, which, among many lucrative education contracts, was awarded a £177 million contract in 2004 for managing the national literacy and numeracy strategies. On occasion, where Ofsted reports identified 'failing' LEAs, central government would commission private contractors to run the local education service, as in Islington managed from 1999 by Cambridge Education Associates (CEA – now Cambridge Education (CE)). The difficulties that such outsourcing might create in terms of accountability was evident in the summer of 2008 when the Secretary of State for Education denied responsibility for chaos in the marking of tests, as this had been contracted out by the Qualifications and Curriculum Authority to an American company, ETS. Policy sociologist Stephen Ball has presented a detailed analysis in his book *Education plc* (2007) questioning the language of 'partnerships with the business community'.

Wales

The Welsh Assembly Government (*Llywodraeth Cynulliad Cymru*) in Cardiff provides for a population of 3 million (5 per cent of the UK population). In 2007, under a new Government of Wales Act, the executive (Welsh Assembly Government) was separated from the legislature (National Assembly for Wales). The result mirrors the relationship between the

UK Government and UK Parliament and that between the Scottish Government and Scottish Parliament. Before devolution, the Welsh school system had been the closest to England in terms of policy and structure. From 1947 to 1987 education policy for England and Wales had been dictated from London, despite the existence of an Education Department at the Welsh Office, as civil servants at the Welsh Office were wary of granting too much autonomy to Welsh LEAs (Phillips 2002). A Department for Children, Education, Lifelong Learning and Skills (DCELLS) is now responsible for education and children's services as an executive body of the Welsh Assembly Government.

Long-standing cultural differences include the use of Welsh language. A significant proportion of children are taught either wholly or largely through the medium of Welsh, with 22 per cent of classes in maintained primary schools using Welsh as the sole or main medium of instruction in 2009. Nevertheless, within Wales there has been a deep cultural divide between the English-speaking majority in South Wales, suspicious of what they see as elitist cultural nationalism in North Wales, West Wales and Mid Wales. Plaid Cymru, the Welsh nationalist party, gained support during the 1980s owing to economic decline, world recession and the Westminster Government's policies in closing the coal-mines. The Labour Party therefore acceded to a policy of devolution as Plaid Cymru became a more effective political rival, and even the centralist Conservative Government under Margaret Thatcher conceded some relative autonomy to Wales from 1987, for example, over the National Curriculum.

In 1998 the vote in favour of devolution, though still reflecting regional tensions between south and north, opened a new era for educational policy-making in Wales. The distinctiveness and difference from England of its education policy was evident in a Welsh 'paving document', *The Learning Country* published in 2001, that was 'fundamentally different in style, approach and articulation of future priorities' (Phillips 2002, 42–43). Ken Jones has underlined the economic as well as the cultural differences of Wales from England in recent decades, where heavy industry was proportionately more dominant, its decline leaving greater levels of poverty. Perhaps because these structural factors are so clear in a relatively small country, in Welsh political discourse schools and teachers are not blamed for poor economic performance, for low skills and qualifications, as they have been by politicians in England. Education is encouraged for its potential in narrowing inequalities between advantaged and disadvantaged areas, groups and individuals, and the 'producerist paradigm' of education for economic recovery is also evident (Jones 2003).

Northern Ireland

The devolved legislature for Northern Ireland, which has a population of slightly less than 2 million or 3 per cent of the UK population, is the Northern Ireland Assembly. The Northern Ireland Executive is a 'consociationalist' or power-sharing government, a form of government involving guaranteed group representation for preserving democracy and managing conflict in deeply divided societies. The Executive's Department of Education is responsible for the country's education policy in relation to pre-school, primary, post-primary and special education, the youth service, promotion of community relations within and between schools, and teacher education and salaries.

Prior to devolution in 1999, a period of Direct Rule lasted from 1971 when the Department of Education, Northern Ireland (DENI) was headed by a British minister. Under Direct Rule, Northern Ireland experienced less change than elsewhere in the UK, lack of action by ministers owing to the multiplicity of other political concerns. A time-honoured tradition of consulting professionals was neglected, and when reform did take place, the tendency was to import policies from England whether appropriate or not, without consultation. Protestant schools had mostly transferred to the state as 'controlled' schools following the partition of Ireland in 1922, and Roman Catholic schools kept their 'maintained' status; education was more politicised than in England because of the alignment of religious and political divisions. Two contrasting perspectives see the troubles as, on the one hand religious, in which case schooling is seen as a potential remedy, or on the other hand political, arising from historic colonisation and partition, and the residual social and economic divisions which are not soluble through education alone. One effect of devolution as Ken Jones has noted was that in order to enable power-sharing and community autonomy and equality under the 1998 Northern Ireland Act, the legal protection of human rights was in advance of other areas of Britain, so that the Department of Education's brief required all educational processes to be subject to scrutiny in respect of equal opportunity on grounds of religion, political opinion, racial group and sexual orientation (Jones 2003).

Scotland

The Scottish Government (*Riaghaltas na h-Alba*) is the executive arm of the devolved government of Scotland, responsible for a population of over 5 million or approximately 8 per cent of the total UK population, with a historically strong nationalist culture. The referendum for self-government in 1997 produced a 3:1 majority in favour, much stronger than that for Wales. Prior to devolution there had been a Scottish Office Education Department under the Westminster Government which had asserted a degree of independence in policy-making, but political responsibility for education at all levels is now vested in the Scottish Parliament, which administers its school system through an Education Department. Schools are supported in delivering the National Guidelines and National Priorities by a body known as Learning and Teaching Scotland, joined in a single executive agency from 2011 with HM Inspectorate of Education, as the Scottish Education Quality and Improvement Agency.

Scotland has a distinctive system of schooling with long historical roots, and in the 1980s successfully resisted or reshaped many education policies of the Conservative Government in London, which were seen as being out of step with Scottish educational principles. There remained, for example, a strong faith in comprehensive education deeply rooted in the Scottish education system, contrasting with the discourse of 'failure' that surrounded comprehensive schools in England, and there was a consequent resistance to the notion that teachers are to blame for 'failure' and must therefore be more tightly managed (Jones 2003, 155). The relative autonomy of the policy process in Scotland meant that the intentions of the Conservative government in London could be modified in ways acceptable to Scottish teachers and parents. In 1983 the Scottish Education Department sponsored a National Committee on Primary Education, and a Committee on a Common Curriculum for ages 10–14 in 1986, which variously recommended 'autonomy within guidelines', and a balance of 'skills, activities and social experiences'. The Conservative Government found this too consensual and tried to introduce a prescribed curriculum for ages 5–14 together with statutory testing at ages 8 and 12, which met with a widespread educational rebellion. An orchestrated campaign saw considerable parental solidarity with teachers in opposing the testing proposals. A subsequent boycott of tests succeeded and as an emollient the curriculum was now described as 'guidelines' rather than as a National Curriculum (Paterson 2003). By contrast with Wales, Scotland's prosperity has advanced to English levels, and more generous funding of schools has been secured by popular protest and through pressure exerted by previous Secretaries of State. Nevertheless, as indicated in a quotation at the start of this chapter, in Scotland, as in England, managerialist approaches have been adopted that deliberately attempted to break from more consensual and gradual processes of change.

Audit culture, assessment and league tables

Audit and globalisation

In a few lines quoted at the beginning of this chapter, Ken Jones conveys the concepts and rationale of performance management as 'a means by which the national agenda can be transmitted to school level . . . with its ambition of achieving a "world-class" education system . . . [and] membership of a global policy community'. This global ambition, with its economic driving force, is found in the national education discourse of all four countries within the UK, though the way it is implemented varies between all four.

Well over a century ago, long before 'globalisation' as we understand it entered educational policy discourse, assessment and testing was introduced as a means of accountability and ensuring value for money in publicly supported education. That was the structure of 'Standards' introduced into elementary education in the mid-nineteenth century, annual testing by inspectors and payment of school grants according to results. With twentieth-century innovations in measuring intelligence, testing came to be seen as a scientifically sound means of assessing children's potential and allocating individuals to appropriate types of secondary school well into the 1950s. The 'Eleven Plus' exam, coming at the end of primary school, also served informally as a measure of a primary school's 'success', though highly questionable and contested in terms of accuracy and fairness. With the subsequent introduction of a non-selective system of comprehensive secondary schools, the 'sorting' function of primary schools became redundant, but testing later re-emerged in the form of 'SATs' as a tool of accountability, for measuring the progress of national and school cohorts.

Accountability and testing culture now needs to be understood in an international perspective, since British education ministers in the 1980s and 1990s followed developments in the USA with its increasing federal control of education policy. President Clinton's administration is sometimes credited with its origins, though the 'standards movement' and 'systemic reform' can be traced back earlier in the 1990s. In turn Clinton's successor, George W. Bush, campaigned for increasing the amount of testing for American schoolchildren. In Chicago, Mayor Daley announced performance on a nationally normed test of basic skills as the criterion for 'promotion' from one grade to the next in the elementary school, replacing 'social promotion' or children moving up with their age cohort. Comparing children's achievement against a national sample put enormous pressure on teachers and pupils to succeed. This policy generated controversy, but received a good deal of public support. Children suffered mind-numbing tests that contributed little to their overall education, while a new atmosphere of accountability and recrimination grew where teachers and schools were judged on the basis of student performance. However, this testing regime also revealed poorer performance of children from poor and disadvantaged backgrounds, and the need to redistribute resources. A policy consequence was the 'No Child Left Behind' programme, which heightened the accountability of individual States required to implement annual testing for all students in elementary schools, and to report the results by race, ethnicity, poverty and disability. Districts and schools failing to make adequate progress were subjected to corrective action. Despite complaints from teachers and educational administrators about the difficulty of achieving performance targets in impoverished urban areas or with groups of ethnic minority or learning-disabled children, the programme continued with bipartisan political support (Rury 2008).

Anthropologist Marilyn Strathern introduced a collection of essays on audit cultures, recognising them as a global phenomenon but also as a distinct 'cultural artefact' (Strathern 2000). In the UK they evolved in the early 1980s when economic pressures operated on government policy and public spending, reinforced by corporate values that gave them international credibility. Audit culture incorporated a vision of how people would relate to 'the market' in education, re-inventing pupils and their parents as 'customers' or 'consumers'. In the case of primary education, the state purchased services on behalf of these customers, and government defined the state's role as a guarantor of value. This value was assessed crudely by measures of 'performance' against a background of constraints on public funding. So the UK Audit Commission was employed to scrutinise local government for 'value for money' but rapidly moved on from its primary concern with finance to a general concern for efficiency. As an instrument of accountability, with the promise of a globalising professional consensus, audit is almost impossible to criticise in principle. Derived from protocols of financial accounting, when applied to public institutions the state's overt concern may at first have been to ensure internal controls and monitoring techniques rather than to impose day-to-day direction.

Audit also becomes represented as a kind of ethics, accountability as a matter of responsibility towards those who will be affected by the outcome of certain actions. It demands 'transparency', making procedures visible, so that administrators in all kinds of professions become more managerial and accountable. However, audit can also be rejected as *unethical*. Transparency of operation is promoted as an outward sign of integrity, yet monitoring schemes are devised and administered by officials who share the same kind of professional background as those whose performance they scrutinise. So children and their families, the supposed beneficiaries of audit, lie outside the closed loop through which professionals demonstrate (to other professionals) their adherence to standards (Strathern 2000).

Onora O'Neill argued from a philosophical perspective that ever-more complex and burdensome mechanisms of accountability were counter-productive as they led paradoxically to *greater mistrust* (O'Neill 2002). She described conscientious professionals and administrators having to work to ever-more exacting standards of practice that quite frequently changed (as with Ofsted's frameworks for inspection), to meet relentless demands to record and report, and subjected to regular ranking and restructuring. She observed how many public sector professionals find that the new demands damage their real work, teachers aiming to teach their pupils, nurses to care for their patients, social workers to help and protect those with difficult lives. Each of these professions has its proper aim, not reducible to a simple set of targets. Requirements and methods of accountability often obstruct the proper aims of education, as tests become more frequent and reduce the time available for children's learning.

Another irony in O'Neill's critique is that for teachers themselves, conflicting demands in accountability procedures often invite compromise and evasion, undermining both professional judgement and institutional autonomy. Performance indicators have a deep effect on professional and institutional behaviour. Even those who devise the indicators know these are at best surrogates for the real objectives, as nobody seriously believes that good test results are the only evidence of good teaching. O'Neill does not deny the desirability and need for accountability, but calls for an 'intelligent accountability' requiring 'more attention to good governance and fewer fantasies about total control'. Reporting is not improved by being wholly standardised or relentlessly detailed, requiring instead substantive and knowledgeable independent judgement about an institution's or a professional's work. 'If we want a culture of public service, professionals and public servants must in the end be free to serve the public rather than their paymasters' (O'Neill 2002).

Assessment

National Curriculum assessment was initiated by an Act of Parliament in 1988, reflecting, as Whetton describes: 'the wider social changes in Britain, and especially the initial Thatcherite distrust of established professional interests and the later Blairite focus on the management mechanisms of accountability and target setting as a means of effecting change in public services' (Whetton 2009, 138). A succession of quangos has been responsible for oversight of the assessment system, beginning with the Schools Examinations and Assessment Council (SEAC) initially separate from the National Curriculum Council (NCC), but then merged in 1993 to form the School Curriculum and Assessment Authority (SCAA), merging with a vocational qualifications council to form the Qualifications and Curriculum Authority (QCA) in 1997, renamed the Qualifications and Curriculum Development Agency (QCDA) in 2008 when a separate regulatory body for examinations and tests was formed under the name of Ofqual. The new Coalition Government announced the closure of QCDA from 2011 as an economy measure. Each organisational change has been in response to a crisis in professional or popular reaction to assessment procedures and/or a significant shift in education policy and reflects the inner dynamic noted by O'Neill whereby audit mechanisms become ever-more complex. The frequent reorganisation and rebranding of major national bodies may itself indicate an inherent weakness of over-elaborate structures subject to political whim. We might question the discursive significance of this constant renaming in the shift from 'council' through 'authority' to 'agency'.

Over a period of time, statutory tests came to serve an increasing number of purposes specified by successive governments, and specialists have pointed to the problems that this poses for validity, as well as the high-stakes nature of some purposes distorting the processes of teaching and learning that are intended to be assessed. It has been argued that a move to more 'intelligent accountability' would allow more prominence (and trust) to be given to teachers' assessment, which would in turn lead to improved 'construct validity'. The case has been made for combining a low-stakes survey for national monitoring, as being more valid and reliable, with local accountability through teacher assessment.

> To develop a national assessment system that is fair to all in a diverse society, provides valid information with great accuracy, supports teaching and learning, raises levels of attainment for children of all backgrounds, provides accountability measures for society, is economically viable, and is accepted by all involved in education, is not just difficult, it is impossible.
>
> (Whetton 2009, 135)

Whetton considers that from a political viewpoint the assessment system has generally been a success, given the original government intention of bringing a measure of accountability to schools, controlling the curriculum and improving standards of achievement. Schools can be seen to acknowledge more readily their responsibilities to pupils, to parents and the community at large, to a far greater extent than had been the case in 1988. Assessment has also contributed to perceptions of raised standards over a period of time, though this was challenged by a Statistics Commission report of 2005 on standards in English primary schools. From an educational viewpoint however the pressure placed on schools is criticised as being counter-productive, narrowing the range of the curriculum and affecting the quality of the learning process. It can be argued that the momentum of raising standards would have been greater through investment in formative or classroom assessment than in a testing regime. Whetton concludes that although it has not satisfied all stakeholders, the testing system 'has not been so bad that it has failed or been completely abolished, but neither has it been so good that it is widely acclaimed' (Whetton 2009, 154–155).

Two reports commissioned by the Coalition Government have reflected on assessment and its procedures. In July 2010, Dame Clare Tickell, Chief Executive of the voluntary organisation Action for Children, was invited to conduct a review of the Early Years Foundation Stage (EYFS) to reduce its bureaucracy and to focus more on learning and development. As a consequence she proposed reducing the sixty-nine learning goals to seventeen and to focus on three prime areas of personal, social and emotional growth, communication and language, and physical development. Lord Bew led a small panel of educationists and primary headteachers to review testing, assessment and accountability at Key Stage 2. His final report in June 2011 argued for a wider range of progress and attainment measures, and more weight to be given to teacher assessment.

League tables

In 2008 the Children, Schools and Families Select Committee (HCCSFC) investigated assessment concluding that testing of 11-year-olds in English, maths and science was 'skewing' their education and advocated 'a root and branch reform of the system'. The committee heard evidence that English schoolchildren were among the most tested in the world and that the government was isolated in its support for the current system. National tests had become increasingly high-stakes because results were used for so many different purposes, ranging from diagnosing learning difficulties to creating school league tables. Evidence examined had pointed to the unreliability of the results. League tables based on test results came in for criticism and the chief executive of the General Teaching Council observed that these high-stakes tables put the reputation of schools and the headteachers on the line in ways that were excessive and unfair. Annual announcements of results were the cause of continuing debate between professionals and government and between politicians of opposing parties. The data invariably allowed conflicting interpretations or outright scepticism, amply illustrating Onora O'Neill's argument that complex and bureaucratic accountability measures serve to heighten mistrust rather than to assuage it.

Attempts to refine the league tables led successively to the calculation of 'value-added' scores (a measure of progress from one Key Stage to the next) and 'contextual value added' (accounting for social background through measures such as free school meals, pupils in care and special needs). The National Association of Head Teachers (NAHT) (which had commissioned independent research on primary value-added tests in 2004) remained opposed to the publication of performance tables also on the grounds that they are misleading and have a strongly negative effect on assessment. Inclusion of pupils with significant learning difficulties, for example, in the calculation of schools results, meant that parents were effectively misinformed by the tables. Value-added information, sensibly interpreted, was seen as helpful to teachers and school leaders in assessing performance, areas of strength and weakness, and as an aid to school improvement. Schools could interpret, with understanding and caution, the statistical reliability of their data, but value-added information lost credibility when published in high-stakes performance tables, taking little or no account of technical flaws such as the reliability of input and output measures or the 'ceiling effect' on high-achieving pupils. Political reputations were so heavily invested in league tables that their abandonment in England was most unlikely, and the Bew review in 2011 reported in favour of their retention but also some refinement to make them fairer and more reliable. Conservative Secretary of State Michael Gove promised inclusion of additional data and 'floor standards', or minimum acceptable levels, to be set for primary schools. The NAHT continued to press for abandoning all forms of performance tables, following the examples of Scotland, Wales and Northern Ireland.

Wales had its own Qualifications, Curriculum and Assessment Authority (ACCAC) from the mid-1990s (later absorbed within DCELLS), which advised Welsh ministers against publishing league tables of Key Stage 2 test results, consequently published only as summaries by LEAs and not national performance tables for individual schools as in England. This distinctive policy environment following devolution was reflected in the policy statement *The Learning Country* (2001) which expressed more trust in teachers' expertise: 'The informed professional judgment of teachers, lecturers and trainers must be celebrated without prejudice to the disciplines of public accountability' (National Assembly for Wales 2001, 11). In the social and political context of Wales, 'marketisation' of state-funded education that induced the drive for test results as school performance measures in England had no place, and cooperation rather than competition was envisaged as the route to improvement in delivery of public services. Key Stage 1 tests were abandoned in 2002 and Assessment for Learning with 'skills profiles' for individual pupils from Year 5 were to contribute to the pattern for curriculum assessment reform. Some research has reported however that reduction in external assessment has led to lowering standards of achievement in Wales. The Northern Ireland Common Curriculum relied on teacher assessment as the main mechanism for evaluating children's attainment at Key Stages 1 and 2. Here the 'Eleven Plus' exam as a high-stakes transfer test was for many years retained for pupils aiming at a grammar school but criticised by the UN Children's Rights Committee; although removed by regulation rather than legislation in 2008 this remained highly controversial and it was continued in practice by many schools. Eleven Plus tests overshadowed Key Stage 2 assessment so that standardised tests were not adopted; through devolved government, policy-making took more account of teachers' professional judgement and rejected the dominance of standardised assessment in core subjects, preferring a focus on thinking skills and cross-curricular skills of communication, applied mathematics and the use of ICT. The Council for Curriculum, Examinations and Assessment (CCEA) of Northern Ireland has also given encouragement to integrate the principles of Assessment for Learning, and a system of reporting children's achievements through seven levels of progression. Scottish resistance to Westminster's testing regime was evident from an early stage when parents supported teachers in the 'SATs boycott' of 1991 to 1992. Parental members of school boards turned out in general to be very respectful of teachers' judgement, resulting in massive popular support in withdrawing children from tests. In some areas as many as 85 per cent of parents withdrew their children and as a result the tests were withdrawn after the 1992 General Election (Paterson 2003).

Inspection

Where the key term in thinking about testing and assessment in its political context was 'audit', with regard to inspection it might be 'quality assurance'. Both activities overlap as means of accountability, but where audit is concerned primarily with computing quantitative measures, inspection traditionally attends to qualitative evidence collected through visiting schools and observing teachers at their work. School inspection and inspectors' reports long preceded written tests and league tables as a way in which government could ensure that the education system was accountable for the national task that it undertook and for the public expenditure entailed. Harold Silver has observed how defining a good school over the centuries, and in different countries and localities, was a question not only of the way a school operated, but of the way its aims had been established, by whom and with what intentions; the variety of purposes that schooling has had meant that judgements have been made from a range of competing viewpoints (Silver 1994). Hence inspection is inherently political.

With regard to publicly funded elementary, later primary, schools in Britain, there has been a common set of purposes defined by the state and stipulated sets of criteria that have changed over time but are common and applied to all primary schools within the system, wherever in the country they might be. In the 1960s an 'educational war on poverty' meant that attention was focused on school systems and their implications for welfare and equality of opportunity, but during the 1970s and 1980s school effectiveness research shifted attention away from social equity and concentrated on detailed internal features of curriculum and teaching.

Over the first half of the twentieth century HMI built a constructive relationship with the local authorities, schools and teachers. A developmental and supportive role for the inspector was implicitly endorsed by the Plowden Report in 1967. HMI's work was increasingly supplemented by LEAs' own inspectors and advisers, and though the organisation and status of national and local inspectorates were quite distinct, both bodies undertook curriculum and professional development with schools and teachers. HMI's principal function continued to be national reporting for the benefit of policy-makers; organised in geographical regions, individually they made many short visits to schools according to need, and working in teams undertook a small number of 'full inspections' of schools each year as the basis for generalised and impressionistic reports submitted to government by the Senior Chief Inspector (Maclure 2000).

Public accountability through inspection was radically advanced by Secretary of State Keith Joseph, who in 1982 put an end to the traditional confidentiality of school inspection reports (Dunford 1998). From 1983 these reports were to be published, foreshadowing New Labour's later policy in 1997, of 'naming and shaming' so-called 'failing schools'. From 1988 onwards the Senior Chief Inspector was also required to produce an annual report on teaching and learning that became a much-publicised exposé of problems faced by the educational system. In 1991, under Conservative Prime Minister John Major, a key policy theme became the 'Citizen's Charter' and subsequent 'Parent's Charter'; inspection was henceforth to act on behalf of the consumer, as a 'regulator' of standards and quality. Thus HMI would have to accept new responsibilities to parents as well as to the Secretary of State, and would need to rethink their relationship with schools. Such policy trends led to the Education Act of 1992, in which fifteen of its seventeen substantive clauses were devoted to inspection; its radical reconstruction of school inspection created the Office of Her Majesty's Chief Inspector of Schools in England, whose task was to commission independent teams of inspectors, operating in a commercial market, to inspect all schools on a four-yearly cycle. 'Ofsted' (Office for Standards in Education) was the acronym coined by the first HMCI Professor Stewart Sutherland.

Chris Woodhead was appointed in 1994 to lead Ofsted, where he initiated a controversial and campaigning role, especially attacking 'progressive' methods and 'incompetent' teachers. His annual report attracted attention as a platform for criticism of policies and practice. In 1995 a revised *Framework for the Inspection of Schools* was issued, including guidance on inspection of nursery and primary schools. From 1996 teachers would be graded on their performance and parental opinion was to be collected as a significant source of data for school inspection. By 1998 all primary schools had been inspected at least once under the new regime and 3,000 inspection reports per year were published, creating an unprecedented database. A great deal of independent research into the process of inspection and school improvement generally was motivated by these new policies and practices, and considerable opposition was generated from teachers and from educational researchers concerning the unreliability of inspection methods and data, and the uses to which it was put.

Ofsted inspections were subject to well-publicised criticism by teachers with negative experiences of the process. An independent group, pointedly named the Office for Standards in Inspection (Ofstin), reviewed the practices of Ofsted. Here Carol Fitz-Gibbon argued that Ofsted's inspection methodology did not meet research standards and that Ofsted had been allowed to operate without adequate validation, with the potential to mislead and distress parents, pupils and teachers, and with apparent faith placed in its findings by politicians. Two major purposes of inspection, school improvement and accountability, were found to be confused but also further complicated by two other purposes – maintenance of minimum standards of quality and collection of standardised national data on school performance. Complexity of the inspection process was seen to put primary schools at a particular disadvantage.

Inspection increasingly embraced the kind of data-gathering discussed above in relation to testing and assessment and audit. New Labour in 1997 established a Standards and Effectiveness Unit at the DFES to encourage and monitor school improvement, with an ever-increasing availability of data, and emphasis on 'value-added' measures. PICSI data (Pre-Inspection Context and School Indicators) were used in early inspections, succeeded by PANDA (Performance and Assessment data) reports issued annually to all schools and local authorities. In 1998, this ability to monitor continuously through statistical data led to increasing the interval of school inspection from four to six years. Data and inspection evidence provided a foundation for HMCI advice to ministers and for public pronouncements.

Widespread concern with inspections and their place within a continuing programme of politically driven educational change led to a House of Commons Select Committee inquiry which reported in 1999. Having taken a great deal of written and oral evidence, amongst many other conclusions it acknowledged the stress that the current programme of inspection placed on teachers, and it proposed reducing the period for notice of inspection from one year to four weeks; it recommended that inspectors take account of self-evaluation procedures used by the school and that HMCI 'should be concerned to improve morale and promote confidence in the teaching profession'.

Chris Woodhead's *Class War* (2002) written shortly after his retirement from almost ten years as HMCI offered some insight into the development of Ofsted in its first decade and rather more insight into his own personality as its leader. He argued that schools should be exposed to external challenge, lacking under the old regime of HMI when inspections of any one school had been very few and far between. His narrative was of the unaccountability of schools under the old regime despite 'years of parent and employer dissatisfaction': 'Nothing and nobody, it seemed, could dent the self-confidence and complacency of the educational establishment. HMI should have blown the whistle and they did not. Ofsted was created to challenge the producer interest.' He attacked the 'progressive establishment' of the teaching profession, and of inspectors, too, 'unable or unwilling to jettison their progressive educational views'. He cast himself as a champion of parents and children, challenging the 'progressive consensus'. Against the criticism that he politicised the inspection process, Woodhead argued that despite its historic claim to independence, HMI had historically always been political: 'Never at any point in its history was HMI wholly or constitutionally independent of government' (Woodhead 2002, 102, 105, 110).

In other parts of the UK, the inspection process was less hostile and less contested. The 1992 Education Act had created a second inspection body alongside Ofsted, namely Estyn for Wales. (Estyn is a Welsh word meaning 'to extend', in the sense of raising quality, but also of extending, or offering, support.) Estyn borrowed heavily from Ofsted handbooks, but a significant difference was its inspection cycle of five years in Wales (compared with every four years in England). In Northern Ireland the tone of inspection undertaken by the Department of Education's own Education and Training Inspectorate has been described as constructive and supportive, including elements of self-evaluation, through planned general inspections, although unannounced inspections are also made in relation to pastoral care and child protection. HMI in Scotland, by contrast with Ofsted in England, worked on the whole in cooperation with the system and not against it. Inspectors in Scotland, for example, played a key role in developing a compromise over the Scottish curriculum to reconcile the political intentions of Westminster with strong professional claims for more autonomy, resulting in a less prescriptive model, described as 'guidelines', by contrast with England and Wales (Paterson 2002).

Chris Woodhead retired as Chief Inspector in 2000 and two years later the role passed to David Bell, himself a former primary teacher and LA director of education. Despite continuing pressure from the Prime Minister's office for school accountability, a more conciliatory tone to inspection became apparent. Research was commissioned for a collaboration between Ofsted itself and independent researchers to evaluate the impact of its work. Schools Minister David Miliband initiated a 'New Relationship' with schools in June 2004, a government policy aimed at improving standards by giving greater autonomy and responsibility within the context of more intelligent accountability and reduced bureaucracy. This was followed by a new School Inspection Framework and guidance on self-evaluation in March 2005.

In 2006 Christine Gilbert succeeded Bell as HMCI and further change in inspection frameworks continued. These changes sometimes appeared ambivalent, for example, in reducing the period of notice that schools would receive. Notice of inspection had already been reduced from two weeks to two days in 2004, and was now removed in preference for 'snap inspections' without warning, with the positive aspiration that this would remove the stress from teachers of preparing for inspection. On the other hand the political right welcomed it as a more punitive approach, preventing schools from allegedly manipulating their results by advance preparation.

Another move, this time towards a more 'data-driven' programme and method of inspecting, began to blur the distinction made earlier in this chapter between auditing and inspection. This has been advocated on pragmatic grounds as being more economical, reducing the cost of accountability, and at the same time it has been defended from a right-wing perspective as leaving 'successful' schools (identified by their test results) more independent of state interference by freeing them from unnecessary inspection. While the Association of School and College Leaders (ASCL) supported the plan of a 'desk audit' to remove the burden of inspection from 'good schools', an alternative professional view was that schools needed to be judged by more qualitative dimensions than simply their statistical outputs. Schools expressed concerns about an inspection regime under which they could not be rated good if their test results were low – regardless of any economic and social factors that might affect their children's performance. Further planned changes to invite expressions of parental concern as a way of triggering inspection of individual schools, and the setting up of a website for parental complaints to facilitate this, were argued against by teacher unions not only as a threat to professionals by troublesome parents, but also on the grounds that such complaints could skew inspection programmes since dissatisfied parents are likely to be more vocal in socially privileged than in socially deprived areas.

Quality assurance procedures have changed and continue to change, to meet shifting cultural and political expectations. Extensive research has adopted different methodologies to explore the national policy implications of Ofsted inspection and its effects nationally and locally on primary schools' curriculum and ethos, on primary teachers' practice, on primary pupils' attitudes and achievement. There has also been international comparative research of inspection practices, notably those that tend towards the adoption of self-evaluation as a component of school inspection (Cunningham and Raymont 2010). In 2007, with the merger at national government and local authority levels of education and children's social services, Ofsted acquired responsibility for inspecting children's social services as well as schools, making it the largest regulating body in England, and controversy about its operation has continued over recent years.

In advance of the General Election in 2010 one outspoken primary head at the NAHT conference expressed the frustration of many. Objecting to continual rewriting of inspection frameworks as a 'constant shifting of the goalposts' he urged that they should:

> no longer tolerate the damage it is doing to schools, school leaders and children. It is our opinion that the current mechanistic, data-driven approach gives rise to limited and inappropriate judgment. The associated demoralisation of schools and their communities must stop.
>
> (*Guardian*, 30 April 2010)

He called for an inspection body more independent of government that would give impartial advice to schools on improvement.

In the Coalition Government White Paper in November 2010, ministers declared that Ofsted would now concentrate its inspections on just four areas: pupil achievement, the quality of teaching, leadership, and children's behaviour and safety, scaling back from twenty-seven headings under the prevailing inspection framework. The White Paper now expressed a wish to allow inspectors to spend 'more of their time observing lessons, giving a more reliable assessment of the quality of education children are receiving'. The new Secretary of State was also keen to reduce monitoring of the best schools, to try to encourage greater independence, so that routine inspections of schools judged outstanding would cease, Ofsted focusing instead on weaker schools.

Conclusion

Monitoring of standards has to be credible and transparent, to provide reliable data and to be supportive of values that reflect both the wide aspirations of parents, and professionals' understandings of primary pupils in relation to their development. Inevitably this means that competing and conflicting claims have to be embraced. That is the stuff of politics. Uncertainties within the testing regime are complicated by the employment of commercial contractors (with consequent operational inconsistencies), by changes of government (with contrasting political stance), and by an economic climate that necessitates reducing costs. Colin Richards (2010), in his commentary on the Cambridge Primary Review, advocates a clearer, simpler, fairer and more informative framework for primary education to provide accountability at three distinct levels in respect of the national system, school performance and the individual child's progress.

The dilemma of reconciling accountability with professional responsibility and a sense of trust is a political problem found in all the public services of a modern welfare state, and indeed within politics itself. It appears that the resolution of this dilemma is evolving differently in different geographical and cultural contexts within Britain, which gives teachers the opportunity to reflect critically on how accountability has worked, how effective it is and what impact it has in our own schools and on teachers' own professional development. National accountability needs clear mechanisms, but is also dependent on culture and politics, as is evident in the differences of practice between England, Wales, Scotland and Northern Ireland.

A healthy research culture in the field of audit and quality assurance should contribute to informed and reasoned argument and the avoidance of doctrinaire posturing. The inspection body needs to be seen as neutral and not campaigning, to gain the trust of the profession and to supply sound and credible data for policy-makers. Above all, accountability, like politics, needs to be balanced by a sense of integrity and value, maintaining professional self-esteem and public confidence.

Key questions for reflection

- What are the purposes of the national accountability of primary schools and in whose interests does it operate? How has it become so politically contentious?
- What are the relative merits of testing and reporting children's progress on the one hand, and school inspection on the other, as a means of accountability?
- What inferences about political imperatives can be drawn from Ofsted's inspection frameworks, from reports on individual schools, and from HMCI annual reports (www.ofsted.gov.uk/)? How effectively do the reports appear to reflect the quality of primary schools or of primary education nationally?

Independent learning tasks

Adopt any one of the above questions as a focus for personal research, and/or the basis for discussion with colleagues.

Choose a relevant House of Commons Committee Report and study it for evidence and critical perspectives on the politics of national accountability. The volumes of oral and written evidence are of particular interest in addition to the Committee's Report. Recent reports that may be of interest in the context of accountability include ones on Ofsted (2011), School Accountability (2010) or Testing and Assessment (2008).

See bibliography at the end of this book for details of relevant reports, or go direct to www.parliament.uk/business/committees/committees-a-z/commons-select/education-committee/

House of Commons Education Committee (HCEC) (2011) *The role and performance of Ofsted* (Second Report Session 2010–2011) HC 570.

House of Commons Children, Schools and Families Committee (HCCSFC) (2010a) *School Accountability* (First Report Session 2009–2010) HC 88.

HCCSFC (2008) *Testing and Assessment* (Third Report Session 2007–2008) HC 169.

Further reading

Alexander, R.J. (ed.) (2010) *Children, Their World, Their Education: Final Report and Recommendations of the Cambridge Primary Review*, London: Routledge.
Discussions relevant to national accountability and the issues addressed in this chapter are to be found in: Chapter 3 (27–49) on policies and legacies, and Chapter 23 (474–482) on central government policy-making; Chapter 16 (311–327) on the strengths and weaknesses of assessment for accountability purposes; and Chapter 17 (336–340) on school inspection.

Chitty, C. (2009) *Education Policy in Britain*, 2nd edn, Basingstoke: Palgrave Macmillan.
A very readable and critical account of key developments is supported by detailed reference to political events. Chapter 3 describes the growth of accountability and centralisation from 1976 to 1997, Chapter 6 describes policy-making over the last half-century including recent developments in Wales and Scotland, and Chapter 5 describes trends towards privatisation from the 1980s onwards.

Cunningham, P. and Raymont, P. (2010) 'Quality Assurance in English Primary Education', in R. Alexander *et al.* (eds) *The Cambridge Primary Review Research Surveys*, London: Routledge, 767–791.
This broad overview of published research on inspection considers national policies and practices as well as consequent experiences of inspection at school level with regard to teachers, curriculum and the trend towards self-evaluation. It also takes account of international and comparative research.

Hall, K. (2004) *Literacy and Schooling: Towards renewal in primary education policy*, Aldershot: Ashgate.
Chapter 1 (5–24) examines the recent politics of primary education and growth of central government control in the context of economic globalisation and the knowledge economy, indicating the international scale of forces operating on educational politics.

Jones, K. (2003) *Education in Britain: 1944 to the Present*, Cambridge: Polity Press.
Chapter 5 (143–174) presents a critical analysis of policy under New Labour, dealing with the discourse of 'decline', 'failure' and 'crisis' in educational policy-making. It sets the policy in historical context and weighs the significance of globalisation, devolution, the cultures of 'business' and 'responsibility'.

Whetton, C. (2009) 'Testing time: A brief history of national curriculum assessment 1989–2008', *Education Research*, 51, 2: 137–159.
A detailed narrative account, by an author closely involved with test development and research, that includes three layers: technical aspects of assessment (very clearly explained), the educational context and the political and social milieu. This article is in a special issue of *Education Research* devoted to national curriculum assessment, with a variety of relevant articles written from different perspectives.

Chapter 8

Local accountability: school, community and local democracy

It is, or ought to be, very simple. Define (and raise, through a reform of the public examination system) expectations of what children should know at different stages of their school careers. Ensure that the school has the resources it needs, and . . . the freedom to determine what needs doing when. Hold the governing body and the headteacher responsible for the school's performance. Intervene when necessary.

Where does the LEA fit into this model of school improvement? It does not. There is no need for an LEA to monitor what is happening in its schools. . . . LEAs pretend that regular school visiting by their advisers is crucial if they are to keep their finger on the pulse, but this is just that: a pretence, and a pretty patronising pretence at that.

Neither is there necessarily any support role. The idea of 'support' is one of the great contemporary education myths.

(Woodhead 2002, 127)

Academies indicate a re-articulation and re-scaling of the state; they are part of a new localism and a new centralism; they encompass new kinds of autonomy and new forms of control: controlled decontrol.

The Academies programme is then a new educational imaginary and microcosm of political transformation and the establishment of a new mode of regulation – constituted within sets of new identities, social relations and institutional orders, that is part of an experimental move and a policy pathfinder towards a new 'fix' and new set of relations between state, market, public sector and civil society organised in relation to global competitiveness.

(Ball 2007, 171, 181)

Introduction

The national accountability procedures of assessments, league tables and inspections discussed in Chapter 7 are the ones that most publicly and politically impinge on primary teachers' work. By contrast, the really meaningful accountabilities for those with a personal investment and commitment to their work are the local and immediate ones, to children and their families in the community. What are the political dimensions of local accountability, and how is it exercised? Chapter 2 illustrated the emergence of democratic local government and its responsibilities for education, established a century ago in the form of LEAs. Until very recent times the role of local authorities remained unchallenged as the main providers and coordinators of state primary schools in their area. They had built up experience and expertise in the role and were often promoters of innovation and improvement, but there were frequent tensions between national and local government, ideological and also financial as public spending was constrained.

We need to examine the contradictions of national policies that more recently have encouraged schools to opt out of local authority control, while continuing to hold local authorities accountable for provision of education in their area. Neo-liberal economists influential in government have advocated a free market in educational provision, with the idea that accountability would be exercised simply through a marketplace of providers and consumers. Accountability also needs to be traced in the relationships between school and its local community and within the school itself.

This chapter considers how accountability operates at local levels, and some of the implications of that accountability: in the wide context of the traditional LEA; in the more intimate context of the school and its local community and the community within the school; and finally, in the policy context of continuing moves to privatise local primary school provision. A key principle is the desirability of democratic participation at every level, the 'politics of action' described by Crick, for a sense of ownership and community involvement.

Local authorities and the tradition of local democracy

Local government structure and democratic principle

Local government can boast a proud history in relation to educational provision. The locally elected School Boards that were created in the 1870s provided a significant advance in democratic governance and were granted considerable powers to raise income through property taxes, and to enforce school attendance. School Boards were replaced in 1902 by LEAs, that were in effect a committee of the county council; a two-tier structure of local government means that some services such as leisure services and street cleaning are delegated to district and borough councils, while the county councils and county borough councils retain responsibility for major services such as social care and education.

Education was the pre-eminent local service and some LEAs gained national reputations for the quality of their provision (Cunningham 1988, 2002b). Local councillors were democratically elected and ultimately responsible for local policy and innovation, though the quality of the service as far as schools and teachers were concerned often depended on the administrative officers, advisory and support staff. For primary education in the decades after the Second World War, certain LEAs, notably Oxfordshire, Leicestershire and the West Riding of Yorkshire, began to set trends and high standards in their progressive and child-centred practices. Local administration was headed by a Director of Education or Chief Education Officer and sometimes these were individuals with a strong educational mission who lent a distinctive ethos to local educational provision. Outstanding examples, who combined creative educational thinking with imaginative and capable provision, include Sir Alec Clegg in West Yorkshire from 1945 to 1972 and Sir Tim Brighouse in Oxfordshire and Birmingham during the 1980s and 1990s. The LEA had responsibility for all state schools in its area, distributing funding, allocating the number of places available at each school and employing most teachers. They supplied schools and teachers with support for professional development, curriculum development, special educational needs, governor training and other services (haughtily dismissed by Chris Woodhead in the quotation at the start of this chapter). Following the 2004 Children Act, local authorities' responsibilities for children's social services, including child protection and liaison with police and health care providers in respect of children, were merged with education and early years provision, to be led by a Director of Children's Services. Local authorities were to fulfil an educational accountability to the children and families that they served and were politically accountable at the ballot box to local ratepayers.

The structures of local government are complex and have been subject to several reorganisations in the recent past. London, because of its size and capital city status, was unique, and in 1965 London County Council was replaced by a Greater London Council (GLC) with an Inner London Education Authority (ILEA) providing for the twelve inner boroughs. The scale and resources of ILEA offered a progressive lead in curriculum and professional development amongst education authorities nationally. In 1974, local government outside London was similarly reorganised. Six large metropolitan counties were created in the large conurbations of the midlands, the north-west, Yorkshire and the north-east and became responsible for education, while elsewhere the county councils in England and Wales continued to serve as LEAs.

The challenge presented to national government by large metropolitan local authorities was unwelcome to the centralising Conservative Government under Margaret Thatcher, and in 1986 the GLC and the metropolitan counties were abolished. ILEA ceased to exist from 1990. These changes left the smaller boroughs and districts in those conurbations to operate as single-tier units, each now responsible for providing education alongside other public services in its locality. Then, in the 1990s, a Local Government Commission for England recommended that other selected areas of the country should be reorganised as single-tier unitary authorities. So, for example, between 1995 and 1998 the Isle of Wight became a unitary authority, the counties of Avon, Cleveland and Humberside were abolished and divided into unitaries, and the city of York was separated from North Yorkshire and given unitary status. Further reorganisation of local government in April 2009 included nine new unitary authorities, five created from existing County Councils absorbing their District Councils, the remaining four through the division of two counties (Bedfordshire and Cheshire) along existing District Council boundaries.

The overall trend in a complex sequence of restructuring local government has been to reduce the political might of local government by dividing it into smaller units, with the proclaimed ideal of devolving decision-making and service provision to local communities. Local government reorganisation has been presented as a constant drive to deliver services more efficiently and more economically. It is also claimed that higher standards of provision will be achieved, more responsive to the needs of 'service users' or 'consumers', which in the case of education means the schools, teachers, parents or carers, families and children. At the same time, on the principle of 'divide and rule', this has served to enhance the power of central government and to weaken the relative power of local democracies.

Wales and Scotland had their local government restructured to single-tier authorities in 1996. Wales has twenty-two unitary authorities for a population of around three million, while Scotland has half as many again (thirty-two) for twice the size of population. In Scotland, the new councils vary widely in size, some modelled on the old counties, such as Clackmannanshire, some on former districts, such as Inverclyde and some on former regions, such as Highland. Latterly there have been thirty-two unitary authorities designated as Councils with councillors elected every four years. Northern Ireland had its two-tier local government system entirely replaced as early as 1973 by a single-tier district council system, but education is separately administered by just five Education and Libraries Boards (ELBs) for a population half the size of Wales. The ELBs are not elected but appointed by the Department of Education, with only two out of five members locally appointed. In addition to the ELBs there is a Council for Catholic Maintained Schools (CCMS) and where each ELB is responsible for staff appointments in its own controlled schools, the CCMS does this for Catholic schools.

Currently there are 152 LAs in England. Sizes of council areas vary widely, one of the most populous in England being Birmingham (a metropolitan borough) with over one million people and 328 primary schools, while the smallest non-metropolitan unitary area, Rutland, has a population of just under 35,000 and seventeen primary schools. These are outliers and most English authorities have a population in the range of 150,000 to 300,000. Northern Ireland's five Boards are in a similar range of size, with Welsh and Scottish LAs being considerably smaller. Statistical analyses, commissioned by the Department for Communities and Local Government (DCLG) in 2006 on Population Size and Local Authority Performance for England, concluded that while the relationship between population and performance is complex, the evidence suggests that performance tends to be better in larger authorities especially as regards consumer satisfaction and value for money.

Funding and services

For teachers the most familiar and immediate impact of local government in their schools has less to do with the political than with the administrative arm of the local authority. In past decades, though subject to policies developed by councillors, the quality of educational administration was dependent on the capacity and imagination of its officers. In their heyday at the time of the Plowden Report certain LEAs were highly regarded for the developmental work of their advisory teams in primary curriculum and its dissemination through teachers' centres. Well known in this respect were Leicestershire, Oxfordshire and the West Riding of Yorkshire with their teams of committed and competent primary advisers. At ILEA in the 1970s many curriculum initiatives, resources and publications provided in effect a national resource for primary education. LEAs provided the means through which teachers and schools could collaborate locally and resources could be pooled. Potential drawbacks were highlighted, however, in Alexander's critical study of curriculum and professional development in Leeds LEA's primary school service in the late 1980s, revealing the dangers of complacency and dogmatism that could develop within a local advisory service. Alexander's report fuelled central government's distrust of local authorities and triggered the 1992 'three wise men' report on curriculum organisation in primary schools, giving rise to a new inspection regime in the form of Ofsted (Chapter 7), and later to centralised control of pedagogy in the National Strategies (Chapter 5). In the last twenty years increased constraints have been imposed by national government on LAs in educational policy.

The problems of funding schools are truly complex, belied by simplistic political rhetoric. Political spin from central government often discredits local government, alleging wasteful bureaucracy and attacking the power that LAs supposedly wield in distributing funds to schools. National government can pretend to take the side of schools against LAs by protesting that too much money is diverted to 'back office' functions in LAs which should be passing more of the education budget direct to schools. That rhetoric conveniently ignores the strict formulae for distribution already in place to which the authorities have to conform.

The new 'pupil premium', for example, promised by the Coalition Government in 2011, a sum of money for every child taking free school meals as a means of providing extra resources for disadvantaged children, is to be distributed to schools via the LA. In addition, many educational functions are statutorily required and leave authorities with relatively little scope for manoeuvre. It also overlooks the valuable additional services a LA can provide in supporting primary schools' curriculum, for example, through provision of libraries, museums and music services. Undoubtedly the quality of services provided by different LAs has been highly variable and this has motivated many schools to support central government policies that provide more direct funding. The last twenty years have seen consistent moves towards Local Management of Schools (LMS) making individual schools responsible for spending their own budgets, introducing an element of flexibility and of democratic control for the school's governing body which can choose which services it procures. The problem this presents for the LA is that a guaranteed level of uptake is needed to sustain provision of services that require a critical mass, and schools making individual choices can undermine the quality or even the viability of these services.

It can be argued that governments allow LAs to continue in existence as a convenient scapegoat for inadequate national funding of education. They can be readily blamed when services are criticised as inadequate. Moreover, despite constant threats to abolish LAs, central government has continued to rely on them for implementing educational reforms, such as New Labour's 'standards agenda'. In some respects the administrative arm of the LA has turned into a local agency for national initiatives, with a consequent deficit for local democracy. New Labour in government introduced a large number of grant-funded initiatives, effectively increasing central funding of schools but using LAs as the medium for distribution. The National Strategies Implementation Programme entailed not only classroom pedagogy, but also school management for improvement and the use of data for monitoring performance. A system of School Improvement Partners (SIPs) was nationally funded but managed by the LA; under new legislation in 2011 SIPs cease to be a funded statutory requirement, their function replaced by NLEs and LLEs trained and accredited by NCSL (Chapter 6) to improve 'failing schools', but LAs remain involved in the process, in this way providing another vehicle of accountability to central government, alongside Ofsted. LAs are in turn assessed annually by Ofsted.

Democratic accountability at the local level may be further diminished not only through increased control by central government, but also through the practice of outsourcing educational services. In the interests of economy, LAs have purchased services from commercial providers. Smaller authorities may be more pressed to do so, the 2006 DCLG analysis referred to above indicating that value for money was better in larger authorities where economies of scale apply. Outsourcing may be influenced by party politics insofar as it may be more commonly, though by no means exclusively, a preference of Conservative authorities. A more fundamental political question however is how far the level of accountability is effectively maintained when commercial providers are involved. Occasionally central government intervention has forced outsourcing on a local authority, doubly undermining any vestige of local participation. This has been the case where Ofsted identified an LA as requiring intervention, so that central government commissioned private contractors to run the local education service, as, for example, in Islington, managed from 1999 onwards by CEA (now renamed Cambridge Education (CE)). The Coalition Government in 2010 announced its intention of encouraging 'new providers' of support services for schools, from the private and voluntary sectors.

The ideal of local government is of local affairs conducted by democratically elected representatives who are familiar with the social, cultural and economic character of the area, responsive to local opinion and understanding of local needs. Ideally this results in local oversight of and accountability for educational provision as a whole, from early childhood through to lifelong learning, schools, libraries, museums, recreational and sports facilities. In addition, the LA structure facilitates networks so that teachers and schools can work not as atomised units but as part of a wider service providing primary education to a neighbourhood. Authorities have served as an umbrella under which clusters of schools can network for mutual support. Reynolds (2008) has offered a critical view of local authorities in Wales where their policies reflected an historical commitment to the use of education to transform society and to achieve social justice for different societal groups, thereby rejecting the 'free market' paradigm adopted in England.

In political culture and mass media, the national increasingly overshadows the local. Organisation of local democratic representation through mainstream political parties blurs a necessary distinction between national and local politics. Increasing voter apathy in local elections has occurred in recent decades as national governments and media collude in presenting a presidential style of politics that casts local politics into the shade. Devolution to smaller scale units, as in the creation of unitary authorities, could potentially encourage greater participation in local politics, but small authorities may lack the critical mass required for effective party organisation and democratic competition in the neighbourhood. Conservative politicians have advocated 'Big Society' ostensibly aimed at 'dismantling the state' but effectively *increasing* state power by requiring more direction from the centre.

Woodhead's antipathy to LEAs (reflected in his words at the beginning of this chapter) can be contrasted with the attitude of Estelle Morris, former Secretary of State for Education from 2001 to 2002. Morris was a reasoned defender of local authorities. Having taught for twenty years in a Coventry comprehensive before entering politics, she recognised the support they could provide to schools, though quite aware too of the undesirable variations in the quality of their services:

> Over the years, there has been a chasm between the performance of different local authorities. Some have been a drain on the energy of headteachers and a burden to endure; others have been the glue that holds the schools together, constantly raising aspirations and sharing best practice.

> (*Guardian*, 22 June 2010)

The debate, she wrote, had too often been about local authorities versus freedom for schools. Instead, the debate should be about what kind of 'middle' we want our education system to have, since there was an undeniable need for someone who administratively keeps the system going and who protects those services that cannot effectively be delivered at school level. Despite repeated criticism and implicit threats of abolition from national politicians at both ends of the political spectrum, local authorities continue to serve essential functions in the education system. The Coalition Government's White Paper in November 2010 described just four functions envisaged for LAs: 'commissioning' excellent education (often from private providers); managing school admissions; championing social justice; and taking responsibility for school improvement. Such a narrowly defined role casts the LA more as an administrative agency of central government than a representative body shaping an education service for its local population.

School and community

Community is both a concept of social organisation and an ideal. It is a powerful and attractive term that can apply equally to the neighbourhood group of families and individuals for whom the school might be a focal institution, and to the organisation and ethos of adults and children within the school itself. Both contexts are considered here to raise questions about accountability.

School within the community

The ideal of a school at the heart of and serving its community had been proposed and experimented with by radical groups early in the nineteenth century, but was not evident in the first state elementary schools. It reappeared following the Second World War, and the Plowden Report in 1967 endorsed this aspect of the primary school's role. Only a decade after Plowden came the notorious disjuncture of William Tyndale junior school (Chapter 5) that led to a good deal of soul-searching about the relationship between primary schools and their local communities. At Tyndale in 1976, the curriculum and pedagogy, and indeed the social organisation of the school itself became an issue of concern amongst many of the parents and the neighbourhood community (Simon 1991, 444–446). That situation was probably not unique except in its extremity and its national exposure, and occasional cases of a breakdown of trust between individual schools and their local communities have been replicated since in the fervid decades of educational debate that followed. The Islington case had immediate effects not only in challenges to the local authority role but also in accelerating reform of school governance.

Understanding the relationship of primary schools to their communities is made difficult by the diversity of school types that have evolved over time. In the first place, the historic partnership of church and state in school provision complicates the accountability of a school to its local community. What are currently called community schools in England and Wales were traditionally managed by the LEA, and the local authority remains responsible for a fair and consistent admissions policy across all its schools, owns the school grounds and buildings, and employs the school staff. These schools coexist in the system alongside several other categories. Voluntary controlled (VC) schools are state-funded schools in England, Wales and Northern Ireland in which a foundation or trust (usually a Christian denomination) has some formal influence in its governance. Their land and buildings are typically owned by a charitable foundation, which also appoints about a quarter of the school governors, but the LA pays all capital costs, employs the school's staff and has primary responsibility for the school's admission arrangements. In England, approximately 15 per cent of all primary schools are voluntary controlled, the great majority associated with the Church of England. Voluntary aided (VA) schools are also state-funded through the LA but have more autonomy than voluntary controlled, and the foundation or trust (usually a religious organisation) has a substantial influence in running the school, appoints a majority of the school governors and owns the school buildings. VA schools receive all their running costs via the local authority and 90 per cent of capital costs. The governing body employs the staff and decides the school's admission arrangements, subject to rules imposed by central government. Pupils follow the National Curriculum, except that faith schools may teach Religious Education according to their own faith. In England, approximately 22 per cent of primary schools are voluntary aided, including all of the Roman Catholic schools and the schools of non-Christian faiths; whilst more than half of the Church of England schools are VC, a substantial number are VA.

Foundation schools arose in 1998 with a change of government. The Education Reform Act of 1988 had attempted to diversify provision and weaken what the Conservative Government saw as the over-powerful influence of LEAs by allowing schools to 'opt out' to Grant Maintained (GM) status, receiving their funds direct from central government, and within ten years 3 per cent of primaries (600 schools) had become GM. After the General Election in 1997, New Labour, committed in principle at that time to continuing LA responsibility for education, fulfilled its election pledge to abolish GM schools and to bring them back within the local authority. Former GM schools were thereby entitled to a new status as Foundation schools. Funded via the LA, their governing body employs the staff and has independent responsibility for admissions to the school (though these have to conform to rules imposed by central government). Approximately 2 per cent of English primary schools are Foundation schools, but the proportion is very much smaller in Wales, where only four primary schools have foundation status.

Confusion and inequity caused by this variety of school types was noted by the House of Commons Children's Schools and Families Committee Report in 2010 (HCCSFC 2009). It observed that foundation and voluntary aided schools (as well as academies, to be discussed in the next section) enjoyed freedom and flexibility to meet the needs of their pupils, whereas community and voluntary controlled schools, together comprising 75 per cent of all main-tained schools, were far more constrained by rules and regulations. The Committee heard calls for much greater emphasis on local determination of the curriculum and responsiveness to parents and pupils, either directly or in partnership with a local authority:

> Missing . . . is the sense of a pull from the consumer or beneficiary. Teachers are well aware of the collective view of the parents but they have not been encouraged or enabled to use that as their driving force. The role of teachers in meeting the needs of parents has effectively been reversed to one of meeting the requirements of the State.
> (HCCSFC 2009, Ev 256, paragraph 9 [Jolly Learning Ltd])

> . . . under the aegis of the National Curriculum, there can be no way in for the notion of education as cultural conversation led by a cultured profession free to express itself in essentially local, small scale environments. In short, politicians have to be persuaded to . . . return [the curriculum] to the care of a revitalised and independent profession working in partnership with a resurrected, well-funded network of local authorities. . . . Along with these reforms there must be a fresh remit [for the QCA] reflecting the needs of children, families and schools – rather than the latest whims of its political masters.
> (HCCSFC 2009, Ev 250, paragraph 6 [Malcolm Ross])

Accountability of schools to their local communities is of a very different kind from the mechanistic and data-led accountabilities exercised at national level (Chapter 7), but is complicated by these conflicting levels and also by the interests of churches and foundations that can be contradictory in their effect. The nature of the community and the ethos of the school are key variables in practice so that a single formula for school–community relations will not work in the same way in different contexts. Indeed, Jim Campbell has warned against complacency in our expectations of community:

> The underlying idea of community responsibility, superficially democratic, hinges on a romanticised and bourgeois conception of 'community' . . . [as] collective, cohesive and mutually supportive . . . in many urban contexts, the catchment areas of schools are riven by conflict, some of it racially motivated, some of it religiously biased, some of it class based, and by competition.
>
> (Campbell 2010, 31)

However great the obstacles, the aspiration must remain of a more organic relationship with its local community than exists between a school and the state or local authority, suggesting the need to strive for democratic participation that nevertheless safeguards a degree of professional autonomy required to secure good-quality teaching and learning.

Community within the school

Currently the formal channel of accountability between the school and its local community is the governing body, with representative parents and local people in its membership. The idea of governors as worthy 'trustees' goes back to the foundation of ancient endowed schools like Eton and Harrow, reappearing in modern guise as representative 'stakeholders'. The schools' teachers are accountable to the governors, who in turn are accountable to the parents and to the state for the good conduct of the school.

Following the 1944 Education Act, primary schools unlike secondary schools had 'managers' rather than 'governors', a sign of their inferior status, and LEAs could set up a single board of managers for a group of schools together. In the 1960s less than half of primary schools still had their own board of managers; in practice much of the decision-making was delegated to the headteacher, and managers were sandwiched between the head and the LEA in their responsibilities. By the 1970s, some of these boards were beginning to include representation of parents and of teachers, reflecting a steady groundswell of public debate about control of education and a desire for more participation, so it was not just the traumatic example of William Tyndale School that prompted government to announce an enquiry into school governance. The Taylor Report *A new partnership for our schools* was published in 1977 and proposed making governing bodies more representative of all those with an interest in the school.

That trend gathered pace so that by the mid-1980s legislative reforms began to promote governing bodies as independent forces, with parents taking a leading role, to improve the work of the school. A government White Paper *Better Schools* in 1985 suggested that governors should be able to determine, with the headteacher, the main policies and lines of development of the school, should participate in the appointment and dismissal of staff, help determine the aims and objectives of the curriculum and be given control over expenditure on certain items. These principles were embodied in legislation in 1986. Despite this devolution of power, placing responsibility on governors' shoulders, the same government imposed a national curriculum only two years later in 1988, undermining a significant freedom that schools had enjoyed. This paradox epitomises the ambivalence of governments in devolving weighty accountabilities to groups of lay people. Governor training was provided by LAs, subsequently with some private sector participation, and the Schools White Paper of 2010 promised a further role for NCSL in developing courses for Chairs of governing bodies.

In Northern Ireland the management of all schools was devolved in 1990 to Boards of Governors and Principals, with responsibility for admissions, discipline and delivery of the

Northern Ireland Curriculum. Financial responsibilities were also devolved under Local Management of Schools (LMS) as in England and Wales, but this met with some criticism because of the limited ability of governors to fulfil their extensive range of duties, often consequently left to the headteacher as a 'chief executive' with a relatively weak 'board of directors'. School Boards were introduced in Scotland in 1988 to encourage parental involvement in schools. Involved in determining the overall policies, objectives and ethos at the school, they had a special duty to promote good relationships between the school, its parents and the community and to form a channel for the flow of information between these groups. They comprised parent, teacher and co-opted members drawn from local business or the community, with parents in the majority; the strength of parental support for teachers in their confrontation with the government was noted in Chapter 7. By the Scottish School Act 2006, they were replaced by a two-tier system of Parent Forums and Parent Councils.

The broadly democratic principle of parental and community involvement in their local primary school is by now well established. Governors came to be held responsible for the quality of a school's practice, though questions might continue to be raised about the limits of accountability that can realistically be imposed on a relatively transient group of non-specialists. Questions have also been raised about how truly representative of the 'stakeholders' governing bodies are. Studies of their composition and working noted the disproportionate presence of white, middle-class males, leaving ethnic minorities, women and lower socio-economic groups under-represented; governing bodies in privileged catchment areas were able to co-opt the professional skills of lawyers and accountants. Furthermore the financial value to the state of such unpaid labour has been calculated in millions, raising the question of whether governors were to be seen, in the words of one study, as active citizens or state volunteers. Political principles of the 'Big Society' might be realised in this arrangement, or alternatively it might be seen as the politics of opportunism, a means of economising in educational administration.

Discussion of the school community might include at one level, accountability of the head, and at another, accountability to pupils. Answerable to the governors, the headteacher is directly accountable for the school's work. There may be some tension in the relationship between head and governors in managing a school, and there is also tension for the head between the different roles of curriculum and professional leadership, monitoring the performance of children and teachers and management of facilities and personnel. Allison's (2010) study compares English and Polish primary headteachers. School directors in Poland do not have responsibilities for managing budgets and premises experienced by their English counterparts. They are simply there to run the school and ensure that children have the best education possible. In addition, it was noted that English heads were fixated on systems and routines to track pupils' attainment and monitor teacher performance, generating much time-consuming and energy-sapping paperwork. This, and fears of being found wanting by Ofsted, can make headteachers unwilling to risk broadening the curriculum and experimenting with pedagogy.

Accountability to pupils in respect of goals for learning is closely stipulated by the state in levels of attainment, but two broader perspectives may be identified in human rights and in 'learning without limits'. Rights-respecting schools not only teach about children's rights founded on the UNCRC as discussed with regard to citizenship education in Chapter 4, but they also model rights and respect in relationships between adults and pupils (UNICEF UK, 2011). Within the school community this requires arrangements for listening to and taking serious account of children's opinions, presenting a challenge to organisation and governance of the school community where mechanisms such as a School Council, for all their good intentions, may still be superficial and tokenistic. Article 12 of the UNCRC states that children have the right to say what they think should happen when adults are making decisions that affect them, and to have their opinions taken into account, Article 13 that they have a right to receive and to share information (as long as the information is not damaging to them or to others). That discipline in schools should respect children's human dignity is laid down in Article 28. Another mode of accountability to individual pupils is embedded in the project of 'learning without limits'. The work of this project in schools has made a powerful contribution in recent years to debates about the effects of ability labelling and ability-focused practices of government-sponsored models embedded in literacy and numeracy strategies, offering alternative pedagogies that recognise and accommodate the individuality of learners (Hart *et al.* 2004; Learning without Limits 2011).

Consumerism or democratic accountability?

Choice and diversity

The model of consumerism in state education proposes more variety and choice. Stable relationships between schools and communities on the other hand would seem to require a more consistent pattern of provision. Department stores, supermarkets and restaurants may excite consumers by their competing attractions, but fail to generate the kind of loyalty, identity and community coherence that might be looked for from a primary school. A steady increase in privatisation would seem to complicate and effectively undermine local accountability.

Private provision of primary education in itself is nothing new, and in some areas has a significant effect on pupil intakes and destinations. Where private alternatives exist locally, it may lead to a more socially segregated group of children within the state school, some children entering at age 7 perhaps having experienced a Montessori or a Steiner pre-school, or leaving the primary for a local prep school at age 8. Where there is choice of publicly funded primary schools, the existence of voluntary church schools alongside maintained schools may also skew the social profiles of pupils in any one school, and the more recent appearance of academies, trust schools and free schools will take this differentiation further in some localities.

The Conservative Government of the 1980s had been bent on freeing schools from the 'grip of local authority control' by creating Grant Maintained (GM) schools. GM status offered direct funding from Whitehall, bypassing the LEA. The process was notionally democratic insofar as proposals to convert had to be agreed in a ballot of parents, but the object was to give competitive advantage to a single school rather than to benefit all schools and children in the neighbourhood. A further incentive, even more divisive within communities, was the freedom to set their own admissions criteria, sometimes at variance with those applied by the LEAs.

Academies

Although the abolition of GM in 1998 was a symbolic rebuff to Tory policy and a reward to Labour LEAs and local electoral support, the urgent imperative of 'modernisation' and reform drove the New Labour Government, like its Conservative predecessor, to bypass the LEAs once more. So just two years after abolishing GM, New Labour introduced a new type of directly funded school, specifically designed to 'rescue failing inner city secondary schools' – the City Academy.

Originally aimed at failing secondary schools, academy regulations allowed for independent sponsors, such as businesses and social entrepreneurs, charitable groups and churches, to found and help finance brand-new schools. Freedoms for academies included the power to set their own pay and conditions for staff, and freedom from the National Curriculum. As the programme gathered pace, it was extended to allow for various kinds of experimentation, including federation of primary schools with their local academy. Aimed at dismantling a so-called 'public sector monopoly' of state education, academies were overtly anti-democratic. Sponsors were originally to provide 10 per cent of costs up to a maximum £2m, to appoint the majority of governors (with only one elected by parents and one LEA governor), to determine the ethos, specialism and uniform of the school and were entitled to select and appoint staff.

The intention of academies was expressed in a powerful policy discourse. They were to address generational poverty and unemployment in deprived areas, by 'challenging a culture of educational under-attainment in localities' and 'breaking the cycle of underachievement', acting as a focus for learning for pupils, families and other local people, and sharing their expertise with other schools and the wider community. This important ideal could equally have been tackled through well-resourced schools democratically accountable to their communities, and indeed through other measures to deal with deprivation. However, their mission also included 'social and economic strategies of regeneration' by 'building partnerships with local community and businesses' and was therefore to move beyond traditional public sector welfare solutions, which were seen as having failed. These propositions were elaborated with rhetorical tropes about business as the key to 'innovation', 'enterprise', 'opportunity' and 'choice', not just the key to local regeneration but also to international economic competitiveness. The spirit of private enterprise, transferred to the school, would encourage the flexibility needed to be innovative, to be creative in curriculum, staffing and governance, and to 'escape from limitations of traditional organisation'.

This linguistic play of rhetoric and reality richly illustrates the political theatricality identified by Kenneth Minogue (Chapter 2), but it also has far-reaching discursive significance. Stephen Ball, in the quotation that opens this chapter, describes how academies re-articulate our notions of localism and centralism, of autonomy and regulation. Academies were promised to increase 'diversity and choice' for parents as consumers in the educational marketplace, but also internally would lead to 'modernisation' of teachers in 'workforce remodelling' under transformational leadership by a new breed of dynamic, visionary, risk-taking, entrepreneurial headteachers. And of greatest relevance to our concern in this chapter, academies would represent a break from traditional roles and structures and relationships of accountability in state education, where sponsors acquired a major role in the governing body and a major say in the ethos of the school. Though sponsors were described as 'partners', some of the most eminent business sponsorships were negotiated not in the locality, but at the highest level of central government including not only the Department for Education but also the Cabinet Office.

Following the General Election in May 2010, an Academies Act, rushed through Parliament, vastly expanded the possibilities for schools to become academies. Academy status was now not just for failing schools, but ultimately for all schools, initially inviting those judged 'outstanding' by Ofsted to apply, and including primary schools in their own right. In June 2011 the Secretary of State went further in announcing a plan to force the

700 worst performing primary schools to become academies through partnership with established secondary or primary academies.

Trust schools

A clear difficulty of relying on business sponsorship for schools is its dependence on continuing prosperity of the business concerned. As the original academies programme progressed it became difficult to find a sufficient number of sponsors willing to put up the large capital sum required, £2m in the early stages, so this was soon relaxed. The Education and Inspections Act in 2006 offered a compromise solution in the form of a trust school, allowing a school to acquire a charitable foundation to support it. The trust might comprise a single school or group of schools with a stronger school assisting a weaker one under a unified governing body. It was proposed that organisations involved in trusts might help to create a culture of innovation and enterprise. Examples of bodies that might enter long-term partnerships with trust schools to improve local education included local charities, businesses, other schools and universities, and specialists in business, sport, education or the arts were expected to make significant improvements for the whole school. The extent of influence an individual business would enjoy in a trust school depended on how many (if any) other members of the trust there are, and how many governors the trust appoints.

Some trust proposals were community focused. One proposal (which didn't come to fruition) was for a shared trust including twelve primary schools and one special school, partnered with the local Primary (Health) Care Trust, a mental health provider, the Salvation Army, Community Police, the County Council, and a partnership for school-centred initial teacher training (intended to increase the number of high-quality teachers within the school cluster). The specific focus in this instance was to contribute to community cohesion, working together to improve services for pupils, students and their families, offering potentional for the kind of social pedagogy discussed in Chapter 5. The trust would share good practice within the cluster of schools, with the aim of raising aspirations and attainment. This collaborative approach could be seen as a means to fulfilling on a small and more local scale one of the traditional roles of a LEA in improving the quality of education provision throughout a locality.

By September 2010 there were almost 400 trust schools of which about one-third were primary, and numbers were expected to rise. However, a boost to the Academies programme by the Coalition Government may have encouraged prospective trust schools to apply for Academy status instead.

Free schools

Free schools were a flagship education policy promised by the Conservative Party in its manifesto for the 2010 General Election, and introduced by an Education Bill of 2011, allowing government to respond to proposals from groups of parents, teachers, charities (religious fundamentalist groups excluded) and businesses. The concept draws on a model from Sweden where it provokes controversy and disputed assessments of its success. In England, so far, the free school must be non-profit-making, though some on the political right advocate profit-making free schools. They are to have the same freedoms as academies, and like academies, would be funded on a comparable basis to other state-funded schools, although large capital sums have been made available for acquisition of buildings and for start-up costs. Like academies they are to be free from following the National Curriculum, but also free to employ unqualified teachers, raising serious questions about the role of both National Curriculum and Qualified Teacher Status within a national system of education.

A paradoxical set of approaches was embedded in the legislation, and introducing it in Parliament, the Secretary of State unwittingly expressed the contradiction:

> The core aim of the Bill was stated to be *to empower schools and teachers to make their own decisions and to reduce bureaucratic burdens.* In addition, *improvements in discipline, inspections and international benchmarking were stated to be vital* to improving educational performance [my emphasis].
>
> (DFE 2011)

The detail of the Bill reveals that whilst the schools are described as 'free', the Secretary of State acquires fifty new powers within the education system.

Proponents of free schools aspire to 'drive up standards' by creating more 'local competition', arguing for greater choice and diversity in the state as in the private sector of independent schools. Many of the earliest proposals promise a curriculum or ethos currently available only in independent schools, arguing that the state system is too narrow or 'monolithic'. Whilst supporters claim that parents should be able to choose according to their preferences or perceived needs of their children, this principle inevitably benefits more privileged parents who have time and expertise to deploy in setting up their own free schools. The disproportionate use of public resources on individual small schools implies that funding will be diverted away from existing schools, especially at a time of cuts in public service budgets. The NUT have warned against a policy fuelling social segregation and undermining local democracy, their survey of parents indicating that free schools are neither wanted nor needed, and an overview of research on the Swedish free schools suggests that whilst the schools have failed to improve pupils' academic achievement overall, those who benefited most were students from more privileged homes.

Free schools, unlike academies, are likely to remain a token few, though their political and ideological significance goes beyond their number. Of the first sixteen proposals accepted by the government, half were for primary schools: two of these were for Jewish faith schools based in Haringey and Barnet, one an Evangelical Anglican primary in Camden, one a Hindu faith school in Leicester, and one in Birmingham proposed by a Sikh education trust open to people of all religions. The others were proposed by the private company ARK for White City in the borough of Hammersmith, two by childcare providers: the Childcare Company in Slough, and a Montessori school in West Sussex. A total of 249 proposals nationally had been received by the Secretary of State by February 2011, and NASUWT leader Chris Keates had already concluded that this low response suggested that the public preferred good local schools run by democratically accountable local councils: 'The Secretary of State suggests that he wants free schools to be engines of social mobility but in many cases the free schools announced so far will only fragment communities and lead to greater social segregation and separation' (BBC News, 6 September 2010). By the summer of 2011 over 300 applications had been made for free schools to begin in September 2012, of which about 50 per cent were expected to succeed, and bids were to include special as well as mainstream schools.

Conclusion

It would be wrong to be nostalgic and uncritical about LEAs as there were certainly flaws and disparities in their functioning, but they were founded on the principle of democratic local accountability for educational provision responsive to local needs, and provided the possibility of a well-resourced service and network of schools and teachers able to offer mutual support rather than an atomised provision of individual small schools. Political discourse emanating from central government over the last twenty years discredited LEAs and local government in general, as a pretext for national imposition, but this can be seen as an attempt to gather more political power to the centre. It is not inconceivable that educational reform could have been realised within a local authority structure.

Central government was also intent on devolving power to individual schools. Under successive legislation since the 1980s, governing bodies gained full responsibility for running their schools, with LEAs responsible for strategic planning of provision throughout a local area, and for providing challenge and support on behalf of national government. Funds passed by central government to local authorities were distributed according to strict funding formulae according to the needs of schools, yet local authorities were still described in the language of 'oppression' as imposing burdens from which schools needed to be relieved. The promise of academies, trust schools and free schools was the notional 'freedom' they would be given, allowing governors, headteachers and teachers 'more control over how they run their schools'. However it was abundantly clear that the constraints under which schools worked by 2010 came far less from local authorities than from central government control.

Political journalist Simon Jenkins summed up the problematics of the Academies policy: 'Transient private corporations or parent groups' sponsoring academies and free schools 'cannot realistically stand proxy for a community, let alone for a town or city'. Whatever was wrong with English schools, it was not governance, he argued. Local developments showed that what most parents wanted was a fair admissions system, run through some sort of local democracy, and that most schools and teachers welcomed support in curriculum and professional development from the local authority, and the opportunities it created for collaboration through clusters of schools. 'The key to better education must lie deep within [the schools] themselves, in their ethos, morale and staffing. Good schools are underpinned not damaged by civic commitment and civic pride' (Jenkins 2010).

The rhetoric of 'freeing schools from local control' was effectively, Jenkins claimed, a cover for greater centralisation. Tony Blair had repeated Margaret Thatcher's oxymoronic aspiration to 'make every school an independent state school', but in effect the more schools had been 'liberated', the more they had been regulated (Jenkins 2010). The underlying issue remains, after this relentless sequence of structuring and restructuring, how a service such as primary education mostly controlled and largely funded through national government, can remain democratically accountable in the locality and responsive to local needs.

Key questions for reflection

- What is the role of the local authority and how does it affect the work of your school? What kinds of support, services or networking with other local schools does it facilitate? What is its role, if any, in securing accountability, and to what extent is politics a significant factor in its educational provision?
- What is the relative role of head and governors in determining a primary school's aims and evaluating its achievements? How do national political priorities affect their work?

How effectively can a governing body take account of and respond to the opinions of pupils and other members of the school community?

- Examine the relationship of your school to its local community. How far is this affected by the kind of school, for example, community, faith, foundation, academy, free school? How representative of the local community and the 'stakeholders' is your school governing body?

Independent learning tasks

Adopt any one of the above questions as a focus for personal research, and/or the basis for discussion with colleagues.

Interview a primary school governor (or if possible two governors of different categories: community, sponsor, parent or teacher). Explore their experiences of primary school governance, their understandings of the principles and operation of accountability, and their perceptions of the political dimensions of school governance. In what ways do they see themselves as accountable, and to whom? How do they rank their accountabilities to children, to parents, carers and families, to the local community, and to the state?

Further reading

Alexander, R.J. (ed.) (2010) *Children, Their World, Their Education: Final Report and Recommendations of the Cambridge Primary Review*, London: Routledge.
Chapter 20 (382–405) traces the recent historical development of integrated services, local authorities and the multiple agencies working with schools for the benefit of young children. Lacking detailed description of the political context, it nevertheless critiques the tensions and difficulties at the heart of policy. Chapter 23 (458–483) describes the structure of governance at national, local and school levels, including opinion and evidence about the roles of LAs and of school governing bodies.

Ball, S. *Education plc: Understanding private sector participation in public sector education*, London: Routledge, 2007.
In Chapter 1 (1–16) Ball discusses the concept and the discourse of privatisation and the sociological thinking to interpret and explain the phenomenon, and Chapter 2 (17–38) provides a full account of recent policy. Chapter 8 (184–191) reflects on the impact and significance of these developments.

House of Commons Children, Schools and Families Committee (HCCSFC) (2010c) *From Baker to Balls: The foundations of the education system* (Ninth Report Session 2009–2010) HC 422.
This report reviews education policies as a whole over the previous twenty years, drawing on oral evidence and discussion by four former Secretaries of State, the most persistent theme being the tension between central and local responsibility and control.

Reynolds, D. (2008) 'New Labour, education and Wales: The devolution decade', *Oxford Review of Education*, 34, 6: 753–765.
This informative and closely argued account of distinctive education policies in Wales after devolution of power in 1999 illustrates the significance of cultural and political context by contrast with England. It focuses on the roles of central state and of local authorities acting in collaboration with educational partners and rejecting the 'consumerist' paradigm, offering a mixed judgement on the outcomes.

Taylor, F. (1997) 'Governors, parents and primary schools', in C. Cullingford (ed.) *The Politics of Primary Education*, Buckingham: Open University Press, 114–124.
Written when parent representation on governing bodies was already well established, but when new mechanisms of accountability were still under development, a few details are dated but the broad issues raised are still highly relevant and incisively discussed.

Chapter 9

Going forward

Going forward we go into the unknown. We have seen the influence of economics in shaping policy, and economics now works on a global scale with heightened unpredictability. Politics and political actors are driven by economic events such as fluctuations in the price of raw materials and manufactured goods and competition in world markets. Culture and economics are in a symbiotic relationship and politicians respond to cultural trends too in their education policies. Social change, slower and fractionally more predictable, also depends on economic and cultural conditions.

Teachers might feel dragged forward by these overpowering forces, powerless before the forces of change. But politics provides a forum for making the professional voice heard. The challenge for teachers and others involved in primary schools lies in campaigning for education and opportunities of a much broader kind for children, while continuing to work conscientiously within the narrow constraints and straitened resources of current policy. To form a coherent message requires reflecting critically on our own experience and acquiring some knowledge and understanding of how policies developed as they did, of what alternative paths might have been taken. The challenge is to go forward with clear ideas and principles for teaching and learning that can be explained and defended in an antagonistic political environment.

The main thrust of this book has been to view primary education policy as a product of deep trends, identifying where politics intervenes. We need to recognise the interplay of long-term cultural change and the more immediate contests of party politics played out week by week in the media. The agency of individuals is part of the story told in the previous chapters and individual actors have featured prominently. Prime Ministers Thatcher and Blair, both with a passion for education, their education ministers Baker and Blunkett, administrators and policy advisers like Woodhead and Barber have all played their roles, but might also be seen as mouthpieces for ideology or creatures of circumstance.

Politics over the last thirty years has demonstrated compromise and continuity between administrations of opposing political parties. Thatcher's policies reflected both neo-liberal and neo-conservative forces within her party, free enterprise alongside a defence of traditional institutions. Blair's project to 'modernise' his party led to the election of a New Labour Government whose policies on education combined neo-liberal measures along Conservative party lines with more traditional social democratic policies of Labour politics based on the role of the state in ensuring social justice and redistribution of wealth. The indecisive outcome of the 2010 General Election produced a coalition government that made great play of distancing itself from its New Labour predecessor, but didn't in effect mark a radical change in direction. Devolution tipped the balance towards social democracy in Scotland and in Wales with coalitions of Labour, Liberal Democrat and nationalist parties in power, though the more limited powers of the Welsh Assembly moderated the effects in Wales. In Northern Ireland, the continued priority of power-sharing in a situation of intractable political and religious conflict inhibited fundamental change in education policy.

A current trend traced in the previous chapters is the commercialisation and privatisation of provision that increasingly affects primary schools. Global economic shifts of power have been accompanied by shifts of balance in the national economy from manufacturing to finance and service industries. Both the global and national dimensions have affected communities and culture, making new demands on primary education. Simultaneously, they have affected government education policies. Commercial culture with its pursuit of profit and competitive marketing is reflected in national mechanisms of accountability based on competition between schools, and the programme of academies and free schools is designed to reduce public spending and create an educational free market based on diversity and consumer choice. The discourse of a 'third way' in New Labour education policy appeared to reconcile the welfare state and the free market, but needs to be treated with caution as multinational corporations compete to win contracts for providing education services. The scale of these developments makes them seemingly unstoppable, but all concerned with primary schools – governors, teachers and other staff, parents and carers – need to be aware of the changes and to strive against their negative effects on the quality of young children's educational experiences.

Hence a theme throughout this book has been the place of democracy as defined by Bernard Crick. An elected national government has a democratic mandate to determine education policy but election on a broad platform of policies cannot automatically be assumed to imply widespread support for specific policies. Other deficits in the democratic process include the role of the media and manipulation of popular opinion. Education policies are frequently far from commanding majority support, and many policies fall short of providing equal educational opportunity or fail to respect rights enshrined in the UNCRC. Locally elected government has often been found deficient in its provision of education, and a good deal of voter apathy exists at the local level. The variability of primary school practice in the past has required the state to step in as a guarantor, in principle at least, of entitlement and quality. But consistent centralisation of policy-making has undermined the participation and sense of ownership that parental and community representation on governing bodies appeared to promise. The political discourse of 'big society' appears to offer more local responsibility for primary schools, but needs to be questioned critically. Smaller units of local authority have less political leverage, fewer resources to support primary schools in their curriculum development and offer limited scope in the networking that benefits professional development of teachers and other staff. Though partnerships and federations are proposed as part of the academies model, a competitive marketplace of academies and free schools is not destined to encourage cooperation between primary schools on an equal basis. And a free-market ethos is unlikely to foster the democratic principles, participation, trust and security, self-esteem and respect for others required for effective personal, social and citizenship education for children within primary schools.

Obstacles to primary teachers' professional autonomy have featured in Chapters 5, 6 and 7 where attempts at micro-management of teachers' practice were seen to have derived from a political conception of the economy's needs. Teachers working on a daily basis with their own class are in a better position to identify and to respond sensitively and appropriately to the individual child's learning needs as against a narrowly prescribed national programme.

Primary teachers need to be trusted to work according to their conscience and good judgement, based on an understanding of child development, while remaining accountable to children, parents and carers and the community. Reviewing the work of pressure groups and think tanks in the chapters above has exposed dogmatism by political pundits on pedagogical issues. Effective pedagogy requires continuing independent research by professionals and educationists, and its transmission through initial teacher education and continuing professional development, with an overriding concern for the progress of individual learners in a collaborative classroom environment. Moreover, teacher autonomy is a prerequisite for empowering pupils, identified over eighty years ago by the government Board of Education in 1927 when it held that 'ideals of self-discipline and self-education for children went hand in hand with a reliance on the individual teacher's judgment'. A state-imposed model of authoritarian teaching also has negative implications for pupil autonomy and for the prospect of children becoming independent learners. Independent learning is a necessary context for the development of citizenship, entailing self-awareness, self-confidence and self-esteem.

A commendable focus of national policy has been to bring children out of the cycle of poverty, at which literacy and numeracy strategies have been aimed. Yet the boredom of passive and routine learning and the frustrations of constant testing and labelling are likely to alienate rather than motivate. Employability will be better achieved by cultivating children's capacity for creativity and imagination and love of learning for its own sake, including the basic skills. Children can't simply be schooled out of poverty, but a constructive curriculum and motivational pedagogy can encourage primary pupils to be partners in their own learning, setting personal targets for achievement. In the words of a primary headteacher on reading a draft of this book:

> The reason we're so far down the international league tables for both attainment and for happy and confident children is that children don't enjoy school as much as they should and don't have enough autonomy and enough encouragement to direct their own studies at their own pace. And of course it's more likely that children will do well in every respect (including passing tests) if they feel that school is enjoyable and learning is meaningful; if their school experiences are cooperative rather than competitive; if they feel that learning is truly personalised rather than regimented.
>
> (Gary Foskett, private communication, 5 April 2011)

The conclusion of this book must be that teachers need to find an effective political voice, a challenge not confined to the UK. In the USA, educationist Diane Ravitch, formerly a prominent adviser to Republican governments in the 1990s, has criticised political attacks on teachers and their unions: 'Destroying the unions will silence the only organised voice that opposes draconian cuts to education budgets. Without that voice, schools can expect larger class sizes and reduced funding for the arts, school nurses, libraries, and other programs' (Ravitch 2011). In political argument an 'educational establishment' often stands accused as the source of education's problems. This 'establishment' supposedly comprises teachers and educationists, caricatured as left-leaning and self-interested, and therefore not to be relied upon for objective views on primary schooling or other related matters. What is described as 'left-leaning' may simply reflect the fact that a primary teacher's role entails commitment to securing the well-being of others, and a primary teacher in close contact with children and their daily lives is likely to see this well-being in more rounded terms than policy-makers focused on narrow test scores. The accusation of 'self-interest', used to discredit professionals whose concerns are for the quality of the service they provide, reflects the fact that teaching young children demands heavy investment of the self, of personal resources such as empathy and imagination.

A broad understanding of education and schooling as political is intended to inform and support a critical consideration of policies for primary education. This calls for a study of past events that has been called a 'usable past'. Interrogating the discourse of current education policy in previous chapters has revealed how governments engrain interpretations of the past as a way of justifying change, in the language of 'modernisation', the need for 'step change', and the dismissal of past educational practices as responsible for inadequate levels of literacy and numeracy, and consequent poor economic performance. An independent study of the past raises questions about the discourse and scepticism about a view of educational reform as simply a technical and managerial approach to narrowly defined problems. A valuable and accessible resource is the collective memory of teachers, subjecting their own experience to critical reflection, locating these in a context of political, economic, social and cultural change. Such activity is, as one historian of education has suggested, to 'restore the broken links between our generation and our predecessors' (McCulloch 2011).

Our aspiration should be for primary teachers to be confident professionals able to make their own decisions about curriculum and teaching method, ready to analyse policy in place of unthinking acceptance, involved in union and other collaborative activities to resist mere imposition, initiating or engaging with opportunities for consultation and democratic debate.

Those who work in, with and for primary schools need to maintain a critical consciousness of the political context, to defend the measure of autonomy required to promote children's development and all-round learning, to respect children's rights and to model habits of good citizenship. We need to remain alert to the political dynamics and be ready to engage in an informed way with parents, local community, and in national debates. That is where the foregoing chapters have aimed to assist by examining the political dimensions to primary teachers' work.

Appendix: Politics and primary education – a recent history 1964–2011

	Politics	Education
	Including Education Acts and policy documents	*Including official reports*
1964	Labour Government Department of Education and Science (DES)	
1965	Teaching Council (Scotland) Act	General Teaching Council for Scotland established Inner London Education Authority established
1967		Plowden Report Gittins Report (Wales)
1969–1975		Black Papers on Education
1969	Northern Ireland 'Troubles'	
1970	Conservative Government	Teacher strikes
1972	NI Parliament abolished White Paper: *Education: A Framework for Expansion*	
1973	Oil crisis, stock market crash	
1974	Labour Government Centre for Policy Studies (Conservative think tank) established	NFER Reading Survey
1974–1976		William Tyndale School troubles
1975	Inflation reaches 25%	Bullock Report: *A Language for Life* on teaching English
1976	PM Callaghan's 'Ruskin speech' 'Great Debate' on education	Neville Bennett survey on *Teaching Styles and Pupil Progress*
1977	DES Green Paper *Education in Schools*	Taylor Report: *A New Partnership for our Schools* on school governance
1978		HMI Primary Survey
1979	Conservative Government Wales and Scotland reject devolution	
1980		ORACLE survey ON *Observational research and classroom learning*
1981	DES: *The School Curriculum*	

	Politics	Education
1982		Cockroft Report on teaching maths
1983		Council for Accreditation of Teacher Education (CATE) Scotland: National Committee on Primary Education Schools Curriculum Development Committee (SCDC)
1986	Education Act Governance of schools	
1987	Teachers' Pay and Conditions Act	
1988	Education Reform Act (National Curriculum, testing, local management of schools) HC Speaker's Commission on Citizenship	National Curriculum Council (NCC) Schools Examination and Assessment Council (SEAC)
1989	United Nations Convention on the Rights of the Child (UNCRC)	
1992	Department for Education (DFE)	'Three Wise Men' Report
1992		Ofsted
1993		Dearing Review: *The National Curriculum and its Assessment* Schools Curriculum and Assessment Authority (SCAA) replaces NCC/SEAC
1994		Teacher Training Agency (TTA)
1995	Department for Education and Employment (DFEE)	
1997		Qualifications and Curriculum Authority (QCA) replaces SCAA
1997	New Labour Government White Paper: *Excellence in Schools*	
1998	Northern Ireland Assembly (Good Friday agreement) Welsh Assembly Scottish Parliament School Standards and Framework Act Teaching and Higher Education Act Green Paper: *Teachers: Meeting the Challenge of Change*	Crick Report: *Education for Citizenship and the Teaching of Democracy in Schools* National Literacy Strategy (NLS) General Teaching Councils (England) and (Wales) established
1999		National Numeracy Strategy (NNS)
2000	UK rule reimposed in Northern Ireland Department of Culture, Media and Sport: *A Sporting Future for All*	
2001	Department for Education and Skills (DFES) National Assembly for Wales: *The Learning Country* World Trade Center attack, 11 September	

	Politics	Education
2003	Green Paper: *Every Child Matters* *Excellence & Enjoyment: A Strategy for Primary Schools* (PNS)	Workforce remodelling
2004	Children Act	
2005	London bombings, 7 July	
2006		Cambridge Primary Review begins
2007	Department for Children, Schools and Families (DCSF) *Children's Plan* policy document published	Ajegbo Report: *Diversity and Citizenship* 'Independent' Rose Review of primary curriculum established by DCSF
2008–2011	International financial crisis	New National Primary Framework
2008		Ofqual (replaces regulatory functions of QCA)
2009		Qualifications and Curriculum Development Agency (QCDA) (reformulation of QCA) *Independent Review of the Primary Curriculum* (Rose Review final report) Reform proposals adopted for implementation in 2011
2010	Conservative–Liberal Coalition Government Department for Education (DFE) Academies Act (including provision for Free Schools) White Paper: *The Importance of Teaching*	Cambridge Primary Review Final Report Primary curriculum reform (Rose Review) abandoned Allen review on Early Intervention Tickell review of EYFS Bew review of Key Stage 2 testing, assessment and accountability
2011	Education Bill 2010–2011 abolishing QCDA, TDA and GTCE Green Paper on special educational needs and disability	National Curriculum Review

Note: Richards (2001) identifies 'four periods': 1965–1974 as an 'age of excitement'; 1974–1988 'age of disillusionment'; 1988–1997 'age of regulation'; 1997– 'age of domination'.

Alexander (2010) sees four phases in which primary education 1967–1976 is largely 'unchallenged'; 1976–1987 'challenged'; 1987–1997 'regulated'; 1997–2009 'dominated'.

Bibliography

Note on web-based official resources: documents previously existing on departmental and official websites may usually be found on the National Archives website when their policy relevance has expired (http://webarchive.nationalarchives.gov.uk/). *Many historic printed official documents can also be found at* www.educationengland.org.uk

Action for Children and nef (2009) *Backing the Future: Why investing in children is good for us all* (www.actionforchildren.org.uk/policy-research/policy-priorities/backing-the-future, accessed 20 June 2011).

Alexander, R. (2000) *Culture and Pedagogy: International Comparisons in Primary Education*, Oxford: Blackwell.

Alexander, R. (2004) 'Still no pedagogy? Principle, pragmatism and compliance in primary education', *Cambridge Journal of Education*, 34, 1: 7–33.

Alexander, R. (ed.) (2010) *Children, Their World, Their Education: Final Report and Recommendations of the Cambridge Primary Review*, London: Routledge.

Alexander, R., Rose, J. and Woodhead, C. (1992) *Curriculum Organisation and Classroom Practice in Primary Schools: A Discussion Paper*, London: DES.

Allison, E.B. (2010) 'Pedagogy – how is it influenced in primary schools? A comparative study of literature about pedagogical influences in primary schools in England and Poland, with a focus on English primary schools', *Education 3–13*, 38, 1: 55–67.

Arthur, J. (2002) 'Roman Catholic Schools', in L. Gearon (ed.) *Education in the United Kingdom*, London: David Fulton.

Ball, S. (2007) *Education plc: Understanding private sector participation in public sector education*, London: Routledge.

Bangs, J., MacBeath, J. and Galton, M. (2011) *Reinventing Schools, Reforming Teaching. From political visions to classroom reality*, London: Routledge.

Barber, M. (2007) *Instruction to Deliver: Tony Blair, public services and the challenge of achieving targets*, London: Politico's.

Beck, J. (2008) *Meritocracy, Citizenship and Education: New Labour's Legacy*, London: Continuum.

Bennett, N. (1976) *Teaching Styles and Pupil Progress*, London: Open Books.

Board of Education (1905) *Suggestions for the consideration of teachers and others concerned in the work of public elementary schools* [Cd. 2638], London: HMSO.

Board of Education (1927) *Handbook of suggestions for the consideration of teachers and others concerned in the work of public elementary schools*, London: HMSO.

Brehony, K. (2005) 'Primary schooling under New Labour: The irresolvable contradiction of excellence and enjoyment', *Oxford Review of Education*, 31, 1: 29–46.

Campbell, R.J. (2001a) 'The colonisation of the primary curriculum', in R. Phillips, and J. Furlong (eds) *Education Reform and the State: Twenty years of politics, policy and practice*, London: Routledge, 31–44.

Campbell, R.J. (2001b) 'Modernising Primary Teaching: Some issues related to performance management', in C. Richards (ed.) *Changing English Primary Education: Retrospect and Prospect*, Stoke on Trent: Trentham, 95–106.

Campbell, R.J. (2010) 'Conservative Curriculum and Partial Pedagogy: A critique of proposals in the Cambridge Primary Review', *Forum*, 52, 1: 25–36.

Campbell, R.J. and St. J. Neill, S.R. (1994) *Primary teachers at work*, London: Routledge.

Chitty, C. (1992) 'The changing role of the state in educational provision', *History of Education*, 21, 1: 1–13.

Chitty, C. (2009) *Education Policy in Britain*, 2nd edn, Basingstoke: Palgrave Macmillan.

Chitty, C. and Simon, B. (eds) (1993) *Education Answers Back: Critical Responses to Government Policy*, London: Lawrence and Wishart.

Conway, M.D. (ed.) (1894) *The Writings of Thomas Paine*, New York and London: G.P. Putnam, 2 vols (http://files.libertyfund.org/files/344/0548-02_Bk.pdf Online Library of Liberty (Liberty Fund Inc., accessed 25 August 2011).

Crick, B. (2000) *In Defence of Politics*, 5th edn, London: Continuum.

Crick, B. (2002) *Democracy: a very short introduction*, Oxford: Oxford University Press.

Cullingford, C. (ed.) (1997) *The Politics of Primary Education*, Buckingham: Open University Press.

Cunningham, M. and Hargreaves, L. (2007) *Minority Ethnic Teachers' Professional Experiences* (DFES Research Report 853), Cambridge: University of Cambridge Faculty of Education.

Cunningham, P. (1988) *Curriculum Change in the Primary School since 1945: Dissemination of the Progressive Ideal*, London: Falmer Press.

Cunningham, P. (2002a) 'Primary Education', in R. Aldrich (ed.) *A Century of Education*, London: Falmer, 9–30.

Cunningham, P. (2002b) 'Progressivism, Decentralisation and Recentralisation: Local Education Authorities and the primary curriculum, 1902–2002', *Oxford Review of Education*, 28, 2 & 3: 217–233.

Cunningham, P. (2007) 'Plowden in History: Popular and professional memory', *Forum*, 49, 1 & 2: 21–31.

Cunningham, P. and Raymont, P. (2010) 'Quality Assurance in English Primary Education', in R. Alexander *et al.* (eds) *The Cambridge Primary Review Research Surveys*, London: Routledge, 767–791.

DCSF (2009) *Independent Review of the Primary Curriculum* (Rose Review) (DCSF-00499-2009) (www.education.gov.uk/publications/standard/, accessed 20 June 2011).

DES (1967) *Children and their Primary Schools* (Plowden Report), London: HMSO.

DES (1975) *A Language for Life* (Bullock Report), London: HMSO.

DES (1978) *Primary education in England: A survey by HM Inspectors of Schools*, London: HMSO.

DES (1981) *The School Curriculum*, London: HMSO.

DFE (2010) website (www.education.gov.uk/schools/teachingandlearning/curriculum, accessed 5 October 2010).

DFE (2011) Press release on Second Reading of the Education Bill in House of Commons on 8 February 2011.

DFES (2003) *Excellence and Enjoyment: A national strategy for primary schools* (DFES-0377-2003).

DFES (2004) *Every Child Matters: Change for Children* (DFES/1081/2004) (www.education.gov.uk/publications/standard/, accessed 20 June 2011).

DFES (2007) *Diversity and Citizenship* (Ajegbo Report) (DFES-00045-2007) (www.education.gov.uk/publications/standard/, accessed 20 June 2011).

Drummond, M.J. (2010) 'BRAVO! and BUT: reading the Cambridge Primary Review', *Forum*, 52, 1: 9–16.

Dunford, J. (1998) *Her Majesty's Inspectorate of Schools since 1944: Standard bearers or turbulent priests?*, London: Woburn Press.

Ecclestone, K. and Hayes, D. (2009) 'Changing the subject: The educational implications of developing emotional well-being', *Oxford Review of Education*, 35, 3: 371–389.

Evans, A. (1985) 'The Welsh Dimension', in M. Plaskow (ed.) *Life and death of the Schools Council*, London: Falmer, 93–103.

Furedi, F. (2009) *Wasted: Why education isn't educating*, London: Continuum.

Furlong, J. (2001) 'Reforming teacher education, re-forming teachers: accountability, professionalism and competence', in R. Phillips and J. Furlong (eds) *Education, Reform and the State: Twenty-five years of politics, policy and practice*, London: Routledge, 118–135.

Galton, M. (2007) *Teaching and Learning in the Primary Classroom*, London: Sage.

Galton, M. and MacBeath, J. (2002) *A life in teaching? The impact of change on primary teachers' working lives*, NUT/University of Cambridge Faculty of Education.

Galton, M. and MacBeath, J. (2008) *Teachers under pressure*, London: NUT/Sage.

Galton, M., Hargreaves, L., Comber, C., Wall, D. with Pell, A. (1999) *Inside the Primary Classroom: 20 Years On*, London: Routledge.

Galton, M., Simon, B. and Croll, P. (1980) *Inside the Primary Classroom*, London: Routledge & Kegan Paul.

Gearon, L. (ed.) (2002) *Education in the United Kingdom*, London: David Fulton.

General Teaching Council for England (2011) website (www.gtce.org.uk/, accessed 20 June 2011).

General Teaching Council for Northern Ireland (2011) website (www.gtcni.org.uk/, accessed 20 June 2011).

General Teaching Council for Scotland (2011) website (www.gtcs.org.uk/home/home.aspx, accessed 20 June 2011).

General Teaching Council for Wales (GTCW) (2011) website (www.gtcw.org.uk/gtcw/, accessed 20 June 2011).

Gilbert, R. (2010) 'Curriculum Reform', in P. Peterson *et al.* (eds) *International Encyclopaedia of Education*, Amsterdam: Elsevier; Oxford: Academic Press, vol. 1, 510.

Gove, M. (2010) Letter to headteachers from Secretary of State, Department for Education, 9 September (www.teachernet.gov.uk/_doc/backtoschool090910.html, accessed 11 September 2010).

Griggs, G. (2007) 'Physical Education: primary matters, secondary importance', *Education 3–13*, 35, 1: 59–69.

Hall, K. (2004) *Literacy and Schooling: Towards renewal in primary education policy*, Aldershot: Ashgate.

Halsey, A.H. and Sylva, K. (eds) (1987) Plowden: History and prospect (Special Issue), *Oxford Review of Education*, 13, 1.

Halstead, J. M. (2002) 'Faith and Diversity in Religious School Provision', in L. Gearon (ed.) *Education in the United Kingdom*, London: David Fulton.

Hart, S., Dixon, A., Drummond, M.J. and McIntyre, D. (2004) *Learning without Limits*, Maidenhead: Open University Press.

Hayes, D. (2001) 'Changing Aspects of Primary Teachers' Professionalism: Driving forward or driven backward?', in C. Richards (ed.) *Changing English Primary Education: Retrospect and Prospect*, Stoke on Trent: Trentham, 139–154.

Hayes, D. (2010) *Encyclopedia of Primary Education*, Abingdon: Routledge.

House of Commons Education and Skills Committee (HCESC) (2007a) *Citizenship Education* (Second Report Session 2006–2007) HC 301.

HCESC (2007b) *The Work of Ofsted* (Sixth Report Session 2006–2007) HC 165.

House of Commons Children, Schools and Families Select Committee (HCCSFC) (2008) *Testing and Assessment* (Third Report Session 2007-8) HC 169.

HCCSFC (2009) *National Curriculum* (Fourth Report Session 2008–9) HC 344.

HCCSFC (2010a) *School Accountability* (First Report Session 2009-10) HC 88.

HCCSFC (2010b) *The Training of Teachers* (Fourth Report Session 2009-10) HC 275.

HCCSFC (2010c) *From Baker to Balls: The foundations of the education system* (Ninth Report Session 2009–10) HC 422.

House of Commons Education Committee (HCEC) (2011) *The role and performance of Ofsted* (Second Report Session 2010–11) HC 570 (www.parliament.uk/business/committees/committees-a-z/

commons-select/education-committee/, accessed 31 May 2011). For previous sessions see www. parliament.uk/business/committees/committees-a-z/commons-select/education-committee/ publications/previous-sessions/, accessed 31 May 2011).

Jenkins, S. (2010) 'Gove's claim to be "freeing" schools is a cloak for more control from the centre', *Guardian*, 27 May 2010.

John, G. (2006) *Taking a stand: Gus John speaks on education, race, social action and civil unrest 1980–2005*, Manchester: Gus John Partnership.

Jones, G.E. and Roderick, G.W. (2003) *A History of Education in Wales*, Cardiff: University of Wales Press.

Jones, K. (2003) *Education in Britain: 1944 to the Present*, Cambridge: Polity Press.

Lankshear, D. (2002) 'Church of England Schools', in L. Gearon (ed.) *Education in the United Kingdom*, London: David Fulton.

Laycock, L. (2002) 'Primary Schools', in L. Gearon (ed.) *Education in the United Kingdom*, London: David Fulton.

Leach, J. and Moon, B. (2008) *The Power of Pedagogy*, London: Sage.

Learning without Limits (2011) website (http://learningwithoutlimits.educ.cam.ac.uk, accessed 31 May 2011).

Maclure, S. (2000) *The inspector's calling: HMI and the shaping of educational policy, 1945–1992*, London: Hodder & Stoughton.

MacConville, R. (ed.) (2007) *Looking at Inclusion: Listening to the voices of young people*, London: Paul Chapman.

McCulloch, G. (2011) *The Struggle for the History of Education*, London: Routledge.

McKinney, S. (ed.) (2008) *Faith Schools in the Twenty-first Century*, Edinburgh: Dunedin Press.

Marshall, T.H. (1950) *Citizenship and social class, and other essays*, Cambridge: Cambridge University Press.

Minogue, K. (2000) *Politics: A very short introduction*, Oxford: Oxford University Press.

Minogue, K. (2007) *Alien Powers: The pure theory of ideology*, 2nd edn, London: Transaction Publishers.

National Assembly for Wales (2001) *The Learning Country: A paving document: A comprehensive education and lifelong learning programme to 2010 in Wales*, Cardiff: NAfW.

NCC (1990a) *Curriculum Guidance 5: Health Education*, London: National Curriculum Council.

NCC (1990b) *Curriculum Guidance 8: Education for Citizenship*, London: National Curriculum Council.

Ofsted (2010a) *Citizenship Established? Citizenship in Schools 2006/9*, London: Ofsted (www.ofsted. gov.uk/publications/090159, accessed 20 June 2011).

Ofsted (2010b) *Steady Progress for Citizenship Education*, (NR-2010-02) (www.ofsted.gov.uk/Ofsted-home/News.Press-and-media/2010/January/, accessed 20 June 2011).

O'Neill, O. (2002) *A Question of Trust* (The BBC Reith Lectures 2002), Cambridge: Cambridge University Press.

Osler, A. (2009) 'Citizenship, democracy and racial justice: Ten years on', *Race Equality Teaching*, 27, 3: 21–27.

Osler, A. and Starkey, H. (2010) *Teachers and Human Rights Education*, Stoke on Trent: Trentham.

Parekh, B. (2000) *Rethinking multiculturalism: Cultural diversity and political theory*, Basingstoke: Palgrave.

Paterson, L. (2002) 'Scotland', in L. Gearon (ed.) *Education in the United Kingdom*, London: David Fulton.

Paterson, L. (2003) *Scottish Education in the Twentieth Century*, Edinburgh: Edinburgh University Press.

Peterson, P., Baker, E. and McGaw, B. (eds) (2010) *International encyclopedia of education*, 3rd edn, Amsterdam: Elsevier; Oxford: Academic Press.

Phillips, R. (2002) 'Wales', in L. Gearon (ed.) *Education in the United Kingdom*, London: David Fulton.

Plaskow, M. (ed.) (1985) *Life and death of the Schools Council*, London: Falmer.

Pollard, A. (2001) 'Towards a new perspective on children's learning', in C. Richards (ed.) *Changing English Primary Education: Retrospect and Prospect*, Stoke on Trent: Trentham, 7–16.

QCA (1998) *Education for citizenship and the teaching of democracy in schools: Final report of the Advisory Group on Citizenship* (Crick Report), London: QCA.

QCDA (2010) National Curriculum website (http://curriculum.qcda.gov.uk/key-stages-1-and-2/Values-aims-and-purposes/index.aspx, accessed 1 November 2010).

Ravitch, D. (2011) 'Obama's War on Schools', *Newsweek*, 20 March.

Reynolds, D. (2008) 'New Labour, education and Wales: The devolution decade', *Oxford Review of Education*, 34, 6: 753–765.

Richards, C. (ed.) (2001) *Changing English Primary Education: Retrospect and Prospect*, Stoke on Trent: Trentham.

Richards, C. (2010) 'A Possible Accountability Framework for Primary Education: Building on (but going beyond) the recommendations of the Cambridge Primary Review', *Forum*, 52, 1, 37–41.

Robinson, W. (2004) *Power to Teach: Learning through practice*, London: RoutledgeFalmer.

Rury, J. (2008) *Education and Social Change: Contours in the History of American Schooling*, London: Routledge.

Schenk, C. (2010) 'A Tale of Two Reviews', *Forum*, 52, 1: 17–23.

Schools Council for Curriculum and Examinations (1981) *The Practical Curriculum* (Schools Council Working Paper No. 70), London: Methuen.

Schools Council for Curriculum and Examinations (1983) *Primary Practice* (Schools Council Working Paper No. 75), London: Methuen.

Silver, H. (1994) *Good schools, effective schools: Judgements and their histories*, London: Cassell.

Simon, B. (1981) 'Why no pedagogy in England?', in B. Simon and W. Taylor (eds) *Education in the eighties: The central issues*, London: Batsford.

Simon, B. (1991) *Education and the Social Order 1940–1990*, London: Lawrence and Wishart.

Simon, B. (1998) *A Life in Education*, London: Lawrence and Wishart.

Soler, J. and Openshaw, R. (2006) *Literacy crises and reading policies: Children still can't read!*, London: Routledge.

Southworth, G. (2001) 'Primary School Management', in C. Richards (ed.) *Changing English Primary Education: Retrospect and Prospect*, Stoke on Trent: Trentham, 107–122.

Strathern, M. (ed.) (2000) *Audit Cultures*, London: Routledge.

Taylor, F. (1997) 'Governors, parents and primary schools', in C. Cullingford (ed.) *The Politics of Primary Education*, Buckingham: Open University Press, 114–124.

TDA (2010) Masters in Teaching and Learning website (www.tda.gov.uk/teacher/masters-in-teaching-and-learning.aspx, accessed 27 October 2010).

Training and Development Agency (TDA) website (www.tda.gov.uk/, accessed 20 June 2011).

UN High Commissioner for Human Rights, Committee on the Rights of the Child (UNCRC) (2008) 49th Session, 15 September to 3 October (www2.ohchr.org/english/bodies/crc/crcs49.htm, accessed 24 May 2011).

UNICEF UK (2011) website: Rights Respecting Schools Award (www.unicef.org.uk/rrsa, accessed 31 May 2011).

Warwick, P. (2007a) 'Echoes of Plowden? Opportunities and pressures evident in teachers' experience of autonomy and accountability in one school community', *Forum*, 49, 1 & 2: 33–38.

Warwick, P. (2007b) 'Hearing pupils' voices: Revealing the need for citizenship education within primary schools', *Education 3–13*, 35, 3: 261–272.

Warwick, P. and Cunningham, P. (2006) 'Progressive Alternatives? Teachers' experience of autonomy and accountability in the school community', *Education 3–13*, 34, 1: 27–36.

Webb, R. and Vulliamy, G. (2006) *Coming full circle? The impact of New Labour's Education Policies on primary school teachers' work*, London: ATL.

Webb, R. and Vulliamy, G. (2007) 'Changing classroom practice at Key Stage 2: The impact of New Labour's national strategies', *Oxford Review of Education*, 33, 5: 561–580.

Whetton, C. (2009) 'Testing time: A brief history of national curriculum assessment 1989–2008', *Education Research*, 51, 2: 137–159.

Woodhead, C. (2002) *Class War*, London: Little, Brown.

Woodhead, C. (2009) *A desolation of learning: Is this the education our children deserve?*, Rake, Sussex: Pencil Sharp.

Woods, P. and Wenham, P. (1995) 'Politics and pedagogy, a case study in appropriation', *Journal of Education Policy*, 10, 2: 119–141.

Wyse, D. (2003) 'The National Literacy Strategy: A critical review of empirical evidence', *British Educational Research Journal*, 29, 6: 903–916.

Wyse, D., McCreery, E. and Torrance, H. (2010) 'The Trajectory and Impact of National Reform: Curriculum and assessment in English primary schools', in Alexander, R. *et al.* (eds) *The Cambridge Primary Review Research Surveys*, London: Routledge, 792–817.

Index